JUDAISM and ETHICS

JUDAISM and ETHICS

edited by

DANIEL JEREMY SILVER

KTAV PUBLISHING HOUSE, INC.

© COPYRIGHT 1970
CENTRAL CONFERENCE OF AMERICAN RABBIS

SBN 87068-010-2

LIBRARY OF CONGRESS CATALOG CARD NUMBER 78-105307
MANUFACTURED IN THE UNITED STATES OF AMERICA

TABLE OF CONTENTS

SOCIAL ACTION

THE MISSION OF ISRAEL

INTRODUCTION

Daniel Jeremy Silver
Editor, CCAR Journal
Rabbi, The Temple
Cleveland, Ohio

These essays have been culled from the pages of the *CCAR Journal*. Each raises questions about moral judgment and ethical standards, critical issues in our times, particularly for a faith whose central obligation is "the yoke of the commandments." Not so long ago Judaism stood in an enviable position as regards questions of moral conduct. Judaism presupposed that "it has been taught thee, O man, what is good and what the Lord doth require of thee. . . ." The Commandments had been revealed, the terms of the Covenant were known and generation upon generation of devoted teachers had explored every possible case and exception and given the response of the Torah tradition. There was a clear well-marked halacha, a way that man should go.

Obedience to the halacha was basic; above it was the *midat hasiduth,* the saintly way. Through legend, biographical incident, and personal example, the tradition and its interpreters suggested a way above and beyond man's normal obligations *lifne ve'lifnim meshurat ha-din.* Traditional Judaism had both a clear structure of duties and an inspiring moral reach. A century ago an anthology such as this would have dealt largely with the exploration of specific cases brought up by the changing conditions of life to be analyzed according to accepted halachic norms. The rabbis explored the tradition and the law for analogies, texts, case decisions, and moral principles which would be helpful in making clear judgments on the issue before them. A few such studies continue to appear in the pages of the *CCAR Journal* and some representative examples are reprinted here.

This traditional approach has been challenged by the postulates of modern thought. A number of articles in this anthology raise questions as to the validity of this time-honored procedure and, indeed, of the entire rabbinic construct on which it depends. The *Zeitgeist* is uneasy with the authority of any specific Commandment, and skeptical of every categorical claim on man's actions. Many today doubt the reality of a specific revelation. Humanism and secularism have made deep inroads into traditional categories of thought.

Many of these articles are by "pulpit" rabbis who are keenly aware that if their congregants are not aware of the depths of the Jewish tradition, they are well acquainted with tales of its shortcoming: the enforced loneliness of the *agunah,* the constrained permission of autopsy, the lack of enthusiasm for birth control. Rabbinic responsa are seen as quibbling rather than bold. On the other hand, thought which is radical and requires a sweeping review of accepted conventions and convictions commands an immediate popularity. Questions abound: On what is the traditional ethic based if significant elements of it must be doubted or denied? What does it mean to teach "traditional" Jewish values? Which are the traditional values and what is their authority?

Liberal Jewish preaching has tried to avoid the dilemma by shifting from discussion of the specifics, à la responsa, to broad sweeping invocations of the passion of Biblical prophecy: "Proclaim freedom unto the land." "Righteousness, righteousness shalt thou pursue." Well and good. But what is freedom? How does one proclaim freedom? Has freedom outer limits? Precision was *the* great virtue of the rabbinic ethical stance. Passion is the staple of current ethical activity, and these oratorical sparks have lit some slumbering fires. But in practice, high themes may be only high sounding, and bold phrases little more than the rationalization for quite mundane concerns or even downright mischief. Governments have long known how to write white papers to rationalize dark deeds. One does not need a long memory to recite chapter and verse of the crimes committed by those who knew in their blood what was right and chanted highflown phrases to cover their evil. Dietrich Bonhoeffer, who lived in an era when Hitler promised a thousand years of peace, has written some perceptive words on the danger of verbal hyperbole in ethical decision making:

Timeless and ethical discourse lacks the concrete warrant which all authentic discourse requires. It is an adolescent, presumptuous and illegitimate declamation of ethical principles, and however intense may be the subjective earnestness with which it is propounded, it is contrary to the essential character of ethical discourse, in a way which is clearly felt even though it may be difficult to define. In such cases it is often impossible to find fault with the process of abstraction and generalization or with the theories advanced. And yet they do not possess the specific gravity of ethical propositions. The words are correct but they have no weight. In the end it must be felt that they are not helpful but chaotic.

Parenthetically, Bonhoeffer continued with some thoughts which are not irrelevant to the immediate situation:

For some obscure but, in the end, undeniable reason it is in the nature of things simply not possible, not in accordance with any true state of affairs, if a youth recites ethical generalities to a circle of experienced and grown men. It will be a sign of maturity or of immaturity whether one perceives or fails to perceive from this experience that what confronts us here is not the stubborn and narrow-minded self-complacency of old age or its fear of allowing youth to assert itself, but it is a question of the safeguarding or the violation of an essential ethical law. Ethical discourse requires a warrant such as the adolescent cannot simply confer upon himself, however pure and earnest may be his ethical conviction. In ethical discourse what matters is not only that the contents of the assertion should be correct, but also that there should be a concrete warrant, and authorization for this assertion. It is not only what is said that matters but also the man who says it.

Those who are quoted in these pages are not of a mind. Some continue traditional studies. Some are impatient with the whole process of ethical casuistry. The time is late and the problems seem too urgent for long study. Yet for many of those who have worked and sacrificed for economic and racial justice the concrete choice between specific alternatives is becoming increasingly difficult. They are among those who seek a more consistent and clear ethical mandate. Intuition or doing your thing provides only an erratic and confusing compass.

In the halcyon days of Reform Judaism some rabbis and many laymen felt that the time had come to be free of the whole concept of halacha. They held that the Torah law no longer was operative. Its authority was challenged. Why lean on a broken reed? Moral values are universal values and known to all reasonable men. The sympathy they felt for the tradition was limited to citations of prophetic ardor and disarming epigrammatic simplicities. They "knew" what was required of them. Hindsight has made it clear that many mistook solid middle-class burgher virtues for a valid ethic, and should make us wonder if we have not mistaken our restive and opinionated social ethic for the good. In any case, a few prophetic *pesukim* do not represent the sum of tradition. If the halacha and the casuistic method are abrogated, how does anyone get down to specifics?

Modern man may be groping toward a new awareness of revelation, one not based on a static, once upon a time, conversation on Sinai, but on the claim of these commandments upon this generation. Perhaps he is learning to see the mitzvah not as a text set down once and for all, to be literally obeyed, but as the whole context of the life of a concerned and devoted Jew.

These essays are intended as a beginning of understanding and not its authoritative conclusion. It is doubtful that there are final and fixed conclusions any more. Revelation is in the encounter. Yet it remains probable that an ignorant man cannot be a saint and that our hell on earth is in part the result of the good intentions of the innocents of our modern and complex society. The beginning of wisdom is get wisdom. To that high purpose these pages are humbly dedicated.

THE ISSUES

SOME CURRENT TRENDS
IN ETHICAL THEORY

Abraham Edel
Professor of Philosophy
The City College of the City of New York
New York City, New York

Ethical theory today is a complex and sometimes forbidding field. Whereas in older days one was likely to stumble on a panegyric of duty in the Kantian vein, with some frequency—which nevertheless served only as a momentary relief from Kantian technicality—today one can come on an almost mathematical treatment of the *ought,* as well as a syntactic treatment of the *good.* It is this technical concern that stands out prominently in the works of the analytical schools, whether formalistic or cast in ordinary language. One has to probe deeply to find the human issues involved. But on the other hand, even in ethical writings today where the heart is touched at first sight—as in Martin Buber's lyrical treatment of the difference between relating to another as *It* and relating as *Thou,* or in many of the existentialist pronouncements—one would go astray if one neglected the depth of technical philosophy built into the concepts. For the history of ethical theory is old, and collectively learned, if not always wise. Intellectual experiments have been tried, and new models press hard on the old. Behind its formulations lie the same human concerns, but it is human life and human knowledge that has been changing, and so the points of focus are shifted, often rapidly, sometimes bewilderingly. In approaching the scene, therefore, one must take technicality and depth for granted. The too frequent charges of triviality in ethical theory which burst occasionally upon the pages of our Sunday supplements or journals of the intellectual establishment, neglect the fact that the commonsense is often the commonplace. The commonsense view of the world and man belongs to the middle range of middle-sized objects. Its categories were themselves an achievement of human construction, not the direct representation of ultimate reality. They will not necessarily do in ethics—any

11

more than in our scientific picture of the world—for micro-problems and for macro-problems. We have come to expect the fashioning of fresh categories in fresh ranges of problems on the basis of accumulated fresh experience.

I should like in what follows to remind you of the traditional concerns of ethical theory, and the kinds of answers it developed; then to pinpoint the major sources of change that burst upon the older schemes, and characterize the reactions that occurred in ethical theory. Then I want briefly to consider four themes in the outcome to see where we now stand. They are: the growth of the conception of moral autonomy, the struggle over the concept of moral law, the outcome in the relation of religion and ethics, and the tension in the relation of science and ethics.

I

Traditional Frameworks and the Impact
of Intellectual Changes

Traditional ethics took hold of familiar moral concepts—good and bad or good and evil, right and wrong, duty and obligation and responsibility, virtue and vice—and analyzed their meanings, criteria for their application, and major forms. It reached out to presuppositions about man and the world that appeared necessary for moral operations, for example, assumptions about free will, and argued over them. If religious in orientation, it presented the divine background; if secular, it gave an account of human nature. Some general themes were recurrent—for example, how far morality was a matter of inner spirit or outer acts, of correct knowledge or right attitude, whether a man could ignore his dependence on material things, how the tensions of individual interest and social well-being could be reconciled, whether responsibilities issued from individual commitment or could be imposed, and so on.

The history of ethics shows at least three major conceptual or theoretical frameworks. One was a human-nature ethics. It saw man as a goal-seeking being, with a definite ground-plan in his aspiration. That at which he aimed was called "the good." Rules of obligation and duty were generalizations about the most effective ways of achieving this, and virtues were appropriate character traits for this quest. Knowledge of the good unified the life of man, whether the good was described in theological terms of eternal bliss, or in Aristotelian terms of happiness, or hedonistic and utilitarian terms of pleasure and avoidance of pain, or naturalistic terms of the maximum harmonious expression of human impulse, drives or instincts.

The second framework was juridical. It saw morality as a system of authoritative laws enjoined on man. It presupposed in man an intellectual capacity for discerning the laws and an effective capacity for respecting or obeying them. Its conception of good character and legitimate goals was framed in terms of the requirements of the moral law. The central ethical concept in this scheme is duty or obligation. In the traditional religious form, the authoritative source of law is divine command; in the Kantian ethics, so influential in modern times, it is the rational self, legislating for the community of selves.

The third framework focused more directly on the self; either in a static way on its character, or in a dynamic sense on its growth and development. Its favored concepts are virtue and vice. Its uses criteria of inner strength and self-control, as did the ancient Stoics, or peace of mind and serenity, as do many moderns, or self-development and self-realization, as in some nineteenth-century Hegelian-influenced conceptions of the moral ideal. Goals of striving, and rules of living, have a derivative place, oriented to the major task.

Such frameworks sample the theoretical structures of the traditional approaches. They do not even suggest the rich analytic power and detailed refinement that went into all of them, nor the sensitivity they displayed in moral elaboration. But our task is to describe trends in theory, not even theories, much less moral delineation.

What shook the foundations of traditional ethics were the tremendous intellectual changes of the last 100 years. Here are some of the strands.

Darwin saw man as the product of the continuing evolution of the animal species. This shot the ground from under the traditional concept of human nature. For that idea had been teleological, and tied together three criteria—what had been the universal direction of human striving, what was inherent in man's makeup or implanted within him and what was the good of his species. After Darwin, the universal comes to represent simply scientific generalization of what man happens to be doing at that stage of his development, a product of his past struggles for survival. His inherent drives and instincts are tendencies that helped out in the past but may be liabilities at present—for example, if he now has natural aggressive tendencies. The tie to the good of the species is broken, and man's good has to be defined on its own. Either ethics is pitted against evolution, as Thomas H. Huxley saw it (the gardener against the encroaching wilderness), or ethics is built up out of the rules and conditions that are necessary for survival and maintenance of man on the globe. It is not surprising that a Nietzsche called for transcending the whole process and basing an ethics on what man could evolve into rather than what he is now; or again, that later writers, like Reinhold Niebuhr, made a mystique out of self-transcendence, man's ability to stand above and appraise himself, as if it took him out of the evolutionary process. But in a self-enclosed evolutionary naturalism such transcendence is deceptive—it is simply some of the dynamic tendencies in man elevating themselves to become the basis of criticizing their fellows, just as the party in power speaking for the national interest is not cut off from its own party roots and interests. Responding to this whole crumbling of the human-nature framework, contemporary ethics has tried out different concepts as a foundation of an account of the good. Some turn to a generalized theory of value, defining value simply as interest, or allying it with purposive behavior, psychologically studied. Some take refuge in an indefinable intuitive quality of goodness. Others give up the attempt to picture a good in terms of any system of ends, making its task, as Dewey has done, to be the development of methods of appraisal.

Just as the Darwinian revolution had a disruptive effect on the human-nature framework in ethics, so Freud had an equally disruptive effect on the juridical framework. For one thing, he pointed to the irrational bases of rationalistic pretensions; and, indeed, the moral law had often been allied with reason. But perhaps more long-range in effect was the psychoanalytic probing into the origin and development of conscience in the individual, into the way in which internalizaton of rules of conduct and feeling takes place in relation to parental figures and how fear is transmuted into guilt and anxiety. This dealt a hard blow to the concept of moral law as itself the object of respect. Robbed of its psychological base, the moral law has gone in different philosophical directions. One is the shift from law to ideal, from binding phenomena to phenomena of aspiration, though these in turn suffer a comparable psychoanalytic fate. Another is to take a social interpretation, so that moral law becomes the recommendation of an institutional pattern—but institutions require less to be commanded than to be justified. Perhaps the only hard core that has remained in philosophical discussions—and it is a lively one today—is the notion of obligation as having a universalistic meaning, that is, that when I say I ought to do something I imply that anyone in such a situation is under similar obligation. But even such a minimal binding is open to different interpretations, and while some philosophers see it as the solid logical base for moral operations, others see it as the crystallization in human attitude of man's long experience with the disastrous consequences of special privilege and exploitation.

It is on such a historical side that the impact of Marxian thought has had a many-sided potential. Man is a historical being through and through, and the forms of his thought as well as the forms of his practical life constitute a response to the socio-historical problems of his day—and these are material problems, changes in the economic life and technology forcing alteration in institutional patterns, making old questions meaningless and forcing new wine into old intellectual bottles. From the point of view of ethical theory Marx, like Freud, could be looked at in two ways—as debunking old modes of thought by showing the class base of supposedly eternal and universal moral systems, or as showing that all theorizing about morality had a socio-historical meaning and was part of the problem of continual refinement of intellectual instruments for social change.

In the twentieth century, the impact of anthropology has been equally great. Its display of the variety of cultural phenomena and cultural patterns has finally brought the realization that culture penetrates not only into our structures and institutions but into all our awareness and responses. The problem that ethical theory was faced with in this array of contrasts was that of justification, and the issue of ethical relativity came for a while to occupy the center of the stage. For example, much of the heat generated by one school of ethical theory in the 1930's and 1940's—the emotive theory which held that moral utterances are not propositions that are true or false, but expressions of emotion—no doubt came from the practical fact that whole systems of life were locked in bitter struggle; the question was raised whether a humanistic ethics facing a Nazi outlook could say nothing better for itself than that its adherents had been shaped in certain emotional patterns. While some of the theoretical energies of philosophers and social scientists went to promoting the search for universal values to act as a base for moral judgment, perhaps the more far-reaching endeavor was to see cultural differences in moral pattern as different answers, hammered out in the experience of peoples, to common human problems, and so to render explicit criteria for adequacy of solution, with the realization, however, that while this narrowed down the fear of arbitrariness in morals it still left open the possibility of major diversities of pattern.

I have still two strands of influence to explore that worked more directly upon the moral philosophers. One is the philosophy of science. Think of the vast changes that have taken place in the progress of science, especially the physical and biological. As the Einsteinian contributions showed, these were also conceptual revolutions. Why should men's thought about good and right and obligation remain cramped in older categories when concepts of simultaneity and space and time and causality had burst their older bonds with all sorts of implications for the nature of even the most general theoretical categories? For basically it showed us that our concepts are human constructions born in the progress of our knowledge and our theory, directed toward practical and theoretical jobs, and open to revision, even abandonment, as our experience and requirements change. As a matter of fact, we can sense conceptual experimentation all about us. We talk less of obligations than commitments, we no longer think of goods so much as values, our touchstone is no longer virtue but authenticity, and our failures are less often felt as sin than as immaturity! There is a great deal built into such conceptual shifts, which it would take us far too long here to explore. There is probably as great a difference as Nietzsche found between good and bad as compared to good and evil, the one an aristocratic ethic, the other a religious ethic.

Although for a while it looked as if the moral philosophers might try to apply the lessons of the philosophy of science, I must confess that they have not on the whole carried this through. There were special reasons I shall touch on in connection with the topic of autonomy later. Or perhaps it was simply that the philosophy of language proved more immediately attractive. This has been one of the most exciting areas of mid-twentieth-century exploration. Many of the old philosophical issues that had been explored in the theory of knowledge as problems about the nature of thought and things now became viewed as questions of how to use words and what we could do with words. And it was to words that a vast part of the energies of moral philosophers was devoted. They conceived of moral philosophy—now removed from the moral fray under the name of "meta-ethics"—as the logical-linguistic analysis of moral terms and moral utterances, how they were used and how they were related to other utterances in the language in processes of justification. Into this analysis they poured the wealth of a much improved modern logic and a rapidly growing science of linguistics. After a few decades, the outcome was a tremendously refined view of moral discourse which swept aside many older assumptions and problems. For example, it could no longer be assumed that because we had a single term "good," therefore there was a single quality *named* by the term, for terms function in countless other ways than naming. This would not prevent a moral philosopher from arguing that there was a single quality of *requiredness* discernible in the phenomenological field of moral experience; but he would have to exhibit this by pheno-

menological analysis and could not assume it on the basis of
our existing moral language. Older doctrines of moral intuition-
ism were thus called on to present their credentials. Again, to
take an illuminating example, we could no longer assume that
"ought" had the same function in all contexts of its use. When
we say "I ought" the context is one of deciding; "you ought" is
prescribing to a person present; "he ought" is neither deciding
nor prescribing, but evaluating. As the contexts differ, the problems differ, and different analyses and criteria are required.
Again, there was an extensive hunt for diversity of uses of moral
language, from expressing emotion, prescribing and advising, to
grading, evaluating, and even to such doing as laying down responsibilities and obligations. It was the old cognitive mode of
morality as knowledge that was being shouldered aside, and an
activist conception of morality as interpersonal influence or
as decision at choice points that was coming to the fore.

But I must not dwell on the specifics. I have tried so far
merely to suggest why the tasks of moral philosophy have been
so vast in the contemporary world. It is not merely that the
problems of change and practice have intensified and assumed
crucial proportions. It is not merely because old habits of
thought hang on as obstacles to reconstruction, sometimes clung
to by older interests and older fears and insecurities. It is
because the whole transformation in our way of looking at the
world, spurred by progress in so many fields of knowledge, has
posed the task of working through to fresh, more adequate concepts and models. This is a theoretical task of the first magnitude.
It is not prompted by ignorance and breakdown, it is made
necessary by intellectual riches in many areas, the promise of
greater riches in others, and by the inadequacy of the older
formulations either to meet the practical problems or to absorb
the advances in knowledge. I am not saying that contemporary
moral philosophy has carried out the task, nor even that it has
faced it with sufficient self-consciousness. It is my interpretation
of what has happened and what is happening in the field that I
am offering. What I do want to say is that I find little that is
trivial or irrelevant to the task. There is much that is narrow, and
does not even see what it is accomplishing—for example, much

that thinks of itself as analyzing ordinary language and does not see that it is at the same time fashioning the way men should look on problems of decision. There is much that is one-sided, that for example looks to the inner consciousness and does not consider whether this may not be the ethnocentric view of a particular tradition. And there could be everywhere a greater consciousness about the field and what it is trying to do, and its relations to the great problems of theory and practice in the contemporary world. But never in the history of thought has a task of such magnitude confronted ethical theory, and it will be a long time before it is out of the woods.

Let us now turn to the four themes that I want to explore. In part they will give some of the common answers I see emerging in ethical theory. In part, they will pose fresh problems, but all of great contemporary concern.

II

The Conception of Moral Autonomy

The demand for an autonomous as against an imposed morality was part of the liberal revolt of the last two centuries. Kant drew the line sharply between an autonomous and a heteronomous ethics. But by autonomy he meant the self-legislation of moral laws for a community of rational selves. Nowadays it means rather decision not determined from outside, whether the decision be law-minded or not. But Kant also turned his concept against an imposed religious morality. Unlike Job who only wanted to know, Kant insisted that the very idea of the goodness of God involved our matching God up against our standard of goodness contained in our moral consciousness. Autonomy thus meant the primacy of ethics, and the demand that religion conform to it.

In twentieth-century ethics the concept of moral autonomy has been used against the encroachment of science as well. In the sharp distinction so taken as axiomatic in ordinary thought and philosophy and social science—that between fact and value—

and in the claims that science is value-free, we find the implication that no scientific picture of man and his world can suffice for determining values and obligations. This was enshrined in ethical theory quite early in the century in George Edward Moore's influential conception of a naturalistic fallacy. This fallacy was committed, he said, when one tried to define ethical terms by reference to terms describing states of existence, for example by saying that "good" meant pleasure, object of desire, being in accordance with God's will or with the course of historical development. (Moore thus attacked metaphysical ethics as well as naturalistic ethics.) Since he put the question as if it were a logical issue of definition and a matter of intellectual fallacy, he loosed a whole torrent of critical philosophizing that has not yet died down. But our present point is simply to note that this extreme claim for autonomy isolated the search for intrinsic value from scientific determination. For Moore, intrinsic value could be grasped only in pure immediate intuitive beholding. To many other philosophers also, it seemed that science, by furnishing causal or deterministic explanations of human behavior, left man no longer the decision-center of his ethics, and so destroyed its autonomy.

I shall look at both the relations of ethics and religion and ethics and science separately soon. But it is clear that the demand for moral autonomy is an extremely complex one. Yet there are many currents in ethical theory today that suggest it is in some sense with us to stay, and on justifiable grounds.

There is first the shift in what is paradigmatic of a moral problem itself. Whereas Kant was worried about following the moral law against the enticements of inclination, Dewey points out that adhering to what we know to be right is theoretically a secondary problem. The real moral problem is the one in which there is a conflict of values or rules, and we have to decide which way is right. And such conflicts we have more and more with us in an increasing number of areas.

Second, there is the existentialist stress on the almost unrestricted scope of decision, tied by them into a view of the absolute character of freedom. For example, Sartre makes it clear that even to follow someone else's advice is to choose the advisor, even to stick by one's own past principles is to reaffirm them in the fresh present situation, and even to overlook a problem and ignore an evil, such as war which is not of your making, as somehow not your concern, is already to choose not to face the question of what you could do to stop it.

Third, even in the refined linguistic analysis of ethical discourse, we see the problem of decision coming to the fore. The problem of justification is central, and it is one of finding good reasons for doing. When the Oxford analyst, R. M. Hare, insists that moral terms should be given a prescriptive meaning primarily, rather than a descriptive meaning—that is, to say something is good is to commend it, not to describe some of its properties—he gives the reason that if we adopt the latter path we will tend to slide along in our decision, whereas if we treat our terms as prescriptive we will constantly be facing decision and so be more sensitive to fresh situations.

Fourth, in philosophical doctrines that have stressed authoritarian obedience—the Catholic doctrine is the best current example—we see the demands for individual conscience and decision breaking through at almost every point.

Fifth, in practical problems we see more and more weight of decision being thrown on individuals, as standards in specific fields break down and traditional modes of guidance prove inadequate or are swept aside. In sexual life, once the domain of the strictest regulation, the individual is now often told to decide for himself, with only the injunction to avoid insincerity, conformity as such, self-deceit or exploitation of others. In the practice of a vocation he meets with constant conflicts that emanate from the social and cultural problems of the day so that there is little guidance. Even the traditional military situation no longer allows us to rest on blind obedience to orders, given the extension of conscience and individual responsibility in the Nuremberg trials; and this has an obvious extension to issues of patriotism and obedience to the state. If such justification by loyalty now risks moral condemnation, is the same true today of justification of action in terms of absolute faith? Would Abraham now be put on trial for his blind intention of sacrificing Isaac, and not even allowed Kierkegaard as a defense attorney?

Now some of this emphasis on individual decision may represent an ethnocentric individualism in the Western world. We are well aware of the rise of individualism to excessive pinnacles in the last two centuries, till nothing seemed to obligate a man unless he freely committed himself to it. Perhaps some of the objections to conforming have this rebellious character; for where something is good, not to go along with it just because others are uniformly doing it would seem a type of folly. And there is sometimes a kind of smugness even in the expression "I'm entitled to my opinion" where it is used to imply that I do not have to know anything about it, I have no responsibility to inquire, I can simply settle by willing, as if opinions were inviolable private property! But to point out ideological uses of individualism is not to gainsay that we have here a moral value of the individual that has been growing, and will abide, even though much of the demand for it may continue to express an outcry against pressures of large-scale corporate regimentation and imposition of uniformity. It will abide, apart from any inherent values, for sociological reasons too, because the complexity of problems will continue to confront men with the situations of choice and decision.

Ethical theory is here faced with tasks of great magnitude it has not yet coped with sufficiently. It has to develop a sound conception of an individual, and the identity of a self. It has to work out standards for decision which take account of the fallible character of all moral reckoning in relation to particular situations. These cannot throw too great a burden of guilt upon the man who comes to realize he made a wrong decision, but the standards must not be so relaxed that any decision goes if it is sincere at the moment. For example, to adapt the traditional model of confession and forgiveness is not adequate, for this was oriented rather to a situation of violating one's standards; a probabilistic view of decision might hope to avoid the buildup of guilt in unavoidable wrong decision. Hartmann, in his *Ethics,* uses a concept of unavoidable guilt which is borne with dignity; this is pointed to the issue of conflict of value and sacrifice of value in decision. On the whole, I think this is an area in which, given the novelty of the problem, new concepts have yet to be worked out, concepts which will help an individual face rather than flee from decision.

Moral autonomy, I suggest then, is part of our emerging morality. But the concept itself needs more thorough working over than it has yet received.

III

The Outcome for Moral Law

Pressures against the concept of law in morals have been building up for a very long time. It is of special interest to religious ethics for the obvious reason that every faith has had its issues between legalism and antinomianism. We need not recapitulate such familiar stories.

In contemporary ethical theory, there is little trace of the old sacredness of law any more than the sanctity of institutions or the greater reality of the collective whole. Men's experiences with the tyranny of totalitarianism have been too bitter, men's sense of alienation as a phenomenon too keen. Law tends to be thought of as abstract, as instrumental in a utilitarian way, not as in some sense intrinsic to the good. If any category beyond the individual has an appeal today, it is that of interpersonal relations, as distinguished from inner feelings on the one hand, or institutional forms on the other. There was a time—in hedonistic theory—when inner satisfaction was the ultimate good. And there was a time when social reality seemed to capture intrinsic value—in the idealist self-realization theories which, under Hegelian influence, looked for the substance of the self in the institutions of the age. I think that Martin Buber struck a responsive note when he took both inner feelings and outer institutions as goals to constitute a flight from the authentic, from the interpersonal mutuality of the *I-Thou* relation. And existentialist attacks upon abstract system in favor of the living concrete have a similar unfavorable impact on the prospects of law as an ultimate ethical category.

I know of only one recent trend in technical ethics which looks as if it attempts to weave law into the substance of morality. It falls within the current analysis of human action as essentially rule-guided and regards morality as a system of practices. It reflects Wittgenstein's influence, especially the preoccupation with games as a model. In playing chess, there are two kinds of rules. One kind is instrumental, telling you, for instance, how to play well. But the other is constitutive, and such rules define the game—otherwise you are not playing chess. If life consists of patterns of rule-guided action, then some rules will be its structure. This has only begun to emerge in the periodical literature, and I do not know how far it can be carried or whether it is more than a *tour de force*. But it would be ironical if something like the older concept of law as the inner texture of morality got restored through treating life as a game. In principle it does not seem to me very different from the ancient model of life as an art, to prove that it must have objective rules. But I think it is too late for such narrow confines in ethical theory. Life can be modelled as an art, and it can be played as a game, but it is richer than all the models and cannot be held long in one.

In general, what has pushed the legislative attitude into the background is partly the whole revolt against absolutism and command historically associated with the concept of moral law, but even more the actual clumsiness of moral law in moral decision, when the problems grow complex, shifting, and even sometimes quite indefinite. The older religious tradition did not live by law alone, but by the spirit of interpretation. Talmudic casuistry, I take it, was oriented to multiplying distinctions for solving problems ingeniously, not evading them in some mechanical jurisprudence. But there is a limit, and it is all a question of the rate of change. Change that used to go unnoticed in one's life, because only a historical view could note it after generations, now takes place in a small fraction of one's lifetime. And so the concept of law as an organizational category is shifted back to more general principle, then to a general method of analysis, and when even that is too specific, there is appeal to some general attitude or virtue or broad objective.

At the extreme point there will be nothing left but the appeal to the courage to be, in Tillich's fashion, little more being asked than that life be taken seriously.

Thus in the detailed structure of morality today, we can expect a diversity of organizational forms, shaped to context. There may be strict laws in a few areas where the need for them is overwhelming; for the rest, probable directives, general methods, broad purposes, will occupy the stage—and justifiably so where the rate of change itself accelerates.

IV

How Religions Relate to Ethics

It is surprising, given the traditional strength of religion in Western civilization, what a small role religious concepts have played for the past two centuries within the inner texture of ethical theorizing. Already in the eighteenth century, even religious thinkers did their ethics in a secular way, although there was often a religious motivation or religious anticipation of cashing in on the results of a secular analysis of human nature. Thus the acute Bishop Butler in the early eighteenth century does not argue from religious premises to establish the principle of authority within the human makeup, but proves such a principle exists by showing how self-love curbs the passions; it is only a further step in introspection to show that conscience is on a higher rung. And Archdeacon Paley, whose American editions of his *Principles of Moral and Political Philosophy* had much influence, after giving definitions of moral notions in religious terms, channels the whole concrete ethics in a utilitarian vein by a proof that God's purpose is the happiness of his creatures. Thereafter it is happiness that serves as the effective criterion.

It was Kant who, as I have suggested in discussing moral autonomy, propounded the great reversal between religion and ethics. Ethics now stood independent in the moral consciousness, and religion got its force from meeting ethical requirements. On such a conception, what we expect to find in religion is the sensitive serious insight into the contours and detail of human hopes and fears, ideals and insecurities—in short, rich moral data. But we would not expect to find an independent standard for the moral. While Kant intended his philosophy to serve as a restoration of faith, the later historian can see its direct relation to subsequent pragmatic and humanistic interpretations of religion. As a historical hypothesis, the relation of religion and ethics may be epitomized in this way: The ethical potential of a religious outlook depends not on the mere assertion of the reality of divinity, but on the kinds of properties assigned to divinity. But the major source of the properties so assigned is precisely the ethics of the age; divinity is given those properties which it must have to yield the ethical results men of the time feel most momentous. Therefore religion reflects ethics and furnishes it no independent standard. It does not help ethics to say that of course men always know the divine only in terms of the stage of their awareness and development at the time; this confirms by explaining, rather than denying the hypothesis.

As I see it, then, contemporary ethics goes on its way no longer fighting the battle of autonomy with religion, and in fact usually oblivious to the question whether a religious or secular interpretation will be taken of its processes and results. For it expects the interpretation will add nothing to its results or give ground for changing them. And I think that in very recent years this attitude has also permeated practice. It used to be assumed that religious morality was stable and secular morality unstable, that religion had moral answers and irreligion moral problems. But now it is quite clear that in practice the same moral problems permeate all outlooks, religious or secular, and require a solution in moral terms. They are equally unsolved in all approaches.

V

How Ethics Relates to Science

The relation of ethics to science, on the other hand, has been one of the great controversial issues of contemporary ethical theory. It has taken the form of intensive dispute as to whether from the study of facts one can get values. The reflection of this problem within ethics has been the sharp distinction of means and ends, and the view that science gives us at best means, but ends have to be selected or taken into commitment, either arbitrarily or dogmatically since they issue from feeling or will. The dominant trend in ethical theory has been separatist in this way, as we saw in discussing moral autonomy. It has used Moore's idea of the naturalistic fallacy and the unbridgeable gulf between fact and value to isolate ethics from science.

In my own view, this isolationism, mistakenly thought necessary for the integrity of moral judgment, has been the greatest shortcoming in contemporary ethical theory. I cannot now enter into a full discussion of what directions the work should take, but perhaps the following brief comments can be indicative.

(i) We worry too much about the alleged unbridgeable gulf. Even if it does exist, which I very much doubt, it does not touch the most serious problems which are not how to extract values from facts or infer obligations from descriptive statements, but to go from some values by means of growing factual knowledge to other values, from a general desire for survival to a well-articulated system of goals that constitute health, from a general desire to get on with our neighbors to a system of mutual respect and shared objectives.

(ii) The great mistake in the relation of science and ethics has been to conceive it in an all-or-none fashion. Scientists too hastily thought to prescribe an ethic from the partial biological picture of man, or the partial picture of some human needs. Ethics found it easy to point out that many of these scientific categories—of needs, and fitness and adjustment—smuggled in ethical values. What is required today is to work out in detail the ways in which the specific results of the sciences make moral judgments increasingly determinate. This calls for a wider cooperative stance than has hitherto existed.

(iii) Our moral judgments seem merely expressive, emotive, arbitrary, as long as we keep them isolated from the scope of growing knowledge in the sciences of man. When we relate them to studies in psychological depth we get more refined and sharper criteria of pertinence, authenticity, maturity. When we relate them to studies of society and history, justice moves from a sentiment of fairness to a system of institutions with appropriate, though developing, principles of distribution of goods and burdens. When we relate them to a deeper cultural understanding, we move from the desire for community to shared modes of expression, communication, and mutual understanding.

I have tried in this account both to give a picture of some major trends and to suggest some directions in which I think ethical theory should move. I hope I have conveyed the general spirit of theoretical hope and not theoretical despair. For I do believe that our older ideas have given way not only because of the intensity of human problems but because they proved too rough, even at best, for the intellectual handling of the complexity, the rapidity of change, and the input of growing knowledge in human life. They need to be reconstructed, if we are to have the intellectual instruments for handling our lives. And if ethics claims moral autonomy in judgment, it also assumes the major responsibility for this reconstruction.

CONTEMPORARY PROBLEMS IN ETHICS FROM A JEWISH PERSPECTIVE

Hans Jonas
Professor of Philosophy
New School for Social Research
New York City, New York

To illustrate the plight of ethics in contemporary philosophy, let me open this paper with a personal reminiscence. When in 1945 I reentered vanquished Germany as a member of the Jewish Brigade in the British army, I had to decide whom of my former teachers in philosophy I could in good conscience visit, and whom not. It turned out that the "no" fell on my main teacher, perhaps the most original and profound, certainly one of the most influential among the philosophers of this century, who by the criteria which then had to govern my choice had failed the human test of the time; whereas the "yes" included the much lesser figure of a rather narrow traditionalist of Kantian persuasion, who meant little to me philosophically but of whose record in those dark years I heard admirable things. When I did visit him and congratulated him on the courage of his principled stand, he said a memorable thing: "Jonas," he said, "I tell you this: Without Kant's teaching I couldn't have done it." Here was a limited man, but sustained in an honorable course of action by the moral force of an outmoded philosophy; and there was the giant of contemporary thought—not hindered, some even say helped, by his philosophy in joining the cause of evil. The point is that this was more than a private failing, just as the other's better bearing was, by his own avowal, more than a private virtue. The tragedy was that the truly twentieth-century thinker of the two, he whose word had stirred the youth of a whole generation after the First World War, had not offered in his philosophy a reason for setting conduct in the noble tradition stemming from Socrates and Plato and ending, perhaps, in Kant.

Thus, there is in this personal experience an indication of the plight of modern philosophy when it comes to ethical norms, which are conspicuously absent from its universe of truth. How are we to explain this vacuum? What, with so different a past, has caused the great Nothing with which philosophy today responds to one of its oldest questions—the question of how we ought to live?

Three interrelated determinants of modern thought have a share in the nihilistic situation, or less dramatically put, in the contemporary impasse of ethical theory—two of them theoretical and the third practical: the modern concept of nature, the modern concept of man, and the fact of modern technology supported by both. All three imply the negation of certain fundamental tenets of the philosophical as well as the religious tradition. Since we are here concerned with gaining a Jewish perspective on the situation, we shall note in particular the biblical propositions that are intrinsically disavowed in those three elements of the modern mind.

I

¶1. First, then, we have the modern, i.e. scientific, concept of nature, which by implication denies a number of things formerly held, and first of these is creation, that is, the first sentence of the Bible: "In the beginning God created the heaven and the earth." To say of the world that it is created is to say that it is not its own ground but proceeds from a will and plan beyond itself—in whatever form one conceptualizes the dependence on such a transcendent "cause." In the view of modern science, by contrast, the world has "made," and is continually making, "itself." It is an ongoing process, activated by the forces at work within it, determined by the laws inherent in its matter, each state of it the effect of its own past and none the implementation of a plan or intended order. The world at every moment is the last word about itself and measured by nothing but itself.

¶2. By the same token, this scientific philosophy denies the further sentence "And God saw everything which He had made, and, behold, it was good." Not that physics holds that the world is bad or evil, that is, in any sense the opposite of good: the world of modern physics is neither "good" nor "bad," it has no reference to either attribute, because it is indifferent to that very distinction. It is a world of fact alien to value. Thus such terms as "good" or "bad," "perfect" or "imperfect," "noble" or "base" do not apply to anything in or of nature. They are human measures entirely.

¶3. A third negation then follows. A nature pronounced "good" by its creator in turn proclaims the goodness of the maker and master. "The heavens tell the glory of God and firmament proclaims His handiwork" (Psalm 19). That is to say, the glory of God, visible in His works, calls forth in man admiration and piety. The modern heavens no longer tell the glory of God. If anything, they proclaim their own mute, mindless, swirling immensity; and what they inspire is not admiration, but dizziness, not piety, but the rejoinder of analysis.

¶4. The disenchanted world is a purposeless world. The absence of values from nature means also the absence of goals or ends from it. We said that the non-created world makes itself blindly and not according to any intention: we must now add that this renders the whole status of intentions and ends in the scheme of things problematical and leaves man as the sole repository of them. How is he qualified for this solitary role, for this ultimate monopoly on intention and goal?

II

With this question we turn to the second theme, from the modern doctrine of nature to the modern doctrine of man, where again we shall look for the negations of biblical views implied in the affirmations of modern theory. We easily discover such negations in the ideas of evolution, of history, and of psychology as they appear in the forms of Darwinism, historicism, and psychoanalysis—three representative aspects of the contemporary concept of man.

¶1. The cardinal biblical statement on the nature of man, let us remember, is contained in the second great pronouncement of the creation story after that of the creation of the universe— the statement, made with particular solemnity, that "God created

man in his own image, in the image of God he created him."
This sentence is the second cornerstone of Jewish doctrine, no
less important than the first supplied by the all-inclusive, opening
sentence of the Bible. And just as the first, concerning nature
as a whole, is denied by the modern doctrine of nature, so the
second, concerning man, is denied by the naturalistic doctrine
of evolution as it applies to the human species.

In the Darwinian view, man bears no eternal "image" but is
part of universal, and in particular of biological, "becoming."
His "being," as it actually turned out, is the unintended (and
variable) product of unconcerned forces whose prolonged inter-
play with circumstances have "evolution" for their joint effect but
nothing (not even evolution as such) for their aim. None of
the forms arising in the process has any validity other than the
factuality of its having "made the grade"; none is terminal either
in meaning or in fact. Man, therefore, does not embody an
abiding or transcendent "image" by which to mold himself. As
the temporal (and possibly temporary) outcome of the chance
transactions of the evolutionary mechanics, with the survival
premium the only selective principle, his being is legitimized by
no valid essence. He is an accident, sanctioned merely by success. Darwinism, in other words, offers an "image-less" image of
man. But, it was the image-idea with its transcendent reference by
whose logic it could be said "Be ye holy for I am holy, the Lord
your God." The evolutionary imperative sounds distinctly different: Be successful in the struggle of life. And since biological
success is, in Darwinian terms, defined by the mere rate of
reproduction, one may say that all imperatives are reduced to
"Be fruitful and multiply."

¶2. Evolution, however, only provides the natural backdrop
for another and uniquely human dimension of becoming, history;
and the modern concept of man is as much determined by
historicism as by Darwinism. Here again it clashes with biblical
lore. As Darwinism finds man to be a product of nature and its
accidents, so historicism finds him to be the continuous product
of his own history and its man-made creations, i.e., of the different and changing cultures, each of which generates and imposes
its own values—as matters of fact, not of truth: as something

whose force consists in the actual hold it has on those who happen to be born into the community in question, not in a claim to ideal validity which might be judged objectively. There are only matters of fact for the positivist creed of which historicism is one form. And, as facts are mutable, so are values; and as historical configurations of fact, i.e., cultures, are many, so are value-systems, i.e., moralities. There is no appeal from the stream of fact to a court of truth.

This historical relativism-and-pluralism obviously negates the biblical tenet of one Torah, its transcendent authority, and its being knowable. "He has told you, O man, what is good": this means that there is one valid good for man, and that its knowledge is granted him—be it through revelation, be it through reason. This is now denied. Relativism—cultural, anthropological, historical—is the order of the day, ousting and replacing any absolutism of former times. Instead of the absolute, there is only the relative in ethics; instead of the universal, only the socially particular; instead of the objective, only the subjective; and instead of the unconditional, only the conditional, conventional, and convenient.

¶3. The finishing touch on all this is put by modern psychology—after evolutionism and historicism the third among the forces shaping the modern concept of man which we have chosen to consider. The psychological argument—because it seems to put the matter to the test of everyone's own verification—has proved to be the most effective way of cutting man down to size and stripping him in his own eyes of every vestige of metaphysical dignity. There has been under way in the West, at the least since Nietzsche's depth-probing into the genealogy of morals, a persistent "unmasking" of man: the exposure of his "higher" aspects as some kind of sham, a "front" and roundabout way of gratification for the most elementary, essentially base drives, out of which the complex, sophisticated psychic system of civilized man is ultimately constructed and by whose energies alone it is moved. The popular success of psychoanalysis, which gave this picture the trappings of a scientific theory, has established it as the most widely accepted view of man's psychical life and thus of the very essence of man. True or not, it has become the common currency of our everyday psychologizing: the higher in man is a disguised form of the lower.

This psychological doctrine denies the authenticity of the spirit, the transcendent accountability of the person. The moral imperative is not the voice of God or the Absolute, but of the superego which speaks with spurious authority—spurious because dissembling its own questionable origin—and this speaker can be put in his place by reminding him of his origin. Note here the reversed meaning which the "reminder of origin" takes on with the reversal of origin itself: it is now forever looked for in the depth, where formerly it was sought in the height. The reductionism, borrowed from natural science, that governs the theory of man, results in the final debunking of man, leaving him in the engulfing miserableness which Christian doctrine had attributed to him as a consequence of the Fall, but now no longer opposed by the "image" to which he might rise again.

Now the paradox of the modern condition is that this reduction of man's stature, the utter humbling of his metaphysical pride, goes hand in hand with his promotion to quasi-God-like privilege and power. The emphasis is on power. For it is not this alone, that he now holds the monopoly on value in a world barren of values; that as the sole source of meaning he finds himself the sovereign author and judge of his own preferences with no heed to an eternal order: this would be a somewhat abstract privilege if he were still severely hemmed in by necessity. It is the tremendous power which modern technology puts into his hands to implement that license, a power therefore which has to be exercised in a vacuum of norms, that creates the main problem for contemporary ethics.

III

Herewith we come to the theme of technology which I had named, together with the theories of nature and man, as the third, and practical, determinant of the present situation. It will be my contention in what follows that the dialectical togetherness of these two facts—the profound demotion of man's metaphysical rank by modern science (both natural and human), and the extreme promotion of his power by modern technology (based on this selfsame science)—constitutes the major ethical challenge of our day, and that Judaism cannot and need not be silent in the face of it.

Modern technology is distinguished from previous, often quite ingenious, technology by its scientific basis. It is a child of natural science: it is that science brought to bear on its object, indifferent nature, in terms of action. Science had made nature "fit," cognitively and emotionally, for the kind of treatment that was eventually applied to it. Under its gaze the nature of things, reduced to the aimlessness of their atoms and causes, was left with no dignity of its own. But that which commands no reverence can be commanded and, released from cosmic sacrosanctity, all things are for unlimited use. If there is nothing terminal in nature, no formation in its production that fulfills an originative intention, then anything can be done with nature without violating its integrity, for there is no integrity to be violated in a nature conceived in the terms of natural science alone—a nature neither created nor creative. If nature is mere object, in no sense subject, if it expresses no creative will, either of its own or of its cause, then man remains as the sole subject and the sole will. The world then, after first having become the object of man's knowledge, becomes the object of his will, and his knowledge is put at the service of his will; and the will is, of course, a will for power over things. That will, once the increased power has overtaken necessity, becomes sheer desire, of which there is no limit.

What is the moral significance of technological power? Let us first consider a psychological effect. The liberties which man can take with a nature made metaphysically neutral by science and no longer accorded an inherent integrity that must be respected as inviolable; the actual and ever increasing extent of the mastery exercised over it; the triumphal remaking and outwitting of creation by man according to his projects; the constant demonstration of what we can do plus the unlimited prospects of what we might yet do; and finally, the utterly mystery-free, businesslike rationality of the methods employed—this whole power experience, certified by cumulative success, dissipates the last vestiges of that reverence for nature, that sense of dependence, awe, and piety, which it had inspired in man throughout the ages, and some of which could still survive the purely theoretical analysis of nature. Kant, sober Newtonian that he was, could still voice the profound admiration with which the starry sky above filled his heart, and could even place it alongside the admiration for the moral law within. "Which one did we put there?" asked the post-Sputnik boy when his father explained to him one of the constellations. Some ineffable quality has gone out of the shape of things when manipulation invades the very sphere which has always stood as a paradigm for what man cannot interfere with. "How is it done? How could we do the same? How could we do it even better?"—The mere question divests the nature of things of a sublimity which might stay our hands.

If it is true that both religion and morality originally drew sustenance from a sense of piety which cosmic mystery and majesty instilled in the soul—a sense of being excelled in the order of things by something not only physically beyond our reach but also in quality beyond our virtue; if the wonder and humility before nature had something to do with a readiness to pay homage also to norms issued in the name of an eternal order—then there must be some moral implication in the loss of this sense, in the nakedness of things without their numinous cloak, offered up for our conquering rape. If reverence or shame has any share in the hold which moral laws may have on us, then the experience of technological power, which expunges reverence and shame, cannot be without consequence for our ethical condition.

IV

But, it may be objected, if nature has lost man's respect and ceased to be an object of his reverence, one might expect his respect for himself to have risen in proportion. Man must have gained in metaphysical status what nature has lost—even what

God has lost: man has stepped into His place as creator, the maker of new worlds, the sovereign refashioner of things. And indeed, admiration for man's achievement after his long ages of helplessness and for the genius behind it is profound and surely not unjust. The collective self-congratulation in which it finds voice sometimes takes the form of humanistic deification: the divine is in man—witness what he can *do*. But here we come before the paradox noted before, viz., that with his very triumph man himself has become engulfed in the metaphysical devaluation which was the premise and the consequence of that triumph. For he must see himself as part of that nature which he has found to be manipulable and which he ever more learns how to manipulate. We have seen before that through modern science he lost the attribute of "image-of-God," as he is not only the subject but also the object of his scientific knowledge—of physics, chemistry, biology, psychology, etc. What we must see now is that he is not merely the theoretical object of his knowledge and of the consequent revision of the image he entertains of himself; he is also the object of his own technological power. He can remake himself as he can nature. Man today, or very soon, can make man "to specification"—today already through socio-political and psychological techniques, tomorrow through biological engineering, eventually perhaps through the juggling of genes.

This last prospect is the most terrifying at all. Against this power of his own, man is as unprotected by an inviolable principle of ultimate, metaphysical integrity as external nature is in its subjection to his desires: those desires themselves he may now undertake to "program" in advance—according to what? According to his desires and expediences, of course—those of the future according to those of the present. And while the conditioning by today's psychological techniques, odious as it may be, is still reversible, that by tomorrow's biological techniques would be irreversible. For the first time, man may be able to determine, not only how he is to live, but what in his constitution he is to be. The accident of his emergence from a blind but age-long dynamic of nature (if accident indeed it was) is to be compounded by what can only be termed an accident of the second power: by man's now taking a hand in his further evolution in the light of his ephemeral concepts.

For let no one confound the presence of a plan with the absence of accident. Its execution may or may not be proof against the intervention of accident; its very conception, as to motives, end and means, must in the nature of things human be thoroughly accidental. The more far-reaching the plan, the greater becomes the disproportion between the range of its effects and the chance nature of its origin. The most foolish, the most deluded, the most shortsighted enterprises—let alone the most wicked—have been carefully planned. The most "far-sighted" plans—farsighted as to the distance of the intended goal—are children of the concepts of the day, of what at the moment is taken for knowledge and approved as desirable; approved so, we must add, by those who happen to be in control. Be their intentions ever so unblemished by self-interest (a most unlikely event), these intentions are still but an option of the shortsighted moment which is to be imposed on an indefinite future. Thus the slow-working accidents of nature, which by the very patience of their small increments, large numbers, and gradual decisions, may well cease to be "accident" in the outcome, are to be replaced by the fast-working accidents of man's hasty and biased decisions, not exposed to the long test of the ages. His uncertain ideas are to set the goals of generations, with a certainty borrowed from the presumptive certainty of the means. The latter presumption is doubtful enough, but this doubtfulness becomes secondary to the prime question that arises when man indeed undertakes to "make himself": in what image of his own devising shall he do so, even granted that he can be sure of the means? In fact, of course, he can be sure of neither, not of the end, nor of the means, once he enters the realm where he plays with the roots of life. Of one thing only he can be sure: of his power to move the foundations and to cause incalculable and irreversible consequences. Never was so much power coupled with so little guidance for its use. Yet there is a compulsion, once the power is there, to use it anyway.

V

Modern ethical theory, or philosophical ethics, has notoriously no answer to this quandary of contemporary man. Pragmatism, emotivism, linguistic analysis deal with the facts, meanings, and expressions of man's goal-setting, but not with the principles of it—denying, indeed, that there are such principles. And existentialism even holds that there ought not to be: man, determining his essence by his free act of existence, must neither be bound nor helped by any once-for-all principles and rules. "At this point," as Brand Blanchard remarks, "the linguistic moralists of Britain make a curious rapprochement with the existentialists of the continent. The ultimate act of choice is, for both alike, an act of will responsible to nothing beyond itself." (*Reason and Goodness,* p. 254.)

To me it is amazing that none of the contemporary schools in ethical theory come to grips with the awesome problem posed by the combination of this anarchy of human choosing with the apocalyptic power of contemporary man—the combination of near-omnipotence with near-emptiness. The question must be asked: Can we afford the happy-go-lucky contingency of subjective ends and preferences when (to put it in Jewish language) the whole future of the divine creation, the very survival of the image of God have come to be placed in our fickle hands? Surely Judaism must take a stand here, and in taking it must not be afraid to challenge some of the cherished beliefs of modernity. So I will dare a few Jewish comments on the contemporary ethical predicament. First a word about the alleged theoretical finality of modern immanence and the death of transcendence, or, the ultimate truth of reductionism. This is very much a matter of the "emperor's clothes" in reverse: "But he has nothing on!" exclaimed the child and with this one flash of innocence dispelled the make-believe, and everybody saw that the emperor was naked. Something of this kind was the feat of the Enlightenment, and it was liberating. But when in the subsequent nihilistic stage—our own—the confirmed reductionist or cynic, no longer the open-eyed child but a dogmatist himself, triumphantly states, "there is nothing there!"—then, lo and behold, once said with the tautological vigor of the positivist dogma behind it, namely that there is only that which science can verify, then, indeed, with eyes so conditioned, or through spectacles so tinted, we do see nothing but the nakedness we are meant to see. And there is nothing more to be seen—for certain things are of a kind that they are visible only to a certain kind of vision and, indeed, vanish from sight when looked at with eyes instructed otherwise. Thus, the bald assertion that the emperor has no clothes on may itself be the cause for the clothes not to be seen anymore; it may itself strip them off; but then its negative truth and our verification of it by our induced blindness are merely self-confirmatory and tautological.

This is the fate suffered by the biblical propositions that God created the heaven and the earth, that He saw that his creation was good, that He created man in his image, that it has been made known to man what is good, that the word is written in his heart. These propositions, i.e., what through the symbolism of their literal meaning they suggest about reality, are of course in no way "refuted" by anything science has found out about the world and ourselves. No discovery about the laws and functions of matter logically affects the possibility that these very laws and functions may subserve a spiritual, creative will. It is, however, the case, as in the reversed story of Andersen, that the psychological climate created by science and reinforced by technology is peculiarly unfavorable to the visibility of that transcendent dimension which the biblical propositions claim for the nature of things. Yet some equivalent of their meaning, however remote from the literalness of their statement, must be preserved if we are still to be Jews and, beyond that special concern of ours, if there is still to be an answer to the moral quest of man. Shall we plead for the protection of a sense of mystery? If nothing more, it will put some restraints on the headlong race of reason in the service of an emancipated, fallible will.

VI

Let us just realize how desperately needed in the field of action such biblical restraints have become by those very triumphs of technology which in the field of thought have made us so particularly indisposed to recognize their authority. By the mere scale of its effects, modern technological power, to which almost anything has become feasible, forces upon us goals of a type that was formerly the preserve of utopias. To put it differently: technological power has turned what ought to be tentative, perhaps enlightening plays of speculative reason, into competing blueprints for projects, and in choosing between them we have to choose between extremes of remote effects. We live in the era of "enormous consequences" of human action (witness the bomb, but also the impending threat of biological engineering)—irreversible consequences that concern the total condition of nature on our globe and the very kind of creatures that shall populate it. The face or image of creation itself, including the image of man, is involved in the explosion of technological might. The older and comforting belief that human nature remains the same and that the image of God in it will assert itself against all defacements by man-made conditions, becomes untrue if we can "engineer" this nature genetically and be the sorcerers (or sorcerer's apprentices) who make the future race of Golems.

In consequence of the inevitably "utopian" scale of modern technology, the salutary gap between everyday and ultimate issues, between occasions for prudence and common decency and occasions for illuminated wisdom is steadily closing. Living constantly now in the shadow of unwanted, automatic utopianism, we are constantly now confronted with issues that require ultimate wisdom—an impossible situation for man in general, because he does not possess that wisdom, and for contemporary man in particular, because he even denies the existence of its object: transcendent truth and absolute value, beyond the relativities of expediency and subjective preference. We need wisdom most when we believe in it least.

VII

It is not my purpose here to argue the "truth" of Judaism in general, or of those biblical propositions in particular which we found to be repudiated by modern beliefs. I rather ask: if we are Jews—and Christians and Muslims must ask a corresponding question—what counsel can we take from the perennial Jewish stance in the pressing dilemma of our time? The first such counsel, I believe, is one of modesty in estimating our own cleverness in relation to our forebears. It is the modern conviction, nourished by the unprecedented progress in our knowledge of things and our consequent power over things, that we know better, not only in this but in every respect, than all the ages before us. Yet nothing justifies the belief that science can teach us everything we need to know, nor the belief that what it does teach us makes us wiser than our ancestors were in discerning the proper ends of life and thus the proper use of the things we now so abundantly control. The arrogance with which the scientifically emboldened reason looks down on past ignorance and, thus blind to past wisdom, assumes confident jurisdiction over the ultimate issues of our existence, is not only terrifying in its possible consequences, i.e., objectionable on grounds of prudence, but also impious as an attitude in lacking the humility that must balance any self-confidence of finite man. Such humility, or modesty, would be willing to lend an ear to what tradition has to say about the transempirical, nondemonstrable meaning of things. Attention to our tradition is a Jewish prescription, directing us, not only to the human wisdom we may pick up here, but also to the voice of revelation we may hear through it. At the least, the modesty of thus listening—a modesty amply justified by our helplessness before the fruits and uses of our acquired powers—may guard us from rashly dismissing the seemingly archaic, biblical views as mere mythology that belongs to the infancy of man and has been outgrown by our maturity. The simple attentiveness of such a stance may help us realize that we are not completely our own masters, still less those of all posterity, but rather trustees of a heritage. If nothing else, the tempering of our presumed superiority by that injection of humility will make us cautious, and caution is the urgent need of the hour. It will make us go slow on disregarding old taboos, on brushing aside in our projects the sacrosanctity of certain domains hitherto surrounded by a sense of mystery, awe, and shame.

VIII

The recovery of that sense, something more positive than the merely negative sense of caution which humility suggests, is the next step. Informed by the idea of creation, it will take the form of reverence for certain inviolable integrities sanctioned by that idea. The doctrine of creation teaches reverence toward nature and toward man, with highly topical, practical applications in both directions.

As to nature, it means especially living nature, and the reverence in question is reverence for life. Immediately we see the practical impact of a creationist view on the choices open to modern technology. God, in the Genesis story, set man over all the other creatures and empowered him to their sovereign use: but they are still his creatures, intended to be and to adorn his earth. Subjection, not biological impoverishment, was man's mandate. Nowhere does the Jewish idea of man's preeminence in the created scheme justify his heedless plundering of this planet. On the contrary, his rulership puts him in the position of a responsible caretaker, and doubly so today, when science and technology have really made him master over this globe— with powers to either uphold or undo the work of creation. While biblical piety saw nature's dependence on God's creative and sustaining will, we now also know its vulnerability to the interferences of our developed powers. This knowledge should heighten our sense of responsibility. Exploit we must the resources of life, for this is the law of life itself and belongs to the order of creation: but we ought to exploit with respect and piety. Care for the integrity of creation should restrain our greed. Even if it means foregoing some abundance or convenience, we must not reduce the wealth of kinds, must not create blanks in the great spectrum of life, not needlessly extinguish any species.

Even if it hurts the interest of the moment, we must, for instance, stop the murder of the great whales.

I say this is a religious or ethical responsibility derived from the idea of creation which sanctions the whole of nature with an intrinsic claim to integrity. It is, of course, also plain utilitarian common sense, putting the long-range advantage of our earth-bound race before the short calculations of present need, greed, or whim. But quite apart from these parallel counsels of prudence (so easily buffeted by the winds of partisan argument, and always conditional upon the conceptions of our advantage and the cogency of our reasoning), it is something absolute, the respect for the manifestation of life on this earth, which should oppose an unconditional "no" to the depletion of the six-day's plenitude—and also, we might add, to its perversion by man-made genetic monstrosities.

IX

With even greater force than for the idea of nature does the idea of creation inspire reverence for man, for he alone is said to be created "in the image of God." Though the ethical implications of this mysterious concept are vast and deserve fuller elaboration, I will indicate only a few. Concerning the "shaping" of this image by man himself, the Jewish posture should be, in the briefest formula: education—yes; genetic manipulation—no. The first kind of shaping is our duty, and of necessity mankind has been doing it, badly or well, since the beginnings of civil society. We may grievously err in the ends and the means of education, but our mistakes can still be redeemed, if not by their victims themselves, then by a coming generation: nothing has been irretrievably prejudged, the potential of human freedom is left intact. At its best, education fosters this very freedom; at worst, it does not preclude a new beginning in which the struggling, true form of man may yet be vindicated.

A different thing is the dream of some of our frontiersmen of science: the genetic remaking of man in some image, or assortment of images, of our own choosing, which in fact would be the scientist's choosing according to his lights. The potentially infinite, transcendent "image" would shrink to charts of desired properties: selected by ideology (or will it be expediency? or fad?); turned into blueprints by computer-aided geneticists; authorized by political power—at last inserted with fateful finality into the future evolution of the species by biological technology. From sperm- and ovary-banks there is only one step to synthetic gene-patterning, with a catalogue of samples to suit different tastes or needs.

Here again, quite apart from the terrible danger of error and shortsightedness inherent in our fallibility, quite apart, that is, from considerations of prudence—we simply must not try to fixate man in any image of our own definition and thereby cut off the as yet unrevealed promises of the image of God. We have not been authorized, so Jewish piety would say, to be makers of a new image, nor can we claim the wisdom and knowledge to arrogate that role. If there is any truth in man's being created in the image of God, then awe and reverence and, yes, utter fear, an ultimate metaphysical shudder, ought to prevent us from meddling with the profound secret of what is man.

Or to take a less apocalyptic or fanciful, and at the moment much more real example, Jewish morality should say: persuasion—yes; but not psychological manipulation such as brainwashing, subliminal conditioning, and what other techniques there are, be they practiced in Peking or New York. I need not elaborate. The reader can easily draw the connection from the idea of the image of God to the principle of respect for the person, his freedom, and his dignity. The protest should always be against turning men into things. My general point is that the idea of creation provides a ground for reverence, and that from this reverence there issue definite ethical precepts in the context of our present situation.

One may object that these precepts, as far as our examples show, are of the restraining or prohibiting kind only, telling us what not to do, but not what to do. True, but it is at least a beginning. Also, we may remember that even the Ten Commandments are mostly don't's and not do's. Moreover, the negative emphasis fits the modern situation, whose problem, as we have seen, is an excess of power to "do" and thus an excess

of offers for doing. Overwhelmed by our own possibilities—an
unprecedented situation this—we need first of all criteria for
rejection. There is reasonable consensus on what decency, honesty, justice, charity bid us to do in given occasions, but great
confusion as to what we are permitted to do of the many things
that have become feasible to us.

X

Let me conclude with one last instance of rejection, which
may not fall on too willing ears among Jews, who notoriously
value length of life. Contemporary biology holds out the promise of indefinite prolongation of individual life. This must seem
glad tidings to those who, in accord with an ever sounded theme
of mankind, consider mortality an evil, a curse, which may yet be
lifted from us, at least be lessened by indefinite delay. But if we
abolish death, we must abolish procreation as well, the birth of
new life, for the latter is life's answer to the former; and so
we would have a world of old age with no youth. But youth is
our hope, the eternal promise of life's retaining its spontaneity.
With their ever new beginning, with all their foolishness and
fumbling, it is the young that ever renew and thus keep alive the
sense of wonder, of relevance, of the unconditional, of ultimate
commitment, which (let's be frank) goes to sleep in us as we
grow older and tired. It is the young, not the old, that are ready
to give their life, to die for a cause.

So let us be Jews also in this. With young life pressing after
us, we can grow old and, sated with days, resign ourselves to
death—giving youth, and therewith life, a new chance. In ac-
knowledging his finitude under God, a Jew, if he still is a Jew,
must be able to say with the Psalmist:

> We bring our years to an end as a tale that is told.
> The days of our years are threescore years and ten,
> Or even by reason of strength fourscore years . . . .
> So teach us to number our days,
> That we may get us a heart of wisdom. (Ps. 90)

WHAT IS THE CONTEMPORARY PROBLEMATIC OF ETHICS IN CHRISTIANITY?

James M. Gustafson
Professor of Christian Ethics
Yale University
New Haven, Connecticut

The contemporary problematic of ethics in Christianity is not a new one, although the forms that it takes are particularly bound to our age. Christians are still dealing with certain fundamental issues that are present in the Scriptures and in the Christian tradition, and are not foreign to the whole humanistic and Western religious history. As a way of stating the basic issue, I turn to a distinction made by Ernst Troeltsch.

In 1902, Ernst Troeltsch published a long review of the theologian Wilhelm Herrmann's *Ethik,* under the title "Grundprobleme der Ethik." [1] In this fruitful essay Troeltsch spades up and turns over a variety of questions that are present in all of ethics, and looks at them particularly in response to what was happening in Christian ethical thought in his time. Among the distinctions he makes there, one, which he and Max Weber used widely, indicates a persistent tension in the ethics of the Christian community. This is the distinction between *Gesinnungsethik* (ethics of disposition, intention, conscience) and *Objektivethik* (ethics of law, norms). The history of Christian ethics, and the contemporary problems among writers in the field can oversimply but usefully be interpreted around these two ideal-types and the relations between them.

In this essay I shall first indicate the ways in which the issues Troeltsch was pointing to are present in the history of ethics in Christianity. Second, I shall indicate with some references to recent writings that the issues are still alive. Finally, I shall state how it seems to me that the problematic ought to be stated in our time.

Disposition and Norm in the History
of Christian Ethics.

Since its inception as an independent religious movement, Christianity has been occupied with the relation of the religious and moral dispositions of persons and the community to authoritative norms, laws, and rules that stand over against the human subjects. A distinction commonly made in textbooks between the teachings of Jesus and those of his contemporary fellow Jews (grossly distorting, like most textbook distinctions), states that Jesus' ethic was one that put primary emphasis on the motives and dispositions of men, while Jewish ethics emphasized the law. To a considerable extent, the Pauline conception of the Christian life is stated in the language of a new life, a new spirit, a new inner freedom, and a new disposition to love. Yet, Paul's polemical powers had to be directed against antinomianism among the early churches. A historical stereotype that one finds on the lips of many untutored Protestants refers crudely to the same general distinction: Catholic ethics are legalistic and authoritarian, and do not arise out of the inner religious life; Protestant ethics are expressions of a living religious faith, they are matters of the heart.

I shall indicate briefly three significant texts in the history of Christian ethics in which we see some of the ways in which disposition, attitude, intention, and spirit seem to be related to law, norms and somewhat objective values. These will illustrate the problematic that is the focus of this essay.

The first is from Paul. The early church in Corinth was filled with dispute over what the proper implications and expressions of their religious life were with reference to matters of ritual practice and morality. One passage, in which Paul addresses their behavior, is pregnant with possibilities for interpreting Christian ethics, namely, I Corinthians 10:23-11:1.[2] Paul's preaching of the gospel had apparently led to a wide expression of spontaneity, freedom, joy, and love. It appears that this freedom had led to breaking some of the accepted rules of sexual behavior, and that some enthusiasts were excessively imbibing the sacramental wine. They were also eating meats that had been sacrificed to the gods of Greece. Paul's response is primarily on a practical level; he had to give a practical moral counsel that was consistent with his religious teachings, and would also guide behavior. Thus he wrote, "All things are lawful," but then he added, "not all things are helpful." "All things are lawful but not all things build up." It appears that some of these Christians were living by the first half of these injunctions, "all things are lawful." They claimed for themselves a new creaturehood, a new manhood, a vivifying spirit. They seemed to assume that their conduct was morally and religiously proper if it was primarily informed by this new life, if it was an immediate expression of their new common spirit. The actual effects of their conduct seemed to be less important than the inner spirit out of which action with moral consequences emerged. An obvious response to the first sentences of the text is this, "What things are helpful?" "What things build up the community?" As if hearing this response, Paul makes clear some guidelines, which particularly deal with the question of eating meats sacrificed to Greek gods, but which also have more general significance. "Let no one seek his own good, but the good of his neighbor." On the one hand, "Why should my liberty be determined by another man's scruples?" on the other, "Give no offense to Jews or to Greeks or to the church of God." "Be imitators of me, as I am of Christ."

The point I wish to make is that while the new life "in Christ" was the primary focus of Paul's message, with its freedom and its love, it became necessary for the apostle to indicate some of the more or less objective directions, norms, patterns, and ends which were consistent with the new life they have claimed as a result of their faith and experience. "Only let your manner of life be worthy of the gospel," (Phil. 1:27) he wrote to the Philippian Christians. Perhaps something near the same point is made in a text that has an interesting history in Christian ethics, Romans 8:2. "For the law of the Spirit of life in Christ Jesus has set me free from the law of sin and death." There is the claim for freedom from "the law of sin and death," but it is the law of the Spirit of life that has made men free. The law of *the Spirit of life* seems to indicate a dynamic impulsion of new life, but it is nonetheless *the law* of the Spirit of life. This principle of life seems to require that Christians ask: What is the proper form, the proper order of life, that is consistent with the newness? What considerations are to be brought to bear in determining how the Spirit of life should be objectified through human action in the order of the world around us?

The second text is from Thomas Aquinas. In the *Summa Theologica,* first part of the second part, beginning with Question 106 and following, Thomas deals with the relation of the "new law" to the "old law." [3] In this passage the "old law" refers particularly to his understanding of Old Testament law, and not simply to the natural law. The passage is significant because it runs counter to some of the more stereotyped impressions of Thomistic ethics. Popular Protestantism has viewed Thomas Aquinas as the fountainhead of natural law thinking in Christian ethics, and this tradition has been confronted primarily in the nineteenth- and twentieth-century forms of a rationalistic rigorism which, accompanied by an authoritarian church, has led to presumably morally unexceptionable answers to such questions as birth control. But Thomas was also a Paulinist and an Augustinian, and this side of his thought comes into relief when he deals with the new law. The new law, Thomas says, is chiefly the grace of the Holy Spirit. It is the Spirit in man; it is a gift of God's gracious love in its primary reference, and only in a derivative sense is it a new written precept. The new law is grace; it is part of God's redemptive work for man which enables man to live in peace with God. As moral teaching the new law does not justify men in the eyes of God. He goes on in Q. 106 and subsequently to indicate that the letter would kill without the healing grace of faith. He is asserting that while there is an objective moral order given in the natural law to which all men are to be conformed, in the Christian life there is also the healing grace of faith, a new spirit. Without this gift of grace, without this "new law" the old law and the new in its written form do not give life, but kill.

In more ethical terms, what is this new law, this Holy Spirit in the heart? It is the law of love. And what is the law of love? It is both a spirit and a commandment. It gives a new disposition and attitude, but in its written form it also requires that man should love God, and love his neighbor as he loves himself. In Thomas we see again the double side: the inner power and the outer demand. The substance of the new law, he asserts, is not contradictory to what is found in the old. The new law reveals the heart of the matter of the old. The Spirit enables man to obey the law freely, whereas formerly he was constrained to obey it; here Thomas follows and cites Augustine. The new law, as well as the old, absolutely prohibits certain things, and absolutely prescribes others, but the grace of the Spirit enables man to have direction in the determination of his conduct in that realm between what is absolutely prohibited and prescribed.

Paul, the champion of liberty, was concerned with what is helpful and edifying. Thomas, the champion of law, is concerned with grace as the dwelling of the Spirit in the believer, as well as with the precepts of the law.

The third reference is to Martin Luther, the celebrator of Christian liberty. It is important to see how the great reformer, whose primary concern was the salvation of man by God, related his proclamation of liberty and love to the realm of moral behavior. Surely morality was not the center of his concern. He sought both to preach and to describe what God's justifying grace did for man to free him from self-justification, and from self-righteousness before his Creator and Redeemer. There was a moral outcome to this, though it is not delineated in scholastic refinement; man was given a new love which led to his concern for the neighbor; "faith active in love" became a repeated note. Indeed, Luther used the metaphor of man as a tube through which the love of God flows out to others in the world. On the side of man's acceptance of God's grace, Luther could say that "a Christian man is a perfectly free lord of all, subject to none." He has been accepted by God in faith. On the side of man's moral expression of this freedom and love, he could say, "a Christian man is a perfectly dutiful servant of all, subject to all." [4] His inner life of faith, love, and freedom are expressed outwardly in service and love of the neighbor. This appears to be the celebration of a new disposition; indeed, Luther was preoccupied with the possibility that specification of the moral expectations of this new life in the form of rules and laws would lead to a new "works-righteousness" which would again jeopardize one's faith in God's grace and love.

But God, for Luther, does not rule the world simply by saving men. Indeed, Christians are at once sinners and justified, and thus need both to repent daily, and to have God's law to give order to their lives. God's law not only makes men aware of a standard before which they recognize themselves as sinners, and thus are moved to repentance; it has a "political use" as well.[5] Inwardly free Christians owe obedience to the magistrates, whether Christian or Moslem, for it is the function of the civil state to preserve the moral order of creation against the pressures of human disobedience. Christians will understand that the magistrates are "masks of God," and that they obey God through obedience to the magistrates. They will not seek to justify themselves before God by their civil moral rectitude, but freely obey what the law requires. Thus again, one sees that the new disposition of freedom and love meets objective laws, and normally it is conformed in external acts to these laws.

But Luther was concerned that in the expression of the new life Christians remember not only to obey the law, but also remember that this life is a gift of Jesus Christ, and that Christ is an example to them, as well as a gift. Christ was to be the pattern of their lives in their relations to others; Christians were to seek the neighbor's good as Christ sought their good. They were to be Christs to their neighbors. It should be noted that in terms of our basic distinction, Christ is primarily a pattern for the inner man, his disposition toward the neighbor, rather than the giver of a new set of moral teachings to be obeyed. The extent to which Christ presents a norm for the ends and values that Christians will seek is a question of debate about Luther's ethics. My opinion is that the Christ who brought the inner life for Luther not only motivates a concern for the neighbor's need, but provides a fundamental pattern and image of how that motive is to be expressed through deeds.

These brief dips into the history of Christian ethics suggest the importance of the Troeltschian distinction. Perhaps against the backdrop of these historical vignettes the problem can be restated. The message of Christianity is primarily one of salvation: God has acted to save men, to bring them into the relationship of fellowship with him. This relationship is expressed not only in praise to God, but in moral life. The moral life is an expression of the Spirit dwelling within man, of the new life he presumably has. Is this all that Christianity has to say about morality? If it is, where is the Christian to find the norms, rules, laws, and values to govern his actions? Do they spring up spontaneously from his new relation to God? Does the Christian simply comply with the existing moral ethos with a new spirit? Does he have insight into the moral order of the world, to obligatory oughts and ends which God has ordained in creation? What is the relation between religion (man's relation to God) and ethics (man's relation to the world)? These questions persist in the contemporary literature of Christian ethics.

The Contemporary Problematic in Christian Ethics

The Troeltschian question takes on new nuances in current discussion. Current discussion, more recently in Catholicism than in Protestantism, has been determined by the prevalence of an anti-legalistic mood. Both thinkers and doers, writers and moral activists, have attended to the negative restrictions on moral activity that seem to be imposed by traditional moral codes and traditional religion. "Legalism" is the most common whipping boy. The term is generally used to refer loosely to two quite different things. On the one hand it refers to an attitude, to what Catholic moral theology calls "excessive scrupulosity." This is an attitude that is overconcerned with the maintenance of an untarnished conscience, with the righteousness of the self, with the desire to have an answer which gives absolute moral certitude under particular situations. The reaction against the legalistic attitude is made on both religious and moral grounds. It seems to deny the primacy of God's gracious love and forgiving mercy in favor of the earning of merit before God. And it cripples creative responses to new and changing moral situations in the human world. Thus Father Bernard Häring and other progressive Catholic moral theologians stress the dynamic morality of love as the antidote to the excessive scrupulosity that non-historical natural-law thinking and juridical conceptions of the church have imposed upon Catholic people. Excessive scrupulosity leads to defensive morality; it cramps in fear of doing a wrong rather than delights in the possibility of doing something right. Protestantism is pervaded with a similar reaction against pietistic Protestant forms of legalistic attitudes. The Reformation themes recur: self-righteousness is to be attacked; the gospel is first a message about God's goodness, and not about the moral demands that are to be met if one is to be justified before God. It offers freedom, joy, and love.

On the other hand, legalism refers to the precise predetermination and pre-conception of what deeds are to be done and what ends are to be achieved in all particular circumstances. The awareness of historical change, of the altering constellations of the human world, and of the complexity of the details of moral issues under unique circumstances have all led to the critique of a morality of absolute commandments and rules, or of the statements of ends and ways of acting that are right in every circumstance. The current term in vogue is "situation ethics," which is too imprecise to suggest more than a very general concern of many Christian moralists. Situations are historically unique, and thus require unique responses: this would be the most extreme characterization of the general drift. Other characterizations would discriminate between what is abiding and what is unique in situations, and thus offer a more refined and discriminating approach to making moral decisions. In Catholicism, the protest is against both platitudinous high-level generalizations of the "natural law" and against the rationalistic deductive process by which priests have moved from the natural law to what individuals are to do. In Protestantism, the protest is often against norms and rules that are believed to be false and absolutistic abstractions removed from an existential involvement in the concrete and the particular.

A series of distinctions drawn from a variety of sources summarizes the mood of contemporary Christian ethics. 1) A dynamic morality in distinction to a static morality. Father Häring writes about a dynamic morality of love, which is man being grasped by love, and being loving toward others, rather than the application of static conceptions to changing historical circumstances. 2) An open morality in distinction to a closed morality. The language is, of course, Bergson's, and is used by Christians to suggest that morality ought not to be restricted by encrusted tradition or anything else that stifles its vitality and its sensibility to the new. 3) A morality of love in distinction to a morality of law. When the point is stated this way it already assumes an antithesis between love and law that is questionable in the eyes of many Christian moralists; love perhaps is used here to refer to a disposition of the self more than to a moral norm. 4) The celebration of the liberty of the individual conscience in distinction to submission to an external, extrinsic morality enforced by external, extrinsic authorities. In Catholicism this has led to new appreciation of the notion of prudence in traditional Catholicism, the virtue that enables men to apprehend what is fitting to the particular situation, and for the liberty of conscience that seemed to get lost in the juridical authority of the church. There is a recognition that many times the church and its priests went beyond the rightful limits of authority in their rules and their judgments. The issue raised freshly, however, the question of what forms the individual's conscience.

5) Orientation toward the future in distinction to orientation by the past. Bultmann's theological ethics would be one example of a stress on being freed from the past, and being open to the future. It is an open future, it is God's future, and men ought not to restrict its possibilities by foreclosures that are determined by past loyalties. The delicate questions, of course, are how one's orientation toward the open future is given direction from the past, and what clues one has to use in deciding which possibilities are better and worse in what is opening into the present. 6) Visceral morality in distinction to cerebral morality. The distinction is drawn from a comment of an exercised student who came to my office and exclaimed, "Mr. Gustafson, the issues are so visceral and you're so damned cerebral." There is a stress among Christians, as among many other young people particularly, on the importance of the depth of one's moral passions,

the extent of one's involvement (which includes emotional involvement), and a reliance in part on one's feelings of indignation or of approval to be the guide to one's action. No doubt there is more latent and manifest ideational content in visceral responses than some persons recognize, and the question has to be raised: what judges between the profound moral feelings of two people or groups (e.g., the far left and the far right) if not rationality and defense of values that can be discussed.

7) The importance of the situational circumstances in distinction to the importance of rational norms. This has been alluded to previously in this paper, and does not require elaboration here.[6] 8) A theological interpretation of God as acting in history, in and through events, commanding, "speaking," involved in the world, in distinction to God as the giver of an immutable law. The theological revolution in Protestantism and Catholicism, which has affirmed the God of the Bible to be active in history, has opened up morality. H. R. Niebuhr, for example, spoke of God acting in all events of which one was a part. The moral response, in turn, is to be determined by one's discernment of what God is doing in these events. We will return to such affirmations again. Protestant theological students for twenty-five years, for example, have learned to interpret the Decalogue not as immutable dictated law, but as an explication of God's covenant with his people. The primary facts are God's calling his people into being, his leading them out of slavery in Egypt, his covenants with them through Abraham and Moses. The Decalogue, then, is interpreted in terms of these affirmed facts. Men are to be morally responsible to what God is doing, has done, and will do, and the Decalogue is a summary of his commandments that is consistent with his actions. Thus one does not read them in a "legalistic" way.

9) A morality of creative responsibility as distinguished from a morality of conformity to law, or from a predefined established order. Indeed, a Swedish theologian, Gustaf Wingren, in his *Creation and Law* uses the word "activity" as a replacement for the word "law." [7] The task of men is to be creatively responding to the activity of God, to God's "ordering" work rather than his "order." A conception of man as a creative and responsive

being, rather than as a conformist to essential orders, meets a conception of God as creative, governing, and redeeming activity, rather than the giver of laws.

Clearly not all of these points can be reduced to Troeltsch's distinction. But that distinction enables one to look at issues that are present in the above effort to delineate the mood of Christian ethicists today. The reader will have to pursue reflection on some on these questions on his own, since this overview does not permit detailed treatment. It is important, however, to indicate where some of the theological well-springs for this mood can be located.

Certainly the mood is congenial in many of its aspects to the theology and ethics of Karl Barth.[8] Barth's well-known efforts in theology were to displace man as the starting point for theological reflection with the revelation of God in Jesus Christ. Similarly, in ethics he replaces the more-or-less natural moral question, "What ought I to do?" with one that has a theological starting point, namely, "What does God command?" Indeed, to start with the human moral question is to limit the possible answers that God can give, and is to rely upon human moral reflection at the center of ethics—a manifestation of unfaith or sin. The ethical question, like the theological one, he asserts, has already been answered in Christ. Thus moral action is witnessing to God's grace revealed in Christ; it is attesting to God's action in Christ, endorsing what God has already done for man there. This leads to an openness, for one will be prepared to hear what the gracious permitting and commanding God requires man to do. Since God's actions and commandments are concrete and not general, one will hear the command of God in the concrete. The most extreme statement about this concreteness follows:

> The command of God as it is given to us at each moment is always and only one possibility in every conceivable particularity of its inner and outer modality. . . . We encounter it in such a way that absolutely nothing either outward or inward, either in the relative secret of our intention or in the unambiguously observable fulfillment of our ac-

tions, is left to chance or to ourselves; or rather in such a way that in every visible or invisible detail He wills us precisely the one thing, and nothing else. . . .[9]

Once one is prepared to hear the objective command of God in the moment, he is permitted to engage in ethical reflection, he reads the Scriptures to find out what God commanded men in other circumstances, and he exercises his rationality in all the ways required. But the answer is not the sum of research and reflection; it will be given in faithful obedience to God's command.

With a different Protestant theology, Bultmann is another writer whose thought is congenial to the mood. He can write, for example, that one who stands in faith, in radical obedience before God, and in love, does not need ethics in terms of general moral principles, or rules which govern the conscience. Love enables one somehow to know what the need of the neighbor is. Put in terms used in this paper, a fundamental disposition to love is the gift of faith, and the claim seems to be that it will cognitively discern what a person ought to do in the immediate situation.[10]

Paul Lehmann uses the notion of the theonomous conscience, a notion also used by Tillich but substantiated with different theological principles. For Lehmann, *"Christian ethics aims, not at morality, but at maturity. The mature life is the fruit of Christian faith. Morality is a by-product of maturity."* This mature life, which is the effect of God's graciousness in the fellowship of the Church, is to give "the believer a clear understanding of the environment and direction of what he is to do." Lehmann asserts that the Christian is characterized by "imagination and behavioral sensitivity to what God is doing in the world to make and to keep human life human, to achieve the maturity of men, that is, the new humanity." The objective moral principle appears to be "what God is doing to make and keep human life human." But one does not discern this through logical methods using absolute moral principles as the first or second premises. Indeed, Lehmann has an extensive polemic against what he calls "absolutist ethics." Rather, he seems to hope for and expect the theonomous conscience, which is "the conscience *immediately sensitive* to the *freedom* of God to do in the *always changing* human situation what his humanizing aims and purposes require. The theonomous conscience is governed and directed by the freedom of God alone (*italics mine*)." [11]

H. Richard Niebuhr, in *The Responsible Self,* develops a view of "man-the-answerer" or responder which he differentiates from "man-the-maker," or "man-the-citizen" or law-obeyer. This model of responding is paralleled by an understanding of God acting creatively and redemptively in the world. The task of the serious moral man, then, is to interpret what is going on in the place where he is called to make a fitting response. This interpretation includes the theological dimensions, and obviously becomes intricate and subtle. The whole thesis is climaxed with this statement: "Responsibility affirms: 'God is acting in all actions upon you. So respond to all actions upon you as to respond to his actions.' " [12]

Finally, Catholic moral theology is being reformed in the light of the biblical theological interpretation of God's acting in and through history. This means that natural law does not emerge as immutable abstract principles discerned by reason as it apprehends the essential structures of being, but rather it emerges in man's changing historical experience. Also, the Pauline and Johannine language of the New Testament about the believer's relation to Christ assume a new centrality in moral theology. Thus Häring can affirm that "Christian morality is life flowing from the victory of Christ"; it is the fruit of the life of faith and devotion to Christ. For a progressive Catholic, however, the ensuing ethics are not as occasionalistic as Barth's, nor as open-ended as Lehmann's view of the theonomous conscience might suggest. Love and law are not antithetical to each other; the Augustinian themes alluded to earlier persist. [13]

The reader will be aware that these citations do far less than justice to the nuances and depths of the writings referred to. They are made to indicate some of the substantial theological and ethical texts which to one degree or another authorize or sustain what I have depicted as the mood of contemporary Christian ethics. Troeltsch's distinction cannot be implanted mechanistically upon these men. But it points to a persisting problem in each of them: Christian faith has a reference to the moral subject: it affects his dispositions and attitudes, his perspective and his intentions. But does it give objective moral guidance? There are "objective ethics" in these writers: it is God's command one is to obey; what one is to do will be disclosed in the human situation; God's humanizing aims are to be endorsed, and so forth. But precision and clarity of rules and principles are on the whole subordinated to a more historical and open-ended view of morality than has sometimes been the case in Christian ethics.

The principal voice in American Protestant ethics that speaks against the stream is that of Paul Ramsey. There are also many conservative Roman Catholics who are critical. Ramsey starts with what he views as the particular Christian contribution to morality, namely the idea of love as it is given in the New Testament. But love does not, for him, provide an automatic guide to right action. It has to be "inprincipled," which is to say that moral men and communities have to develop those principles which are derived from love and in turn are to be applied to complex moral situations. Ramsey believes that the just-war theory in the history of Christian ethics is one such effort. For example, the principle of noncombatant immunity in war is one of the principles that is inferred from love. Increasingly in his writings, Ramsey is concerned to stipulate rules at various degrees of specificity that he believes to be binding on the moral actions of Christians. Objective ethics is both a possibility and a necessity in this view. But Ramsey also has to attend to the more open-ended and dynamic element that is present in Christian thought. Thus he can write, after vigorously showing the need for rules in the "wastelands of relativism," that Protestant ethics has become:

> These rules are opened for review and radical revision in the instant *agape* controls. . . .
> Christian love, which often acts within the law and lays down rules or principles for the guidance of action, still continues to exert free and sovereign pressure—since Jesus

Christ is Lord—toward fresh determination of what should
be done in situations not rightly covered by law, natural
justice, or even by its own former articulation in principle.[14]

The consensus in contemporary Christian ethics seems to
affirm that ethical reflection begins with openness provided by
grace, by the historical nature of existence, and by the nature
of man as responder, and then has to find some way to discern
what the proper objective moral target is. The champion of an
objective ethics of rules and principles has to avoid static fore-
closure and permit love to review and revise, or freshly to determine in the situation what is required. The problematic of contemporary Christian ethics is not very different from the problematic in Pauline ethics.

How Ought the Problematic in Christian
Ethics to Be Stated Today?

Within the limits of space, I can only suggest approaches that
may make more precise some of the issues that have to be
formed within the persistent problematic of Christian ethics.[15]
I have no radically different one to stipulate. It seems to me to
be theologically, historically, sociologically, and psychologically
appropriate in our time to view moral existence as initiating and
responding activity in a changing field of action, with all of its
interactions, and all of its dynamics, change, and structures. It
is healthy to view oneself as the creative and responsible participant in the ongoing development of history and even nature, as
an actor who together with others is giving direction and order
to the events of the times in which we live. Freedom, whether
claimed as a gift of grace or a psychological necessity, is on
the whole healthy. The questions within this that need more
precise work at the present time are two.

The first deals with the formation of the person who claims
his freedom and accepts his responsibility as a moral actor. If
one is to use the word conscience, the questions can be asked:
What forms the conscience that is to govern choices, responses,
and acts? What loyalties and values will be at the center of the

integrity of the conscience? What communities will not only proclaim values that we could affirm as morally sound for all men,
but how will these communities function so that these values
can be internalized? If the language of dispositions and fundamental intentionalities is used, the questions would be similar.
In particularistic Christian terms: how does a Christian loving
disposition come into being? What kind of religious community
life engenders and sustains it? If Christians intend to be disciples
of Christ, imitating him with wholeness and joy, how is this intention formed in pluralistic societies, in rapidly changing times?
I suspect there is a parallel issue confronting Judaism today as
well.

The second deals with the task of developing some objectivity
to our ethics. If impulses, visceral reactions, and intuitions are
not sufficient, what more is needed? If formed consciences, dispositions and intentions are not sufficient in themselves, from
where does some direction come? We can no longer be funda-
mentalists who have a literally divinely-authorized Scripture to
give direction to moral action. We recognize that reason does
not apprehend and disclose the moral structures of the world in
a simple way, and if it did the difficulties of relating the univer-
sals to the particulars, of course, remain. I believe a number
of steps need to be taken. Within the Western religious communities we can discern what human values are recognized and
supported by our Biblical and religious traditions, what significance is given to man and his activities. With awareness of our
own historical location, we can reflect carefully under the light of
the Biblical texts what God seems to be enabling and requiring
us to be and to do. We need to be sophisticated in gaining
and interpreting the factual information that is pertinent to the
moral issue at hand. With the use of our religious resources, our
reason, and our factual information, perhaps we can begin to
come closer to the best solutions to the complex moral issues
of the day.

NOTES

1 Troeltsch, "Grundprobleme der Ethik," *Gesammelte Schriften,* Vol. II, Tübingen: J. C. B. Mohr (Paul Siebeck), 1913, pp. 552-672.

2 The Revised Standard Version is used here.

3 Thomas Aquinas, *Summa Theologica,* First Part of the Second Part, Questions 106-108, in A. C. Pegis, ed., *Basic Writings of St. Thomas,* Vol. II, New York: Random House, 1945, pp. 949-78.

4 Martin Luther, "A Treatise on Christian Liberty," in *Three Treatises,* Philadelphia: Muhlenberg Press, 1, 1943, p. 251.

5 Martin Luther, *A Commentary on St. Paul's Epistle to the Galatians* (1535), London: James Clarke, 1953, pp. 297ff.

6 See J. M. Gustafson, "Context vs. Principles: A Misplaced Debate in Christian Ethics," reprinted in M. E. Marty and D. Peerman, eds., *New Theology No. 3,* New York: Macmillan, 1966, pp. 69–102.

7 Gustaf Wingren, *Creation and Law,* Philadelphia: Muhlenberg, 1961, p. 152, and elsewhere.

8 Karl Barth, *Church Dogmatics,* II/2, Edinburgh: T. & T. Clark, 1957, pp. 509-781.

9 *Ibid.,* p. 663-64.

10 R. Bultmann, "The Meaning of the Christian Faith in Creation," in *Existence and Faith,* New York: Meridian Books, 1960, p. 222. See also, p. 182, p. 261, and elsewhere.

11 Paul Lehmann, *Ethics in a Christian Context,* New York: Harper and Row, 1963. Quotations are from p. 54, p. 116, p. 117, and pp. 358-59.

12 H. R. Niebuhr, *The Responsible Self,* New York: Harper and Row. 1963, p. 126.

13 Bernard Häring, C.S.S.R., *The Law of Christ,* Vol. I, Westminster, Md.: The Newman Press, 1963. The quotation is from p. vii.

14 Paul Ramsey, *War and the Christian Conscience,* Durham, N. C., 1961, p. 179, p. 190. See also his *Deeds and Rules in Christian Ethics,* New York: Scribners, 1967.

15 See J. M. Gustafson, "Theology and Ethics" in D. T. Jenkins, ed., *The Scope of Theology,* Cleveland: World Pub. Co., 1965, pp. 111–32, and *Christ and the Moral Life,* New York: Harper and Row, 1968, the last chapter.

MODERN IMAGES OF MAN

Julian N. Hartt
Noah Porter Professor
of Philosophic Theology
Yale University, The Divinity School
New Haven, Connecticut

I

This paper deals with a fragment of the story generally identified as the conflict between the sacred and the secular in the modern world. It is the part of the story in which the imagination is the battleground, and the triumph of the secular is grasped as the ascendancy of images of man, in which his autonomy vis-à-vis any power and value greater than he is expressed. Before we treat these images we ought to be as clear as possible on the fundamental conflict between the secular and the sacred. I shall begin with several suggestions about this subject. Then a number of images in the conflict will pass in review. In an epilogue a question is raised about the possibility of a reforming of the image of man.

Sociologists and other theologians largely agree that we are living in the Age of the Secular. Religious people, who do not recognize this and adjust the forms of the religious life appropriately, live under that awful threat, Irrelevancy. Progressive religious thinkers, on the other hand, hail the secular spirit as a major advance into the kingdom of light. For the latter secularism seems to signify the attainment of maturity for Western man after an unnaturally prolonged and complicated adolescence: Man has at last come of age, let us rejoice that he has put away childish fears and hopes. What then is this spiritual condition for and in which the sacred retreats before the irresistible advance of the secular? Here are some unsystematic suggestions:

(1) It does not help very much to confuse civil and secular

with each other; or religious and sacred. The civil state has taken over many public services once the preserve of religious communities, for example, care of the indigent and education of the young. These are hardly illustrations of the triumph of the secular. They are cases of things grown too massive for efficient and equitable management by any agent other than the state itself. Moreover it is possible to talk meaningfully about a civil religion, as Professor Robert N. Bellah has done in his famous essay, "Civil Religion in America" (*Daedalus* WINTER 1967). Some sense of the sacred is invoked in that religion, such as the covenant in which we are bound with all who have fought the good fight and kept faith with that God who demands of this nation that it make freedom, justice, and equality available for all who live in it.

In other ways the sense of the sacred slips away from the precincts of the religious forms which once governed it. One might think here of the "sacredness of human life," felt by many to be a more certain bulwark against the triumph of scientifically sophisticated brutality than the traditional forms of religion.

(2) The tension between the sacred and the secular begins to come into its own when the sacred appears as the *inviolable* and the secular as the *manipulable*.

We begin by supposing that objects and places are the prime instances of the inviolable: the Holy of Holies, the Ark of the Covenant, the elements of the sacrament, etc. This is a foreshortened view of the matter. Places and objects are designated vehicles and condensations of sacred power; and they are designated by the sacred power itself, not by mere men. Accordingly, what is sacred by divine designation—places, objects, persons—can be violated, de facto. A temple can be burned, befouled, in a word, *desecrated*. But if one believes that the temple is sacred by divine designation one would say, I suppose, that it cannot be violated with impunity. Vengeance is mine, I will repay, says the Lord.

Are people greatly impressed by this threat of divine reprisal for sacrilege? That is a kind of social psychological question; and I am just enough of a theologian to be interested in it. So I judge that people are not so much impressed by this threat as their parents were. If that is the case, is it part of the triumph of the secular?

An unequivocal answer to that question would be difficult to defend. We would have to know several other things before we got on to that. For one, how has the inviolability of divine power been understood? With the metaphor of the river that spreads destruction all around when it is dammed? As an obligation enforced by profound guilt and anxiety when it is denied practical expression? As a punishment that gathers terror the longer its execution is postponed?

Other possibilities come to mind. One of them is remarkably close to a salient theme in contemporary philosophical religiousness: the silence of God. Out of the Biblical past comes the word against those who have violated the inviolable, "Though you call upon me on that day, I will not answer, for your sins are multitudinous and you are unrepentant." Happily this is still a long ways from a classical Christian doctrine, namely that God withdraws his sustaining grace from the wretched sinners in Eden, and they cannot therefore but be confirmed in sin and guilt until God Himself in mysterious mercy lets His grace again abound. Even so, the prophetic threat is sufficiently terrible because it means that though God takes notice of his people's plight, he will not speak the saving word. From the immensity of the punishment we learn more about the enormity of the offense than its commission alone would have provided.

Now again the silence of God has become a philosophical religious theme. It is in Heidegger, notably. It appears in radical Protestant theologians who are considerably more instructed by the achievements of secularism than they are by the profundities of Heidegger. The note of inviolability of divine power is missing from both: the divine silence is not an expression of divine judgment. Yet Heidegger believes that modern man is wandering in a dense thicket, a creature in a fair way to lose his soul beneath the ever mounting pile of thing acquisitions or in the ever deepening cloud of anonymity emitted from mass culture. Thus something inviolable in the order of being takes shape, whether or not we are licensed to call it divine. If, that is, we say that the conditions of authentic existence cannot be violated with impunity, we are at the least saying being will not let us have it both ways: I cannot will both to be myself and to be your instrument; if I am the master of my destiny, up to death, then I cannot blame my lot on you or upon society, fate or any other god. Put it paradoxically and say that the requirements of freedom are inviolable and the penalty for violating them is—bondage. A poor bargain. To make it poor and inescapable a divine enforcer would seem to be unnecessary. That latter discovery does not clearly or simply redound to the greater glory of the secular spirit.

That spirit begins to take on substance when the question, Do we need to suppose that anything is absolute and therefore inviolable? receives an automatic negative. Heraclitus said, "Flux is king." He believed, also, that there is an eternal rational order. That sentiment excludes him from the spirit of secularity. Against the background of historic religion and philosophy in the Western world the secular spirit stands forth as the intent to lay hands on human life and make something suitable of it without fear or expectation of interference or assistance from beyond. So disposed, men learn quickly that nature, too, is a malleable thing. Thereafter nature is soon sliding down the order of being into pure instrumentality for human aggrandizement. If thereafter man were induced to see himself as a being entirely immersed in nature, what would prevent him from going down the chute into pure instrumentality? We can throw off the subjunctive and say that modern man is in that descent. The doctrine of the sacredness of human life floats out behind like a small and tattered parachute, insufficient for anything except to mark the place where he lands, in case anybody misses him.

(3) The sacred is the ultimately mysterious. The secular is the essentially resolvable.

Mysterious does not mean obscure or unknowable. There is nothing necessarily obscure or knowledge-defeating about love. If love be not palpable wherefore should we call it love? Yet love is a mystery in two fundamental senses: one, it resists assimilation or reduction to anything else; and this is the primordial wisdom in calling love itself divine. Two, love has its own "reasons." What question is more common and less manageable than "Why do you love me?" Love is a great begetter of Why's; but it is begotten by none.

So far as the secular is the comprehensive imperium of the modern world it seeks to resolve all mystery into the operationally manageable. Thus life was for many epochs looked upon as mysterious in its source. Now science is close to producing the real thing synthetically. Once the mystery of amino acids was resolved the great door to the creation of living matter began to swing open. The vista thus disclosed contains a more comprehensive control of human life than even oldtime gods would have imagined for themselves. Having it they would not have risked sharing it with mere men.

Reverence, then, is an emotion of dubious import for the secular spirit. For reverence casts an aura of transcendental value around some aspect or form of being; and whatever is thus endowed cannot be modified or reduced but must be humbly acknowledged and its graces devoutly petitioned and patiently awaited. There may be things in the secular imperium that ought to be fairly respected; but all boundaries therein and thereof are provisional. They may hold us up today. Tomorrow, or on some tomorrow, those boundaries will be penetrated and incorporated by the imperium of scientific man.

Two illustrations of this mentality come to mind. One is the drive to bring outer space within human utility. The other is the systematic penetration and reduction of personal privacy. In both directions the notion of immovable boundaries is an offense to the secular spirit. The power is not yet available to spread human ordure throughout the cosmos. The age has made splendid progress in persuading more and more people that the love of privacy for any purpose, defecation, copulation or celestial meditation, is a destructive residue of ancient religion, and, thank God, can at last itself be destroyed by the technological wizardry of the mass media. Why save your genitals for private consumption when millions can be blessed by a fearless demonstration coast to coast?

There is something odd about this situation. The mass media, which make possible the generalization of social protest from one place to many with the speed of light, nearly, are an indispensable part of a manipulative and exploitive social system. The movement which makes the dedicated use of four letter words the key to existential freedom presupposes a system that makes nothing of the free exercise of reason. From which it appears that the only way to make a case is to be one.

(4) The sacred relates man to transcendent being and value. The secular impulse is to deny either the reality of a transcendent realm or its accessibility. If that realm cannot be reached why should we worry about it? The rhetorical question is an answer. Epicurus put it thus: If the gods exist and are aware of us, they would wish us well. To which we can properly add: Thanks for nothing.

"Transcendent" does not necessarily argue "religious." There are religions of immanence, celebrations of the here-and-now indifferent to what might be yonder and later. And there are intuitions of transcendence, the sense of magnitudes looming above the earthly scene that command loyalty but make no promises.

Nonetheless one religious community or another has been native ground for the sense of the transcendent until now. We should hardly doubt that there it has too often mingled with obscurantist suspicions of rapid and inclusive social change. This may partially account for secularistic attacks on every transcendental element in religion, and for a spirit of toleration for religious understood as devotion to the human ideal, as well.

From this one might too swiftly conclude that *secular* and *humanistic* are properly synonomous. In fact the sense of the transcendent does not rule out even the most evangelical affirmation of the importance of being human; and so far as the secular spirit is committed to the manipulation of human life its humaneness may legitimately be questioned. Furthermore we have come too far down that road to feel profoundly reassured when told that the human engineering now possible will surely be applied to man for his improvement. How wonderful it would be if all the hideous torments heaped upon human life in this century were but nightmares, diabolical dreams; and soon we should wake and thankfully shake off that horrid sleep. It is salty comfort to realize that far worse can be done than has been done.

It is in this area that the principal issue between the sacred and the secular is joined. The question is whether there are limits, both cosmic and personal, beyond which man may not pass and live, neither the intruder nor his posterity if they build upon his sacrilege. Hard upon that comes the next question: Are those limits observed, held, that is, in full survey from the other side or above; and enforced by transcendent power? Or is it just that man, going too far too fast, is bound to run out of steam, and collapse, not in some place ordained for his execution, thither lured by some cunning observant god, but rather, accidentally, beside the road in the desert?

Whatever one's religious disposition such questions unleash anxiety. For that there is no help in returning to believe again in vengeful Deity. That is a misdirected sense of the transcendent. It bespeaks a God who enters the human picture only to punish. Before such a being we might have to grovel; but we could not worship him, we would not worship him so long as any vital sense of human worth remained.

So the contest is for the imagination of man and for his loyalty. For his imagination because he must have a vivid perception of his being, and of his value if he is to stand tall among the other creatures of dust and claim his inheritance. But the contest between sacred and secular is for his loyalty, too. If he has no interests other than his own to serve, the sense of the transcendent can only confuse him; and he has enough to do to determine what he owes of earth's store and the blood's to generations yet unborn. If, however, he grasps in the mind's eye conjunctions of his interests with those of beings all around and beyond, then he ought to act as befits a steward rather than an absolute owner; for what he does matters everywhere and forever.

II

So much for a general account of the conflict of the sacred and the secular. We have now to consider eruptions of this conflict in the realm of images. This we do convinced that as the image goes so goes the man. I do not intend to argue here the merits of that philosophical anthropological assumption.

The Darling. One of the hardiest of religious images of man, this one has been as severely bruised as any in its career in the modern world. It survived the heavy storms which battered the traditional forms of the religious life from the fifteenth century on; but it had to take up life as part of philosophical system and lore. Thus Biblical man was the darling of God. Created in the image of God he was destined to endure divine judgment and finally to enjoy divine favor without stint. "Whom the Lord loves he also chastens": the Maker of the heavens and the earth cares infinitely for his darling, so He will not always be angry; and in due season He will bless him with riches past imagining. But when the philosophical creators of the modern world could no longer embrace such an image they were ready with conceptual surrogates. The Ego of the Cartesian system, Spinoza's intellectual lover of God, Kant's noumenal self, bodied forth as the rational moral agent who is entitled to hope for immortality—a perfection of happiness and virtue in a realm transcending the limitations of the world of space, time, and flesh: each in its own way makes man a special case in the cosmos.

The first half of the nineteenth century saw even greater triumphs for the human ideal. Now man stands forth as the crux of the world dialectical process. He is microcosmos, as he wags so wags the world. Religious imagery having been overcome on the high plateaus of philosophic system, man's self-realization is just as firmly as ever believed to be the grand business of reality.

Then the storms broke; and the image of man as the darling and paradigm of the cosmic process was shattered. Darwinism sealed man back into the animal kingdom and made Chance king therein. Nietzsche proclaimed "God is dead!" and ripped the amiable religious disguises away from man's infinite capacities for deceit, resentment, and self-aggrandizement. Freud reduced the sense of the transcendent to an illusion at the far end of neurotic feeling-projections, and piously scanned the future for an end to the sorry business. And two world wars have made it very easy to believe that the veneer of civilization is terribly thin and brittle. So the erstwhile darling is diminished to a naked ape whose capacities for hell-raising have latterly assumed a cosmic magnitude. In that respect alone man seems now to have transcendental properties.

The Victim. The successor of the Darling seems to be the Victim. This is the image of man trapped inextricably in a system. Whatever the system is it destroys freedom, integrity, hope, dignity—in a word, humanity. If the system fails in this fell but purblind intent, it is as much an accident as a triumph of human courage or wit.

This image may not strike you as being wholly modern. Powerful expressions of the theme do certainly come to mind. There is Sophocles' Oedipus. Is he not a victim of a cosmic system, against the decrees of which he struggles in vain? But we cannot ignore the fact that in Sophocles' theology the cosmic system is committed to justice; or the equally compelling fact that Oedipus implicates himself in his fate. Moreover Oedipus is made finally to stand as a ward of a special divine providence: the curse under which he lives and dies is intended to be a blessing for many.

A more likely candidate for Victim in the imagination of the ancient world is the figure of Pentheus in *The Bacchae* of Euripides. He is the earnest young man whose evangelical zeal for abolishing immoral and irrational religion arouses the fury of Dionysus, whose cult is the target of Pentheus' reforming passion. The radical theologian is destroyed by his own mother in a peculiarly horrible way. But brutal as it is to say so, Pentheus asked for his terrible fate. Indeed in *The Bacchae* there is far less cosmic machinery to overtake overweening pride than in Sophocles' liturgical dramas; and far more emphasis on what we should call the dynamics of personality. Pentheus is truly a victim; but the way in which his character is his fate is supposed to be instructive to the beholder. "What he suffers, he suffers justly." From our lofty position in the moral universe we may lament that notion of justice. There are hints that old Euripides was not wholly happy with it.

And what about Job? There is a mighty image, but should we

call him Victim? He is ground into the dust in a terribly systematic way. He is the capital figure of a man upon whom unmerited suffering is heaped up with a prodigality the Book will not allow to be set down as accidental. But God never loses sight of him; and on his side of the strange transaction Job holds fast to his integrity. In the end God provides ample evidence that Job is still his darling. This theological literary turn is an undying offense to modern theological wisdom.

Our world has produced a variety of persuasive images of the Victim that have little connection with these great figures of the past. Here is Camus' Meursault, who can as easily be called the Victim as *The Stranger*. For him the deadly system is reality itself. It seduces man into loving and seeking happiness and then suspends the sword of death over every moment; so that every achievement of happiness is given a rotten heart. Here too is Hemingway's Frederick Henry of *Farewell to Arms*. For him the First World War is the commanding symbol of the System: it is a monstrously random and reckless dealer of the cards of life, love, and death. With her last breath his beloved Catherine tells it like it is: "It's just a dirty trick." We remember, too, Heller's Yossarian of *Catch-22*. Again war and the military mind are symbolic condensations of a system of reality that is quite literally mad. Heller encourages us to laugh at his antics; but we know all along that his dedicated program for living forever will not protect him from the knife. Are we uplifted at the end to realize that the System does not particularly care who gets it? If you can't win what sort of a fool is the man who keeps trying? Not in the same league with *The Idiot* of Dostoievski; but then the mad Russian was religious.

So far the Victim does seem to have a sense of the transcendent. He is haunted by a boundary and a power he cannot pass through or effectively resist. But neither the limit nor the power of death adds anything of nobility, anything of meaningfulness. Death is simply the last and greatest of brute facts.

Kafka's rendition of the Victim is a somewhat different case. In his view the System has transcendental nuances running beyond random and unbeatable death. K (or Joseph K) cannot help believing that the System knows a good deal about him and has something in mind for him. He is therefore committed to cracking the secret. Like Job he wants a fair hearing. Unlike Job he never gets it. All he gets are cryptic signals from beyond. They do not save him from dying—"like a dog."

These literary allusions are not intended to suggest that creative writers in our time are the only ones obsessed with the image of the Victim. The contemporary world reeks and reels with this image. Here is the man—his name is Legion—who sees himself trapped in the economic system. He is too thoroughly boxed in, buttoned down, tied up, over-committed, and under-motivated to break out. The System has swallowed him whole, all that he is and ever hopes to be. Not even death carries the value of transcendence. It simply marks the end of the book in which every chapter is just more of the same old life. Life in the squirrel cage is just one damned thing after another. But who knows what it's like outside?

Thus are we led to represent ourselves as depotentialized and dehumanized by the massive structures and unremitting demands of society. The Victim cries, "What can *I* do against such might and cunning? Nothing! So it is better for all concerned, for me and my loved ones, to adjust, fit in smoothly, and make no ripples."

This is a plausible plea. Secular society generates a powerful sense in the individual of being an easily replaceable part of a huge machine that has a will of its own. This is what we mean by the instrumentalizing of human life. We are hard pressed to find a loftier epitaph for the good citizen than "His was a useful life." In his natural lifetime the Victim knows that he is used. He does not know that he is loved as a singular person whether or not he is a good tool.

Where this sense of being depotentialized by the System prevails personalistic religion surely has its work cut out. If the overpowering social system calls all of the shots upon which my visible success in this world depends, how real can an appeal to a transcendently wise, powerful, and solicitous God possibly be? He is often invoked as the divine friend of the system. Why should I think he has any interest in me if I am hostile to the system?

The Stranger. This image may seem somewhat less harsh than the Victim. Perhaps this is because it seems to grow out of a long and distinguished religious history. The ancient Israelite is enjoined to remember that he, too, was once an alien in a strange and heathenish land, and his father was a wandering Aramean. The Christian for many centuries saw himself as a pilgrim, a stranger in the world here below, waiting to be summoned to his true and heavenly home; and in the meantime warned to be on guard against the wiles of the world, the flesh and the devil.

No doubt these versions of the Stranger differed from each other in important ways. Nevertheless they made common cause against every cultural and psychological inducement to render ultimate loyalty to any social order that professed not to fear God and thus was free to dispose of human life as some human want might suggest. Thus these religious versions of the Stranger were both steeped in transcendental power; and they were both therefore able to generate acute discomfort in the hearts of those who did indeed bow the knee and submit the will to cultural gods.

The image of the Stranger has largely lost that power. Such discomposure as now grips the men of this age is no longer clearly related to a vision of a kingdom of messianic beauty grasped as the true homeland of the spirit. The Stranger is now likely to express one or the other of two strikingly different formations of alienation. The first of these is an alienation from self brought on by anxiety about missing one's share of the goodies so lavishly displayed in our society. Many people seem to find something morally dubious about a man who does not perform—read "produce"—up to standard. The fact that he is missing out on some of the goodies packaged for men of his rank is ample proof that he is not doing his best. So he is condemned to live in a cloud of anxiety and self-accusation. If the nearest of kin and community do not add their reproaches to his own, he is unusually fortunate. "How *could* you think of settling down *here* when with proper effort from you we could live where we really belong?" Today for uncounted millions that is the existential question.

The other shadow cast by the Stranger is very different from this; it is indeed quite alienated from it. This is an idealistic recoil from the standard expectations and payoffs of the social system. It is a prophetic convulsion of disgust with the callousness towards the very misery produced by the system; and with the self-excuses and self-righteousness of the people who represent themselves as Victims of the system and yet pick off most of the goodies. This sense of shattering failure, and a complementary anxiety lest restitution and amendment be delayed too long, are the products of the intuited requirements of the ideal ethical commonwealth. Much of the power of this Stranger comes from his burning conviction that he is thus in touch with a transcendent realm of value. It is interesting that he is likely to reject the offices of traditional religion as in any way necessary for ascertaining what his forefathers would have called the perfect will of God. His gnosis of the real good is intuitive, personal, invincible, complete. He has been appointed to tear down the walls of the evil City of Man. Some time after he has finished persons of like purity may be able to build a blessed community in its place.

Here then is the image of the idealistic prophet who is a stranger by choice and transcendental vocation, a stranger in his own land and among his own people. Unkempt, girt about with leathern garb, fiery-eyed, ready with thunderous denunciation of a crooked and corrupt generation: he is decidedly not a reed quaking in the tepid blast of middle-class disapproval. Forearmed with sophisticated theories about ideology and class structure he knows that every defense of the System is tainted with mortal corruption; and so every penitential gesture short of reaching for the blow-torch is phony.

I suggest that the unavoidable and so far unresolvable social phenomenon of the age, the shattering confrontation of adult and youth, is best understood as a violent conflict of images. The adult generations make much of the Victim; and particularly the Victim of the social system. They say: "We would have made the important changes, for we too dreamed dreams and saw visions of a better world for all. But the system in the end was too much for us. And now all we ask is a little understanding and some peace and quiet. Let now thy servant depart in peace. Anyway, what's so terrible about the General Motors way of life? It has kept you in college in creature comfort for lo these many many moons." To which the prophetic Stranger makes reply: "In behalf of true humanity we spurn your good life of meaningless and expensive baubles. It stinks of hypocrisy and sell-out. You ask for peace but seek to perfect the uses of violence. Your home is a prison and you are trapped in it. Your church is a museum and a graveyard of high hopes, honest love, and humane faith."

There are doctrinal factors in this conflict but they are secondary. There are philosophical arguments but they are indecisive. The main thing is a brutal clash of images.

The Player. This image takes wing and flies to the antipodes, far far away from the embattled scene just surveyed and perhaps from all the other images considered so far. For here man appears as the creature of make-believe. He draws out of imagination a world that never was on land or sea and for nothing but his own delight.

Four elements of this image will bear inspection. One: It is not an accident that man lives in a world created by imagination. Two: The make-believe world is able to take man into itself despite the commonsensical prejudice that the imaginary is subjective and private. Three: Therefore the make-believe world is something into which man can escape either to avoid or to transcend the factual order of things. Four: The fictional world is intrinsically interesting and valuable whether or not life in the factual order of things is directly improved by it.

One. Human creativity begins in and with the imagination; and this is the singular faculty for apprehending the nonexistent. Imagination grasps all of the modalities of the contrary-to-fact: the not-here-but-elsewhere; the once-but-no-longer; the not-yet-but-sometime-coming. This is a remarkable power. The sense of the transcendent lives in it.

Two. The make-believe world is able to internalize man, it can ingest him and thereby take him out of himself. For art this is the phenomenon of identification with a character of fiction. For religion this is the phenomenon of participation in a community that reaches back into a past much deeper and richer than my individual past, and opens out upon a future I shall never occupy in my own person.

Three. Therefore I can plot a course that will carry me out of the agonies and blandishments of the factual order of things into a vastly richer world of make-believe. I can convert all or the gist of life into a game, and confess that the rules thereof are set by a mysterious Player to whom the game belongs even though he may not appear in it in his own form. Thus one of the most persuasive summons to embrace harsh realistic duty is "Play up, man, and play out the game!"

Four. Enjoying the form and power of the Game, I may reasonably suppose that the factual order, at its very best, is only a part of it and quite the least significant part at that. The transcendent Player did that with his left hand. Why then should I treat the System with the deadly seriousness it ordains?

The secular spirit holds the make-believe in deathly serious suspicion. So the self-alienated Stranger is compelled to invent sober excuses for playing. And the prophetic Stranger is compelled to give his games a divinely explosive metaphysical warhead. In both cases we may begin to suspect that someone is taking hold of the factual order with the pincers of unstated dogma at the behest of uncriticized image. The dogma is that reality is a joyless affair. The image is that of man condemned to work incessantly at an impossible task in a strange and hostile land. Thus are the Victim and the Stranger jumbled together in a barbarous unlovely package: an unholy marriage. No wonder the offspring look upon the Player as a man from Nowhere with a bag of implausible magic.

The Plastic Man. With this image we pass from the modern to the mod. It is the furthest out; and it is therefore the quintessentially contemporary.

The Plastic Man comes in two shapes. One is merely modern, he has, that is, some connections with earlier ages. We may call him Transitional Man. The other is mod, his connections are with the future. We may call him the infinite adapter.

Transitional Man is a creature linking an earlier state of

human development and a later one. What he is in himself does not matter so much as his being a stage on the way to something better. So far this image has a connection with earlier representations of those generations of mankind which lived towards a consummation not available to them. "All of these, though well attested by their faith, did not receive what was promised, since God had foreseen something better for us, that apart from us they should not be made perfect" (Hebrews 11:39, 40. RSV). The man who wrote this and the people for whom he wrote it believed that the time of consummation was at hand; and *they* were therefore not transitional: in them history was about to be fulfilled, not of themselves or for themselves but through God and for his glory. The modern image of Transitional Man has left these religious dimensions behind. Nietzsche is the great prophet of this change. That admirable creature he calls the Free Spirit is a "bridge to the future." And even of Superman Nietzsche proclaims: "He exists to be overcome." Not, of course, by pygmies but by still greater realizations of creative power. The triumph of evolutionism forced an overcoming of Nietzsche's vision of Time as an eternal self-enclosed circle. Thus Transitional Man faces a really open future. There is no end in sight because there is no end. But this means that man is not the end, either. He is not the cherished objective of some purpose, dim or bright, latent in the cosmic process. He is a happy accident, though no one else laughs.

So the connections Transitional Man has with eschatological man are not all that rich. The Darling has a future bright with glorious promise because God has his eye and his hand on him. Whether or not this creature has a home beyond the skies makes no difference to his status in the flow of history: his fulfillment is assured; and time has then an end. So eschatological man is grounded and crowned in transcendence. At the center of his being there is an invincible divine summons to seek a country where God is all in all, the perfecter of human life. For God is the potter, human life is his clay, and he is fashioning something beautiful in his own sight.

Transitional Man is not such a summons. He is a product of a creative élan wholly within nature which only in man knows the score and cares about the outcome. Only in man does nature care. But can man's caring make a difference in the direction of the evolutionary process? Granted that Transitional Man is secular—he answers to no Outsider. Does he have the right as clearly as he has the power to change the genetic stock, to throw the switch and send humanity off on quite a different track in a trackless field of possibility?

The question is formidable. How can we answer it wisely unless we know what images of himself Transitional Man has? Does he cast himself in the role of Lord of all he surveys? Is he, rather, the pragmatic utilitarian Engineer, ready to build what others design? Or does he still contend with a desperate sense of being a servant of a higher purpose to which he must answer now for his intention and later for the far-flung consequences?

Transitional Man is not all the way out from under that transcendental sense. Plastic Man in his mod formation, has made it: The Infinite Adapter. This is the image of man as sheer possibility.

The Infinite Adapter has radically reoriented the eschatological horizons of human existence. For him there is no single all-encompassing goal upon which all lines converge. Even death has been reoriented: it is something that happens to people who deserve it, the aged, the rigid, the structured. Otherwise it is a pointless accident, a cancellation of possibility rather than a possibility in the infinite field.

Personal identity also requires reorientation for the flowing purposes of the Infinite Adapter, the mod version of Plastic Man. He is by definition a multitude: I am many, not one or two. I am not what I was. I shall become, if I want, what I am not. That is the backward-forward plurality of the Infinite Adapter. There is also the lateral plurality: I am this and that and these and those and here and there, all at once. I am everything and nothing. I am on the road but not to anywhere in particular. Send not to ask who I am because by the time you get through I will be something else.

The image of the Infinite Adapter is something more than the creature who rotates through a select number of life-styles, either in imagination or in the factual order. He is a being with many masks each of which has as good a claim as any other to being authentic. But there is nothing behind the shifting masks except the will to be various. This and nothing else is the real I of the Infinite Adapter, this desire to play at being all things. The object of the play is not to deceive. The object is to taste the essence of the part, so far as this can be procured by projection rather than by condensation or concentration of self into one thing. Thus he does not stretch towards some form of existence that would be the ideal completion of destiny. He assumes that he will have time enough to enjoy the essence of the pluriform life. Beyond that lie the dismal plains of uniform existence, undistinguishable at the far edge from the motionless salt sea of death.

In his own sight therefore Plastic Man in his mod version is the maker and molder of his own pluriform life. That is the ideal. I think that the cultural realities are not unambiguous. The social system needed plastic, a cheap synthetic fabric adaptable to a multitude of purposes; and without value or interest in itself. Thence to the metaphor: The System heats, twists, beats, massages, molds, synthesizes human life into an incredible variety of roles and functions, none of which has an intrinsic value or interest in itself. If we take the next step and construe the image of the System cybernetically we can very well make the Prophetic Stranger a function of the System itself: that moment in its operation when a malfunction lights up a panel and circuitry, sophisticated beyond all comparison with ancient magic, begins at once to resolve the block, discharge the tension, and go on to glory.

Undoubtedly this image of the System is profoundly distasteful for the moment to the self-idealization of Plastic Man in his mod version. He sees himself as potent to make of himself anything he wants. He is the self-creating creature. And he is therefore, in his own image, perilously godlike. His essence is sheer possibility. Yet he lives in a system that will not admit that there is any possibility beyond its control.

Thus the latest image out stands in a puzzling relationship to the social system. The system needs a high degree of plasticity

in its human constituents. Some of its constituents imagine
that this plasticity is a metaphysical freedom with which they
are mysteriously endowed. To others it seems to be the antithesis of freedom because it assumes a systematic right and
power to manipulate human life without respect to ultimate
ends. If therefore Plastic Man is the best the age can produce
as the image of creative personal freedom we may wonder
whether the triumph of secularism is a solid victory for man.

III

Here then are samples from the bag of images we carry
about as children of modernity. I have a final question to
pose: Are images reformable? Or put in religious terms: Is
the imagination redeemable? In both forms the question assumes
that re-formation is or might be desirable. Many will deny that
a re-formation of images is now desirable. I suspect that many
would deny that it is possible. In our time that is more likely
to be a triumph of the social system than of metaphysical intuition and argument.

Let us take a case in point, and suppose that Plastic Man, or
The Victim, for that matter, seems to us to be a deficient image.
It strikes us, let us say, as clearly faithful to some aspects of our
existence but it distorts others. Perhaps many people see themselves as Plastic. But we say to them, "That's not good enough!
You cannot really be all things, either in succession or simultaneously. If you are versatile you can work and play at many
things successfully. But that very bundle of diverse accomplish-
ments is a product of high standards of performance rigorously
applied by a self in command at the center. *That* is the real self,
the real you; for without it your life would be a random clutch
of interesting fragments."

I believe that this sermonette is fundamentally sound. We may
nonetheless reasonably doubt that sermons, short or long, accomplish anything other than the self-vindication of the
preacher when things go wrong on schedule. If they are to
accomplish anything meatier our sermons must also draw on

viable and vivid images. Rail at Plastic Man if he arouses a
holy ire. But do not expect him to wither under philosophical
attack. He will yield ground, if not crown, to a more commanding image expressed and conveyed in fable, song, drama, dance,
liturgy, through which some deep spring of humane passion
is released.

"Some deep spring of humane passion" bespeaks a theological
view of man: in the depths, at the core, of his being man is a
creature of humane passions. This doctrine is a stranger in
the councils of the learned today and an alien in the haunts of
mod culture. In high and low places the ruling image of man
is that of a creature loaded by nature with animal drives that
must be tamed and transformed. That is the arduous and costly
business of civilization. The ferocious paradox of civilization,
on those terms, is clear indeed. The process of humanizing the
naked ape may give him access both to instruments that geo-
metrically augment his capability for destructiveness and to
high-level principles justifying his exercise of this capability.

What are the images with which to oppose and best these
low estimates of man? I think they are the cluster called the
Player. There is the creature capable of spontaneous joy and
sorrow. He can summon a world from the depths of his being
as spirit; and use it as a test of sanity of the factual order of
things; and beyond that as divining-rod to probe for richer kingdoms than eye has yet seen. True, the Player is an illusionist.
But he can set a play "to catch the conscience of a king." He
can spin a yarn first to engross King David and then to spring
the trap of awful guilt beneath his feet.

So I lament a world that makes preachers of clowns rather
than clowns of preachers. I lament a world that insists on making laughter self-accusative, and every tear a reflex of guilt. It
is high time again to dance before the Lord; and not as a puppet
jiggling madly on the end of the string but as a free spirit leaping
in unbridled joy to greet the undying radiance of the Eternal.

Will that image stick? We may doubt it, saying, "It is too
frivolous for a world so sick and tormented." So let us remember
that man is not redeemed from sin and suffering by "the spirit

of heaviness." He does not get on with his proper business in a mood of unrelenting self-seriousness.

Contemporary culture lays that mood upon us all. That is a major triumph of secularism as a paradoxically religious force. For if there is no one else to keep an eye on our interests we cannot afford ever to close both eyes or even wink promiscuously. That is what I call self-seriousness.

I do not of course know whether the Player can cure this dis-ease of the spirit of modern man. Nonetheless we should send for him.

IS THERE A COMMON JUDAEO-CHRISTIAN ETHICAL TRADITION?

Irwin M. Blank
Rabbi, Temple Sinai
Tenafly, New Jersey

A. J. Ayer[1], in discussing the way of the logical positivists, proposes the following formulation of the standards by which the logical positivists evaluate the possibility of knowledge. They are, in part, as follows:

1. All knowledge is empirical and is derived from the sense-continuum.

2. The meaning of an empirical proposition is the mode of its verification. In other words, I must be able to make the observations in order to verify and I must know what kind of data I need in order to make and to verify the statement.

The proposition with which we are directly concerned has to do with whether or not Judaism and Christianity share a common core of ethical concepts. Several kinds of data are available to us. Such data will include what Jews and Christians say about their ethical systems and what Jews and Christians do about their ethical systems. What they say about their ethical systems will reveal similarities and discrepancies of meaning. What is done, subsequently designated as history, may reveal either the extent to which the meanings are not realized and/or the extent to which meanings and responses are positively or negatively correlated.

One might wish to conclude that if the record of vicious and brutal treatment which Jews have received from Christians is any indication, then we cannot be said to share any common ethical core. But this would be an unwarranted conclusion because the record may be a record of alienation of Christians from Jews rather than an alienation of Christianity from Juda-

ism. This last mode of reasoning is, in effect, that expressed in the
Vatican II statement on anti-Semitism. Insofar as ethics express
the nature of the "ought" we cannot argue from history for we
do not know what Judaism would consider the "ought" given the
same conditions. Given the condition of extensive sovereignty
what would the Jewish "ought" consist of and what would Jews
do with reference to that "ought"?

Ayer suggests that there are four classes of statements made
by ethical philosophers: There are propositions which express
definitions of ethical terms, viz., sin is x, y, z, virtue is a, b, c;
or judgments about the legitimacy or possibility of certain definitions, viz., while sin is x, y, z, we may have a condition where
x, y, z, are present but the action will not be considered as sinful
because of the presence of another factor—what Catholics are
saying when they speak of objective and subjective guilt; or a,
b, c, which normally define virtue may be present but because
of the presence of some other factor to do that which is normally
considered as virtuous may actually be sinning in this instance.
It should be possible to evaluate Jewish and Christian ethical
systems in terms of definitions and the range within which those
definitions apply.

The second type of proposition proposed by Ayer is the
description of the phenomena of moral experience and their
causes, viz., with reference to the sex drive, the nature of an
ethic of sexuality will be determined in part by the concept of
its source.

The third type of proposition is the exhortation of moral virtue, viz., "Do justly, love mercy and walk humbly with thy God."
"By faith shall you be saved."

The last category is that of actual ethical judgments, viz., he
who does such and so, or does not do such and so shall be ad-
judged virtuous or sinful as the case may be, viz., "To think
adultery is to commit adultery." It should be possible first to
categorize Jewish and Christian propositions in terms of these
four categories and then match the categories to note their correspondence or divergence.

But, there is the problem of history. In Alvin Reines' formulation of the concept of polydox Judaism which, crudely stated,

claims that there are Judaisms not a Judaism, he, we believe, would insist that for each concept under discussion we must ask when was this so and was anything else being said at that time? Any statement as to the normativeness of a concept will have to be validated by demonstrating that nothing to the contrary was being said at that time, or if it was being said clearly was being rejected. Otherwise, an assertion of normativeness is simply an "emotive ejaculation."

In *The Nature and Destiny of Man,* Reinhold Niebuhr says the same of Christianity when he cites the existence of Hellenistic Christianity, Pauline-Augustinian Christianity, Lutheran Christianity, to say nothing of Pre-Reformation and Post-Reformation Catholicism as larger categories.

Paul Lehmann in *Ethics in a Christian Context* notes that "the literature of Christian ethics is one of the most important pieces of evidence for the fact that New Testament ethics and Christian ethics are not identical" (p. 28).

The same can be said of the way in which the rabbinic hermeneutic rules work with Scripture as their raw material as compared with the responses of Solomon Freehof.

There are those who might insist that a consideration of Judaic morality must necessarily be based on orthodox belief and practice to the exclusion of progressives, reforming as well as liberal, and of conservatives, because the liberal or conservative formulations are heresies.

Nevertheless, there have been efforts to evaluate the extent to which Judaism and Christianity do or do not share the same ethical tradition. Primarily they are conceptual rather than historical analyses.

Using Herbert Spencer's categories of social utilitarianism (altruism) and private utilitarianism (egoism), Ahad Ha'am attempted to classify Judaism as egoistic and Christianity as altruistic.[2] Ahad Ha'am's argument begins with the proposition that Israel's ethic is primarily a national ethic of which the individual partakes, but that its thrust is primarily towards the establishment of a holy people as contrasted with the thrust towards personal salvation. The heart of his thesis, however, lies in the claim that "the moral law of the Gospels asks the natural man to reverse his natural attitude towards himself and others, and to put the other before the self" (p. 262)—that is, to replace straightforward egoism by inverted egoism. "The altruism of the Gospels is neither more nor less than inverted egoism" (p. 262). Ahad Ha'am based his claim on an examination of the teaching of Hillel, "Do not unto your neighbor what you would not have him do unto you," and of this rule's formulation in the Gospels: "Whatsoever ye would that men should do unto you, do ye even so to them." Insofar as there is a good in both of these formulations it is clearly utilitarian in nature—different sides of the same coin. Ahad Ha'am claims that a concept of justice which stands at a distance from all parties is at the root of Hillel's formulation. The "I" takes its place as an equal amongst all involved. It is neither superior nor inferior. Unfortunately, he falls into the justice-love cliché which seems to support the notion that Judaism's ethic is pragmatic and self-serving while the Christian ethic is selfless and idealistic. Thus, he cancels his original perception concerning straightforward egoism and inverted egoism. Had he operated with the Christian concept of grace, joining it with the rejection of man's naturalness, his original, and we believe correct, perception of inverted egoism would remain valid. The Christian's self-sacrificing is an effort to give up his naturalness and thus make himself more accessible to God's grace. The Jew insists on justice for himself because he is part of a society and justice must be universal if society is to endure. That he should benefit from the application of a justice applicable to all is his right. That he should demand justice for himself is his duty. Otherwise subjectivism rules the day defeating the possibility of community, albeit retaining the possibility of personal salvation.

Measured against the criteria of utilitarianism and egoism, Christianity and Judaism share a common core. Ahad Ha'am's designation of Christianity as altruistic and Judaism as egoistic does not appear to be valid. In their ethical systems Christianity and Judaism are both egoistic. The "I" is present in both. Are they both altruistic? We lack objective criteria for making this determination. Insofar as any concept of Messianism includes a concept of redemption, it is egoistic. If it can be demonstrated that there is an ethical task in either commitment which is absolutely unrelated to Messianism, hence devoid of any relationship to redemption, then we can make a determination. We suspect that neither Judaism nor Christianity is altruistic.

Leo Baeck's categories for considering the nature of the Jewish and Christian ethic are the categories of mystery and commandment. For Baeck, mystery is the sense of the unifying principle which gives life its meaning for all time, the awareness of that "which embraces" man, "the arms of eternity." [3] Commandment is the manifestation of mystery in time, God's presence in the finite now. The fulfillment of the commandment is the occasion for man's creative engagement with existence. "The foundation of life is the mystery; the way of life (commandment) is the revealed." Baeck insists that in Judaism, mystery and commandment are fused. Every awareness of the mystery carries with it a commandment and every commandment reveals a mystery. Thus, the eternal is expressed in the transitory, and the finite expresses the infinite. "Judaism lacks any foundation for the conflict between transcendence and immanence" (p. 197). "Hence," Baeck tells us, "any opposition between mysticism and ethics has no place" (p. 198). This, he would have us understand, is in direct contrast to Paulinian Christianity in which mystery became everything. Insofar as it became everything it "finally had to become for him (Paul) something tangible, namely, sacraments, and something that can be molded, namely, dogma" (p. 198). Baeck thereby clarifies for us why historically Christianity focused on the development of a systematic theology whereas its ethical system remained ambiguous. This in contrast to Jewish life in which the ethical system takes on an inner orderliness by dint of the hermeneutic rules whereas theology as a discipline remains unsystematic.[4]

Emil Brunner in *The Divine Imperative* noted the lack of systematic ethics, particularly in the pre-Reformation period. But, because of his own fears that the Christian ethic will deteriorate to Pharisaic legalism, his efforts at developing a systematic ethic are inhibited and, ultimately, fail. "The Good is that which God does; the goodness of man can be no other than letting himself be placed within the activity of God. This is what believing means in the New Testament. And this faith is the principle of ethics" (p. 55). Contrast this with Baeck's insistence that faith is expressed in the belief that God is revealed in the commandment. Brunner is explicit when he says "To let God have His way within me means to base my life in its depths on Jesus Christ; it means believing in the gracious Divine Word uttered in Jesus Christ; it means to be crucified and raised with Him" (p. 55).

Within the framework of Jewish thought we would say "To let God have His way within me means to base my life on His commandments, believing in the gracious Divine Word revealed at Sinai, and informed by the history of the Jewish people to stand again at the foot of Sinai and to covenant with Him."

Baeck acknowledges that the Law can be degraded, be reduced to secular ethics, rather than retain its function as an instrument of revelation. For Baeck "The boundary of Judaism was crossed by Paul only at the point where mystery wanted to prevail without commandment, and faith without law" (p. 200). Baeck's meaning is clear. The Judaeo-Christian tradition came to an end with Paul once the interrelatedness of mystery and commandment was negated. With Paul, the mystery was to be expressed in the sacraments and dogma rather than through a systematic ethic.

Lehmann claims "With one or two possible exceptions, the literature of the church through the fourth century had no systematic Christian ethics" (p. 32), citing as examples *Letters to the Corinthians, The Didache, The Shepherd of Hermas.* Lehmann defines the nature of these ethical works with the generalization that "Till the fourth century writings on ethical subjects are all specific and on separate matters" (p. 35). It is not until 361 A.D. that the term "ethics" is used in a Christian treatise by Basil of Caesarea in *The Principles of Ethics,* which consists of eighty rules for the Christian life. In 391 it is used by Bishop Ambrose of Milan in a treatise, *Duties of the Clergy.* Neither volume suggests a systematic approach to ethics. One might add that this is still a characteristic of contemporary casuistic literature written in the manner of the questions and answers of Aquinas. Bishop Nygren agrees essentially with

Brunner: "The whole of the Christian life becomes essentially *meditatio vitae Christi,* in which the emphasis is laid on the suffering and death, with a view to an *imitatio Christi* which shall transform the whole life" (*Agape and Eros,* p. 670).

It would appear that the death and resurrection which are at the heart of the mystery appear to be known whereas the nature of the imitative act, which would be the way in which man, in history, imitates Christ, is unknown. In Judaism the source of the commandment is unknown but His commandments are known. Hence, the chain of tradition recorded in Pirke Avot #1 legitimizing the hermeneutic method, joined with a variation of case law technique   תורות . Lehmann noted that the reformation introduced the question as to whether a systematic synthesis of divergent ethical presuppositions can be developed in contrast to the legalistic morality of the early Christian period which was primarily ascetic and mystical. "Christian thinking about ethics since the Reformation appears to have been divided between the continuation, though not without considerable adaptation, of the medieval way of dealing with ethical matters on the part of Roman Catholic moralists and the attempt on the part of Protestant theologians to work out the ethical reorientation inaugurated by Luther" (p. 42).

R. H. Snape marshals impressive evidence to support his thesis that "Down to approximately 250, Christian ethics were in the main Judaic." [5] His claim that "Changes of time and of place left, it would seem, small trace upon the thought of the Rabbis, it was, with small allowance for personal differences of character and opinion, in the main of one piece" can be justified insofar as the Rabbis functioned within an established system of logic. "It is unfortunately not possible so to regard the ethical writings of the Fathers of the Church. Second century or third, Greek or Latin, Alexandrian or Syrian or African, are questions that must be answered before we can handle the material which the Fathers provide" (p. 617).

Snape explains in this manner his rejection of Paul as the turning point in the splitting asunder of the Judaeo-Christian construct: "In this world (the world of the Greek mysteries) came Christianity, offering among other things the Old Testament, the Law and the Prophets together. The Pauline 'Gospel about Jesus,' setting the historic Jesus within the scope of a great cosmic drama, offered, like the mystery religions, immortality and a divine life; and, though these religions had an ethical side, it offered a great gift, a share in a divine love and holiness which implied an incessant moral demand, and a complete surrender of self to Jesus. The gospel of Jesus, therefore, was implied in Paulinism, and this gospel of the church which would not, and did not, separate from the Law and the Prophets the belief that the Old Testament, through and through, was divine and perfect, was taken over bodily from Judaism" (p. 624).

Judaism and Christianity are allied against the pagan world of Greek culture. "Before the middle of the third century, it may be said, Christianity was fighting not only its own battle, but that of Judaism also" (p. 636). 250 is the turning point for Snape because "The period after 250 is marked by the gradual inclusion in the church of the highly educated classes as well as the rank and file of heathendom. The last great persecution ended with the official toleration of Christianity. It was accompanied by State assistance in the persecution and suppression of heresy, and before the end of the fourth century pagan religion was proscribed" (p. 636).

In *Two Types of Faith*, Buber uses a conceptual framework in which Judaism is categorized as a faith based on relationship, on the need to believe in *someone* with absolute trust and on the need to believe in The One, although unsupported by reason. Christianity, for Buber, is based on the need to believe in *something* as true. The Torah is proof of God's existence and the observance of His commandments establishes His immanence. Belief in the death and resurrection of Jesus establishes immanence. Therefore, the need to "be converted" to believe in the occasions which establish his being. Sacraments and dogmas establish the truth of his being by defining the nature and meaning of the occasions on which one is most near him and by defining the nature and significance of his being. We believe, Buber would interpret Paul as saying when he negates the Torah, that it is at best questionable whether God can be immanent in the affairs of men to the extent that he can be immanent only in man's knowledge of Him.

Judaism would say that where the *mitzvah* is fulfilled, there God is confronted. Here is the essential difference between the Jewish *emunah* and Christian *pistis*.

The problem as to what constitutes the primary ethical task is nicely illustrated by the following midrash:

> Six hundred and thirteen commandments were given to Moses.
>
> Three hundred and sixty-five "Thou shalt nots," the number of the days of the solar year;
>
> And two hundred and forty-eight "Thou shalts,"
> Corresponding to the parts of the body.
>
> David came and brought them down to eleven;
> as it is written:
>
> "Lord, who shall sojourn in Thy tabernacle? . . .
> He that walketh uprightly, and worketh righteousness,
> And speaketh truth in his heart;
> That hath no slander upon his tongue,
> Nor doeth evil to his fellow,
> Nor taketh up a reproach against his neighbor;
> In whose eyes a vile person is despised,
> But he honoureth them that fear the Lord;
> He that sweareth to his own hurt, and changeth not;
> He that putteth not out his money on interest,
> Nor taketh a bribe against the innocent" (Ps. 15:1-5).
>
> Isaiah came and brought them down to six;
> as it is written:
>
> "He that walketh righteously and speaketh uprightly; he that despiseth the gain of oppressions, that shaketh his hands from holding of bribes, that stoppeth his ears from hearing of blood, and shutteth his eyes from looking upon evil" (Isa. 33:15).
>
> Micah came and brought them down to three;
> as it is written:
>
> "It hath been told thee, O man, what is good. . . . Only to do justly, and to love mercy, and to walk humbly with thy God" (Mic. 6:8).

Isaiah came again and brought them down to two;
as it is said:
"Thus saith the Lord,
Keep ye justice, and do righteousness" (Isa. 56:1).
Amos came and brought them down to one;
as it is said:
"For thus saith the Lord unto the house of Israel:
Seek ye Me, and live" (Amos 5:4).
Rav Nahman bar Isaac (died 356 c.e.) objected:
"Seek ye me"—may it not mean: in all the Torah?
Rather, Habakkuk came and brought them down to one;
as it is said:
"But the righteous shall live by his faith" (Hab. 2:4).

This midrash anticipated both Buber and Baeck. "Seek ye Me" which could conceivably be interpreted as *pistis* despite Rav Nahman's objection is superseded by Habakkuk's admonition in which the key word is "live." To live by one's faith is interpreted as the commitment to the commandment.

The emphasis upon the need to know the nature of God (*pistis*), hence the focus upon dogma, seems to be related to the approach of the intuitionists who assert that "good" is doing the will of God. Therefore, the knowledge of good must be based on a prior study of what is ultimately real as the ground of the Universe (the disciples who after the death and resurrection ask Jesus the meaning of the death and resurrection)[6] which means the urgent need to know the nature of God. It may be further asserted that without a prior knowledge of what is truly real one cannot know what is actually good. When Moses pressed God for His name and the privilege of seeing Him face to face, God was prepared to present to Moses not His face but His glory. The Torah, if you will, is His glory. To believe is to know that the Torah is His, and to obey it. Jesus "shows his face" in his death and resurrection. Judaism and Christianity are making different and irreconcilable assertions about what it is possible to know about God. Therefore, their answer to the question, what if anything can man do to bring good into the universe, will be in disagreement. For Christians the ultimately real is already the embodiment of the good. Therefore, man can only bring some good into the universe.[7]

For the Jew, Torah expresses whatever can be known of the ultimate reality.

Man can know and fulfill its requirements. Therefore, the "ought" is not to know God, which is impossible, because he is the Unique One, but to do His Torah. It must follow that where the sense of both the "ought" and the concept of the "good" do not correspond, the ethical systems which flow from them will manifest this lack of correspondence.

Lehmann crystallizes this in saying "The messianic image which emerges from the biblical story is, as we have seen, the crucial image, which illuminates what God is doing in the world. . . . The politics of God give to the Church's concern with and about dogma a christological focus and to Christian thinking about ethics a christological foundation" (p. 104). Having previously formulated "the prior question" as "What is Christian ethics and what are the context and structure of Christian behavior," (p. 44), Lehmann leaves no doubts as to the context. We can assume that the "ought" of Christian ethics has to do with completing God's political program by waiting for His return. Within the Jewish context, completing His political program would consist of understanding the meanings of His Law, and doing it. Whether or not the political program includes universalizing all aspects of that law or being content with some of us observing the Noachian laws while others assume additional ethical responsibilities is a question for another occasion.

Emil Brunner asks: "Could we possibly conceive that the ethic of Buddhism or of Brahmanism, with its world-denying tendency, should not be wholly different from the system of morality which has grown up in China, with its emphasis upon ancestor-worship? How can the morality of the mystic who renounces the life of the world be the same as that of the Parsee or the Mushin who seeks to conquer the world? How can the morality of the deeply serious religion of Egypt be the same as that of Greece with its delight in culture" (p. 33)? "To try to discover an 'original moral common sense' behind these influences of the various religions is simply a wild-goose chase. It is as futile as it would be to try to discover the common element in religion, the religion of reason, behind all the individual faiths" (p. 33).

Abba Hillel Silver in *Where Judaism Differed* demonstrates the accuracy of Brunner's observation by observing the life styles which emerge from these different contexts, illustrating the extent to which these different contexts, in which both the "ought" and the "good" are basically different, produce divergent attitudes on questions having to do with the nature of man, the enjoyment of life, the concept of community, the meaning of history, the nature of law and resistance to evil.

The difference in life styles and in value systems as expressed in notions as to the nature of the "ought" can be attributed not only to the emphasis upon "death and resurrection," but to real differences in the quality of response to the nature of those laws which conceivably Judaism and Christianity might share as a common core, notably the Ten Commandments. It is readily apparent that the meanings attributed to the covenant as expressed in the first commandment, and reinforced by the Sabbath, are substantially different. More than enough has been said elsewhere concerning these differences. Silver has demonstrated the way in which these differences are expressed in different life styles. Differences in meaning flow not from any logical structuring of arguments which might legitimize new definitions or the establishment of new limits within which meanings are valid, but from a completely new set of experiences. Christ as the second Adam begins a new creation. The law which may be cast in the shape of the old law is in fact a new law which, therefore, cannot be said to relate in essence to the old, though it relates in form. Therefore, there is no continuation of meaning. Not only is the meaning completely new, but the nature of law itself is completely new.

Brunner rejects the proposition that the law is for the sake of man. In his view, such a belief leads to the "eudaemonistic ethic of culture, utility and welfare which must degenerate into hedonism and vitalism" (p. 66). "The course of the law," he writes "further manifests itself in the tragedy of the wandering Jew, which is the tragedy of every human being, in the restlessness of his existence, God challenges him in his independence. Now then, if you can do the good by your own efforts, well do it" (p. 673). The words of Deuteronomy "It is not too far off for thee . . ." have new meaning. They now refer to God's grace rather than to God's law. Legalism is to be dreaded because it shifts the focus from the death and resurrection. "Therefore, the chief emphasis of the Scriptural ethic must not be in victory over lawlessness, but in the fight against legalism" (p. 71). Christian ethics cannot tell what one "ought to do" because that would require presuppositions and abstract principles verging on legalism. The Catholic Church may say what one "ought to do" because in contrast to the subjective individualism of Protestantism it accepts the concept of the teaching authority of the church in addition to its responsibility to counsel.

Thus, one must distinguish between form and essence. For even where the forms are the same, the essence is different as in the new creation and the appearance of the second Adam who brings with him the new law. It is a process which in the light of Alexandrian allegorical method predates Christianity and is known to Judaism, finding considerable expression in *aggadic* material.

Niebuhr underscores the uniqueness of these new experiences (*An Interpretation of Christian Ethics,* p. 39). "The absolutism and perfectionism of Jesus' love ethic sets itself uncompromisingly not only against the natural self-regarding impulses, but against the necessary prudent defenses of the self, required because of the egoism of others." The love ethic is in uncompromising opposition to *law* because law and egoism are bound up one with the other.

This opposition is as uncompromising as was the opposition between emergent Judaism and Babylonian religion in which the myths of creation, flood and conflict between the shepherd god and the farmer god were given new meanings. Schechter may have regarded higher criticism as higher anti-Semitism because it suggested for him the attempt to establish a Judaeo-Babylonian tradition or a Judaeo-Egyptian etc., tradition in which the Judaic tradition was simply an extension of Babylonian myth without giving sufficient recognition to those areas in which

Judaism gave essentially new meaning to basic perceptions such as creation, law, sacrifice.

Christianity has done the same vis-à-vis Judaism (*viz.,* the fall of man.) It may be that the guardedness of some of us in our response to Buber's emphasis upon encounter is based upon the suspicion that while reaffirming the Chassidic conviction that confrontation with God is possible, he has not sufficiently, if at all, reaffirmed other aspects of the Chassidic "way," namely the commitment to the commandment. Chassidism is a special case of Judaism. Its commitment to the commandment maintains the relationship.

Beyond the third century Christianity is not a special case of Judaism. Where specific ethical responses coincide, they are coincidental.

The evidence appears to establish that the term Judaeo-Christian which posits the concept of a common core designates that period in which the conceptual framework of Judaism and Christianity were contiguous. That period has long since come to an end.

NOTES

1 *Contemporary Ethical Theories,* ed. by I. J. Binkley, p. 70.

2 *Selected Essays of Ahad Haam,* ed. by J. Neumann, Tarbuth Foundation Inc., 1967, p. 265 f., "Divided Opinion."

3 *Mystery and Commandment in Contemporary Jewish Thought,* ed. by S. Novick, B'nai B'rith Adult Education.

4 Cf. Solomon Schechter's *Some Aspects of Rabbinic Theology.*

5 "Rabbinical and Early Christian Ethics" in *A Rabbinic Anthology,* ed. Newman, p. 635.

6 Acts 1.6-8. The death and resurrection have already taken place; the world apparently remains unchanged. Therefore, the disciples have to know its meaning. When the Law is given, nothing changes because the world awaits the fulfillment of the Law. Therefore, the task is to fulfill the Law.

7 *The Divine Imperative,* Brunner, p. 71.

PROBLEMATICS OF JEWISH ETHICS

Michael A. Meyer
Associate Professor of
Jewish History
Hebrew Union College—Jewish Institute of Religion
Cincinnati, Ohio

The contemporary Reform Jew who seeks moral guidance from a religiously based Jewish ethics encounters a complex of problems, both religious and historical. He seeks an ethic grounded in God, but cannot accept Torah as verbal revelation; he seeks a religious moral imperative, but wants to remain open to the demands of each new situation; he seeks to link his own moral acts with the morality of Jewish tradition, but finds that Jewish history has spawned varying, even conflicting moral points of view. On specific matters he sometimes finds the halakha quite out of keeping with his own moral sensibilities. Yet we in the Reform movement would like to claim that our feelings about war and race relations as well as those decisions which are more completely in our own hands are the products of our Jewish religious consciousness.

Judging by the interest which the problematics of Jewish ethics recently has elicited, it seems to be of great present concern.[1] It is not my primary purpose, however, to deal directly with the methodological problems involved in constructing a contemporary Jewish ethics, but only to clarify them by analyzing their earlier manifestations. Their origins go back at least two hundred years. Specifically, I shall limit my discussion to certain ethical writings which emerged from liberal Jewish circles, especially in Germany, during the nineteenth and very early twentieth centuries. While this subject may be principally of historical interest, I shall in the end suggest certain implications for the present.

Before the modern period in Jewish history there was little endeavor to write a Jewish ethics in the sense of a philosophical and historical exposition. Certainly Jewish philosophers dealt with ethics, but generally as a part of their theology. Certainly there were also Jewish moralists who exhorted their readers to lives of piety, humility, and sanctity. But the medieval moral literature, down to Moses Hayyim Luzzatto's *Mesilat Yesharim,* tends to be instructive, not descriptive. "It is entirely possible," wrote Luzzatto in 1740, "that the reader will find he has learned little that he did not know before his reading." Luzzatto wanted only to reinforce moral tendencies which were already present. He wrote for fellow Jews who were still entirely within the tradition and had not begun to measure it by external standards. It is beyond his purview to consider that his own other-worldly values might conflict with those held by Jews in other times and places, or that they might lack divine sanction.

Only with the European acculturation of the Jew did the need arise to write descriptively about Jewish morality. In the first place, gentiles began to ask whether Jewish morals were compatible with social integration into non-Jewish society and with the acceptance of civic duties and responsibilities. And second, with advancing cultural integration, the Jew himself began increasingly to doubt that Judaism possessed any moral significance not already absorbed by European culture. Jewish leadership responded to this situation with a literature descriptive of Jewish morality, intended to convince gentiles that the Jew was morally acceptable and to convince the Jew that his tradition had moral relevance.

The apologetic strain in Jewish ethical writings is prominent all through the nineteenth century. The opponents of Jewish political equality charged that Jews distinguished moral obligations to fellow Jews from those owed non-Jews. And, in response, Jewish apologetes time and again raised up the passage from Tosefta Sanhedrin, which they quoted as: חסידי אומות העולם יש להם חלק לעולם הבא . Clearly, they argued, universalism was characteristic not only of modern, but also of classical Judaism. And how much ink was spilled to prove that ואהבת לרעך כמוך did not refer only to one's Jewish neighbor!

What I regard as the culmination of this sustained apologetics came in a tiny eight-page pamphlet entitled *Principles of Jewish Morality,* published by the Deutsch-Israelitischer Gemeindebund in 1885. The first of the fifteen principles strikes the universal note: "Judaism teaches the unity of the human race." It further teaches love of neighbor (regardless of religion or nationality), respect for private property and for the religion of others, and concern for the material welfare of non-Jews. It holds physical and mental labor in high regard, demands humility and conscientious obedience to the laws of the state. It commands giving honor to governmental authority as well as loving and willingly dying for the fatherland. Conversely, it forbids financial dishonesty, usury, exploitation, defamation of the religion of others, laziness, arrogance, ostentation, and resistance to the government.

Three hundred and fifty rabbis and Jewish scholars signed the document, indicating thereby that these principles and their negative correlates were grounded in Jewish religious teaching. In addition, the signatures of 270 German and Austrian Jewish jurists testified to the fact that these principles "correspond to the present moral consciousness of German Jewry." Such a morality, affirmed as normative for both past and present by the signatures of experts, would have to make the Jew a model German citizen. Not surprisingly, the little brochure was intended for wide distribution among non-Jews.

But when they wrote for themselves, the newly emancipated Jews were not so sure. The fact of the matter was that obligations to the gentile had not always been regarded as equivalent to those owed the fellow Jew and that, even in the present, Yisroel and Goi were not viewed with undifferentiated compassion. (That may be why the Israelitischer Gemeindebund sent copies of its principles also to Jewish schools.) The official explanation for this gap between alleged moral theory and actual practice was the historical suffering of the Jew which had necessarily driven him to a reciprocal contempt for his oppressor. But admitting the existence of certain non-universal and hence nonacceptable statements within the tradition necessarily raised the question of determining which statements are authoritative and which are not. With increasing historical awareness came the realization that different ethical norms had prevailed at different periods of Jewish history and that countervailing points of view had not been cancelled out to create a single authoritative tradition. Was it at all possible to say: "Judaism teaches . . ." or only, Deuteronomy teaches . . .," "Hillel teaches . . .," "Maimonides teaches . . ."?

If the latter be true, then the only way in which Jewish morality could be presented historically would be with due regard for differences in substance and nuance between moral dicta expressed within various currents of Jewish thought. But such a history of Jewish morality was not written. What was done frequently—and is still being done—was to cull excerpts, "gems," from Bible, Talmud, and later moralists and to arrange them chronologically within subject categories. The problem with this anthologizing lies in the selectivity: the editor filters out those dicta which he does not favor but neglects to set forth explicit criteria for his choice. He avoids the problem of contradiction within the tradition and with the present by merely displaying the still acceptable. He does not explain why certain elements of the tradition are to be considered authoritative while others are not.

Some nineteenth-century writers did try to establish continuity with the Jewish past while preserving an awareness of its internal variety. But they did not entirely agree on what they could link up with. The Bible would seem to be central, yet even here certain provisions—an eye for an eye, a tooth for a tooth—had to be explained away according to historical context. The Talmud as a source of morals was variously regarded. Few were as vehement as Samuel Holdheim in opposing it as a source of modern morality. For this radical reformer the moral basis of the Talmud—its legalism and particularism—was generally, and he thought correctly, recognized as "reprehensible." [2] Most writers, however, took a selective view. And in the course of time the pendulum swung the other way. Moses Bloch, in his *Die Ethik in der Halacha,* carried on in modern form the traditional discipline of seeking moral justifications for the halakha. And in 1913 Jacob Lauterbach, Professor of Talmud at Hebrew Union College, argued before the CCAR that the Rabbis represented a distinct advance over the Torah, reinterpreting its laws to "measure up to their [higher] ethical standards."[3] Lauterbach believed that the entire halakha, ritual as well as civil law, served moral ends.

The Talmud was not the only segment of the Jewish tradition which proved problematic to nineteenth-century Jewish thinkers. There were other obstacles to moral continuity. Samuel David Luzzatto, an original thinker and the leading scholar of Italian Jewry in this period, found a different obstruction.[4] He refused to include medieval Jewish philosophers among the representatives of what he considered genuine Jewish morality. These men—especially Maimonides—because of their addiction to Aristotelian-Arabic philosophy, had favored an intellectualism that derogated from the moral value of the non-philosopher and spawned intolerance for non-Jews and heretics. For Luzzatto it was not the Talmud but certain of the medieval philosophers who deviated from the high road of Jewish universalism. Moreover, in favoring a strict asceticism, they proposed a kind of life hardly suited to the average man, especially in the modern age. The Bible and Talmud, with their "divine simplicity," provided a much better source for modern Jewish morality.

The task of seeking continuity with the past was paralleled by the quest for differentiation in the present. The apologetic strain in Jewish ethical writing, with its innocuous statement of commonly held values, was intended to prove the Jew as moral as the Christian. Certainly it was not intended to point up any differences. Yet in the course of the nineteenth century Jewish leaders concerned with the preservation of Judaism were forced to devote attention to the question of difference. They wanted to provide a rationale for remaining Jewish drawn from the intrinsic value of Jewish morality and not merely from the rejection of Christian dogma. It became necessary, moreover, to distinguish Jewish morality not only from Christianity but also from the Ethical Culture movement which was making headway in America and Europe during the last decades of the century. Vis-à-vis Christianity the question was: Is Jewish morality still significantly different from Christian? Vis-à-vis proponents of natural morality, the question was: Is religion of any kind essential for the moral man?

Max Joseph, a rabbi in Pomerania and, interestingly enough, an early Zionist, was one of the few to deal with the question of Christianity in a work specifically devoted to Jewish morality.[5] Joseph readily admitted that modern Christianity preached a morality similar to that of Judaism but stressed that it had not always been so. Christianity had neither consistently taught love of the non-Christian neighbor nor favored cultural endeavor. It had been repressive of human passions while Judaism had sought to channel them. Nonascetic modern morality was more a product of the Jewish tradition than the Christian. The apologetic motive here gives way to the self-assertive. Joseph is not trying to show that Judaism is as moral as Christianity but that historical Christianity, at any rate, does not conform to modern humanitarian, this-worldly morality. According to Joseph, the modern view is more Jewish than Christian. It was left to Leo Baeck, writing principally after our period, to differentiate more basically between Judaism, for which ethics is essence, and predominantly romantic Christianity in which, according to Baeck, the mystery of the sacrament rendered ethics "all but superfluous."

In America the Ethical Culture movement presented the main challenge. Not surprisingly, it possessed a great attraction for liberal Jews—and not only because its founder had been the son of a liberal rabbi. Reform Judaism had stressed the central importance of morality in religion to the point where it seemed to be the totality of the religious heritage. Religion, it could now be argued, was only a formative matrix which had become an unneeded shell. Having fulfilled its task, it might readily be discarded. In a speech delivered in 1887 Kaufmann Kohler put it this way: "Ethics is the dame of fashion, much courted now, the pet-child of the age. Religion—poor thing!—is declared to be very old. Her bright days are said to be over." [6] How could Jewish religion reclaim her ethical daughter? Two arguments were used in favor of reconciliation: first, that natural morality, lacking divine sanction, gives way in practice to narrow self-interest: selfish inclinations overcome the sense of obligation to fellow man and society. And, second, only the belief in God can provide a highest ideal of perfection against which man may measure his moral actions. We shall have to return to this second argument a little later. Certainly the various speeches and pamphlets did little but indicate awareness of the problem.

By the end of the nineteenth century numerous writings had dealt with Jewish morality: some apologetic, some anthological, some expository. To a certain extent they touched upon the principal issues—contradiction, continuity, uniqueness, divine authority—but they all lacked scope and sustained reflection upon the problematics taken as a whole. And not one of them presented an encompassing solution.

Not until the end of the nineteenth century was the attempt made to write a comprehensive and systematic ethics of Judaism. The formidable task required a scholar with extensive knowledge of the Jewish sources of all periods combined with sensitivity to the philosophical and historical problems involved. Moritz Lazarus, who spent the last twenty years of his life in the production of such a work, was excellently equipped for the task. He combined a mastery of Hebraic sources, retained and deepened from a traditional childhood education, with a creative career in ethno-psychology (a discipline he pioneered) and in philosophy. Within the Jewish community he had taken the lead in German Jewry's defense efforts against anti-Semitism and had played the most significant role of any layman in the Reform movement. In 1898 he published a sizable first volume entitled *Die Ethik des Judentums,* which was translated into English two years later. Lazarus died in 1903 before he could complete the second volume. It finally appeared, edited by Winter and Wünsche, in 1911, but has never been translated.[7] What makes Lazarus' work especially significant in terms of our topic is the author's remarkable awareness of the problems inherent in his task and his self-conscious attempt to come to grips with each of them.

Though it dwells in part upon Jewish universalism and quotes extensively from traditional sources, Lazarus' work can be classified as neither apologetics nor anthology. It is a much more ambitious project: the transformation of scattered moral dicta,

laws, and customs from the Bible and rabbinic literature into
a system which possesses logical order and sequence. In understanding the Jewish texts Lazarus claimed that he had been
aided but not prejudiced by the tools of philosophy. The contents
were drawn entirely from Jewish sources; only form was imposed
in order to provide a coherence not easily apparent in the scattered contexts. Yet even the form did not have a distinctively
foreign origin. He did not wish to share the failing of Maimonides and certain contemporary Jewish writers who modeled
their ethics on foreign patterns and used Jewish sources only
as proof texts. Although Lazarus recognized that some measure
of individuality would necessarily remain—and found precedent
for it even in the rabbinic literature—he intended to minimize
subjectivity.

The focus of Jewish morality, according to Lazarus, is the
ideal of holiness conceived as moral perfection. In subjugating
personal desire to moral law, Jewish morality seeks sanctification
of life through interpenetration of the spiritual and the material.
Lazarus divides the specifics of Jewish morality into "the way"
דרך , including both virtues מדות and duties חובות , and
the nature of the societal institutions which they are to sustain
ישוב . The latter range from the family as the smallest unit
to humanity as the largest. Into his structure Lazarus manages
to fit the wide range of relevant texts, integrating them into a
discussion of each of the specific subjects involved or drawing
upon them without specific reference. The structure as a whole
was intended to be both a historical presentation of classical
Jewish ethics and a guide for the moral conduct of the contemporary Jew.

We must now ask how adequately Lazarus was able to deal
with those problems which, as we have seen, beset any attempt
to present a normative ethics of Judaism. Let us take first the
matter of contradiction. The issue is both historical, insofar as
it involves a selection between divergent texts, and contemporary, insofar as certain texts, morally offensive to modern sensibilities, must be explained away in order to avoid creating a
hiatus between the contemporary Jew and the tradition. Lazarus
was cognizant of these problems and made a firm attempt to re-

solve them. To begin with, certain texts could be dismissed as jests, not to be taken seriously; for example, that discussion dealing with whether it is permissible to slaughter an *am ha-arets* on a Yom Kippur that falls on the Sabbath or only to stab him to death since *shechita* requires a blessing.[8] Others must be seen as deplorable but nevertheless understandable responses to persecution. Here Lazarus specifically mentions Simeon bar Yohai's dictum, so well known to anti-Semites: טוב שבגויים הרוג.[9] Medieval Jewish asceticism with its rejection of the pleasures of this world is explained away in the same fashion, though the historical grounds for regarding it as mere response to difficult times are rather dubious. A third possibility for rejection is given by the obscurity of the author or the opposition which the majority offered his viewpoint. Greater weight must be given to what the community accepted and what gained currency than to what was uttered by a single individual. And here Lazarus draws not only upon dicta but institutions, such as the charitable תמחוי and קפה as well as the numerous חברות instituted for the common welfare. But Lazarus is not willing to rest with this latter, relatively objective historical approach. On the side of the acceptable he wants to allow for the single opinion which stands in advance of the majority. One must pay heed ultimately not to the majority, he says, but to the best, and not to deeds but to unrealized ideals.

Lazarus was well aware that we are thus thrown back upon our own internalized criteria of judgment. By these we evaluate the tradition. The tradition does not judge us. But he claimed that there was ample precedent for this freedom. Akiba and Tarfon, for example, in Lazarus' opinion, had become convinced that capital punishment may have been fitting for an earlier period but was no longer so in their own day. The Talmudic law, moreover, expanded and modified the Biblical to include areas of human sensitivity untouched by the earlier legislation. Since the Rabbis themselves had sifted and refined the tradition in each age, modern Jews were justified in continuing the process, acting according to the lights of their own insight and conscience. The tradition was and is, in Lazarus' words, "to guide but not to shackle conscience, to whet the spirit not to blunt it." [10]

But if present conscience is the final judge of tradition, do the results of this sifting process leave us with a coherent morality? Is there a common substance which unites the elements in the Jewish morality of a particular age and which also provides continuity with past and future, bridging the span from the Bible to the present? Lazarus insists that there is. Despite internal contradictions with regard to specific and occasional aberrant points of view, Jewish moral literature is permeated by a *Gesamtgeist,* a common spirit which is transmitted from age to age. The Rabbis, imbued with the spirit of the Biblical writers, were able to build harmoniously on the Biblical foundation. Specifics changed but the common spirit remained essentially the same. It was thus possible for Lazarus to speak of a Jewish ethics rather than only of separate Biblical, Talmudic, medieval, and modern norms.

One must conclude from Lazarus' discussion that the task of the modern writer on Jewish ethics, seeking out the common spirit, would have to be basically intuitive. Lazarus himself put it this way:

> The ultimate source [of Jewish ethics] is not the spirit pervading the collective literature but the common spirit of the people and the religious community. Just as the literature pours forth from the folk soul, so too a description of Jewish ethics must ultimately draw its substance from the inmost sources of the people's character, at the same time noting historical changes and developments. The task is to listen for even the faintest stirrings of the public consciousness, apprehend with delicately trained senses the imponderable elements of the ethical spirit, and to provide conceptual and verbal form for what moves the hearts of the people only as dim notion and ideal longing.[11]

Lazarus believed that it was possible for the modern Jew to enter into this spirit (*einleben*) and thus close the gap between the generations. It was what he hoped his own work had accomplished.

But Lazarus' personal Judaism lacked a good deal of what had characterized the past: the ceremonial laws possessed value to him only as ethical symbols, and when this value was no longer apparent, they could and should be cast off. He shared Geiger's notion that these laws had acted as a preservative shell guarding an ethical kernel no longer in need of protection. In a statement surprisingly critical of the past, Lazarus pointed specifically to the various charitable organizations of his own Berlin Jewish community, agencies of which "our forefathers had not the slightest idea." [12] But given no more than this ethical kernel and given the development of the Christian tradition, was Jewish ethics still unique in the modern age? Lazarus refuses to dwell on specific differences because of a professed aversion to polemics, yet his general characterization of Jewish morality is unquestionably meant to set it apart even from modern Christianity. Jewish ethics, he insists repeatedly, is *Sozialethik,* social ethics. This was true from Biblical times down to the present age. The idea of morality in Judaism is the idea of the moral society. Aside from God, no individual can be considered holy; only the group can become holy. Jewish morality is characterized by a high degree of concern for the welfare of the community; it is replete with social legislation to ameliorate the lot of the poor; it has created a panoply of institutions to relieve social distress and promote communal harmony. As the ultimate social unit is mankind, its final aim is universal, however much particularism may be viewed as a necessary means to that end. The social spirit is Lazarus' most specific characterization of the collective spirit of Jewish morality which he believed had pervaded all periods of Jewish history. It not only provides continuity in the midst of seeming diversity but also characterizes and differentiates Jewish morality in the present.

We are left finally with what must be the most difficult problem for Jewish—or any religious—ethics: the question of ultimate authority. Does it repose in the individual alone, making him a free moral agent but at the same time divorcing morality from religion, or does it repose in God, providing a religious basis but robbing man of his moral autonomy? Kant had wrestled with this question, resolved it for himself, but declared that Judaism was merely a code of statutory laws and as such heteronomous.[13] Lazarus, very much a Kantian, was obliged to argue the autonomy of Jewish ethics. In the introduction to his second volume he added moral autonomy (the subject of an earlier chapter) to social concern as the second basic characteristic of Biblical and Rabbinic ethics.

In Lazarus' view Jewish morality has its origin in the individual Jew; it was not created by the Sinaitic legislation. "The feeling of duty," he says in agreement with Kant, "is the autonomous source of the ethical." [14] Jewish morality does not consist of obedience to externally given laws, but of Jewish responses to the inner feeling of duty. As evidence Lazarus cites Onkelos' unusual rendering of Genesis 3:22, הן האדם היה כאחד ממנו לדעת טוב ורע as, "See, man is unique, of himself knowing good and evil." [15] Far from being incompatible, the basic principles of Kant and of the Jewish spirit are identical. And because of this identity the writer on Jewish ethics, trained in Kant, possesses a deeper understanding of the Rabbis—according to Lazarus, a better understanding even than they had of themselves. Jewish ethics is deontological, concerned with the fulfillment of obligation not the seeking after individual happiness. Therefore it is inimical to both utilitarianism and eudaemonism, each of which nullifies the moral character of an act. Jewish ethics does not seek a chief good to be obtained by man but the right path for him to follow. Johanan ben Zakkai did not ask his disciples to seek the good, but the good way to which a man should cleave.

God, as Lazarus repeatedly tells us, is "the source and archetype of the moral idea. He is morality personified and realized, or, rather, the moral idea itself." [16] Lazarus, who considered himself a theist, of course rejected the conclusion which some might draw: that man therefore creates God. He insisted that "only a fool supposed himself the creator of his own [moral] nature." [17] But he avoided dealing with the question here, arguing that the ethical discipline begins with man's moral powers as given. The question of their origins is not ethical, but metaphysical.

Reading Lazarus' work today, half a century after its appearance, one becomes aware of the futility of his task. For all of his professed attempt to avoid subjectivity, the passing of two generations lays bare the time-limitedness of his work. The psychology upon which he built now seems shallow and naive; the values those of a civilized elderly German gentleman; his underlying belief in the evolutionary advance of morality overly sanguine. Reflecting on Lazarus, one despairs of ever finding a Jewish *Gesamtgeist* which is not in large measure a projection backward of one's own morality. The effort involved in trying to construct a normative Jewish ethics seems better spent on genuinely historical studies. By not seeking to impose unity where it is absent, these inquiries can provide a truer picture of Jewish morality in all of its variations and contradictions. Not the imposition of a system but carefully tracing the diverse currents of development in their contexts would seem the only fruitful approach.

Yet if this conclusion is correct, does it leave any basis for Jewish ethics in the present? My belief is that it does, but that we err when we focus on the past. A Jewish moral tradition fraught with contradictions, in part repugnant to our own moral sensibilities, and for many of us lacking the sanction of revelation, can be instructive only as history. It is close to us because it is our own history, but it carries no authority for our present moral decisions. Yet though the past offers no hope of moral impulse, I believe that the future does. It is in this connection that I must touch briefly on Lazarus' better-known contemporary, Hermann Cohen.

Cohen's ethical position was similar to that of Lazarus. Both men were ethical idealists in the Kantian tradition; both were severe critics of eudaemonism. Perhaps in part because of this near agreement, Cohen in a lengthy review, could be so viciously critical of Lazarus' work.[18] His main argument was that Lazarus incorrectly separated ethics from philosophy of religion and therefore virtually excluded Jewish philosophers, such as Cohen's favorite, Maimonides, because they did not make this false distinction. According to Cohen, a systematic ethics must be part of a philosophy and hence also include logic. Since Judaism was not a philosophical system, Jewish ethics could not be systematic ethics. It could only be the religious philosophy governing Jewish morals and as such was inseparable from theology. Lazarus should not have neglected to discuss the Jewish concept of God, for, according to Cohen, God's very essence is morality. For Lazarus, as we have seen, God was indeed virtually identical with morality, but he had chosen to focus upon what the Jews did with their sense of moral obligation. He had intended to do little more than analyze and organize the materials of the past.

In the last years of his life Cohen himself embarked upon the task which he claimed Lazarus had misunderstood. His post-humously published *Religion of Reason out of the Sources of Judaism* presents a systematic conception of the Jewish religion, relating ethics to the major issues of theology. It would go beyond the limits of this paper—and my own competence— to subject Cohen's system to philosophical critique. Suffice it to say from the perspective of the historian that insofar as Cohen deals with traditional Jewish sources he is every bit as guilty as Lazarus of shaping them to fit his own purposes. He too imposes his own concepts and his own order. He too takes insufficient account of the variety of Jewish thought, regarding Jewish religion, for all its vicissitudes, as the "uniform product of the Jewish *Volksgeist*." [19]

But there is a strikingly different element in Cohen's work which gives it great significance in terms of our subject: the prominence which Cohen gives to the future. According to Cohen, religious institutions do not derive value by precedent from the past, but only through the endeavor to achieve what is not yet realized. Put in terms of the individual, personal relig-ious conviction implies a messianic religious consciousness which provides perspective on the present. Lazarus devoted very little attention to messianism; but for Cohen it is central. It is "the most significant and original product of the Jewish spirit" and the "culminating point of Judaism." [20]

The prophets, who created this "goal-idea," brought about a new direction in morality. In the universality of their concep-tion of mankind they drew a necessary consequence from their belief in the one and universal God. The messianic kingdom, which is the Kingdom of God, implies no less than the absolute victory of the good in terms of the relations between both nations and individual human beings. Thus conceived, the messianic idea assures the independence of religion, its freedom from domination by the state and its rejection of the status of a mere agent of social control. It is a most timely virtue of messianism that it provides the basis for an independent religious critique of society: "The political idea of the messianic future," Cohen wrote, "directs thought beyond all laws, statutes, and political states of present reality. This is the meaning of the Kingdom of God as the ideal of world history." [21]

By removing our focus from the past to the future, I believe, Cohen provides us with the basis for a viable contemporary Jewish ethics: a messianic ethics. The messianic ideal points the direction for moral advance; it becomes the criterion for judgment and decision. The only norm is the norm of the future, its value as a measuring rod not at all diminished by the poor approximation which can at best be rendered it in the present. Its significance lies in the moral striving which it creates out of the tension between what is and what might be.

Messianism, as the heart of a contemporary Jewish ethics, avoids the pitfalls to which a Jewish ethics based on past morality is subject. It is certainly not quietistic like the earlier apologetic works; quite to the contrary, it makes demands which may prove most unpopular in their execution. The problem of contradiction loses its relevance when the resolution of conflicting tendencies is no longer essential for the sake of establishing a single common spirit. Continuity with the Jewish past is provided by the link to the Hebrew prophets as the original source of the messianic vision and by regarding the history of Jewish moral activity as our people's manifestation of various degrees of messianic awareness. As for differentiation from Christianity in the present, Cohen argued—and I think the argument is valid today—that Jesus remains the redeemer of the individual whereas the Jewish Messiah (however reinterpreted) redeems the society of mankind. Finally, the link between morality and religion is firmly established when the idea of God is related to the moral ideal not yet realized. The nature of this relationship is a theological question which may be solved in a variety of ways. But, in some sense, the demands imposed by the vision become the commands of God.

How would a messianically oriented ethics function in the actual process of individual moral decision? The term "situation ethics" is popular today to represent a Christian approach to this subject. In Fletcher's version, it seeks to apply a calculus of agapeic love to determine the moral course of action.[22] There must be no preconceived maxims, only the unhindered application of love to the realities of the situation. The weakness in such an approach, it seems to me, lies in its failure to provide a goal for action. In its dread of "legalism" it sets forth no definite ideal which love is to serve; it achieves freedom from constraint at the price of indirection. Messianically oriented ethics must, indeed, also take full account of the circumstances of each unique situation, and it may draw freely upon the moral wisdom of the Jewish past, but its aim and motivation remains the moral ideal: the genuine community of mankind. The ideal is applicable to taking a moral position on relations between nations and between races. It can serve, as well, as a guide to personal conduct. The ideal determines the direction; the situation determines the specific course. Such an ethic is both flexible in detail and uncompromising in demand. It is open to the needs of the moment but spurred by the vision of the future. In messianic ethics, I submit, lies the best solution to the problematics outlined in this paper and the best hope for a relevant Jewish morality.

NOTES

1 See, for example, the January 1968 issue of the *CCAR Journal;* also Jacob Neusner, "What is Normative in Jewish Ethics?" *Judaism,* Winter 1967.

2 *Über Auflösbarkeit der Eide* (Hamburg, 1845), 48.

3 *The Ethics of the Halakhah* (reprint from *CCAR Year Book,* 1913), 32.

4 *Israelitische Moral-Theologie* (Breslau, 1870).

5 *Zur Sittenlehre des Judentums* (Berlin, 1902). Another was the traditionalist Italian rabbi, Elie Benamozegh, who as early as 1867 had argued in his *Morale Juive et Morale Chrétienne* that Pharisaic morality was both anterior and superior to Christian morality; Pharisaism combined justice and charity while Christianity dwelt one-sidedly on charity alone.

6 *The Ethical Basis of Judaism* (New York, 1887), p. 4.

7 The first German volume appeared as two volumes in English, rather inaccurately translated by Henrietta Szold. Citation here will be by the paragraph numbers, which correspond in the German and English texts.

8 Appendix to para. 48a.

9 Para. 49.

10 Para. 53.

11 Para. 66.

12 Para. 361.

13 See Nathan Rotenstreich, *The Recurring Pattern* (London, 1963), 23-47.

14 Para. 112.

15 Para. 97.

16 Para. 183.

17 Para. 102.

18 "Das Problem der jüdischen Sittenlehre," *Jüdische Schriften* (Berlin, 1924), III, 1-35.

19 *Religion der Vernunft aus den Quellen des Judentums* (2nd ed.; Frankfurt, 1929), 35.

20 "Autonomie und Freiheit," *Jüdische Schriften,* III, 41; *Religion der Vernunft,* Preface.

21 "Das Gottesreich," *Jüdische Schriften,* III, 174.

22 Joseph Fletcher, *Situation Ethics: The New Morality* (Philadelphia, 1966).

REVEALED MORALITY
AND MODERN THOUGHT

Norbert Samuelson
Rabbi, Director Hillel Foundation
Princeton University
Princeton, New Jersey

Within the classical or mediaeval tradition of Jewish philosophy the study of man centered around two questions, how is man a knowing agent, and how is man a moral agent. This paper is an attempt to answer the latter question.

Many contemporary American intellectuals are caught in a strange ethical dilemma. On one hand they unqualifiedly assert through their public actions that civil rights are good and the war in Viet Nam is bad. They are equally convinced that Nazi hate was bad but (at least in some circles) love is good. On the other hand these same intellectuals are as committed conceptually to one or more of the various forms of ethical subjectivism that are current today. When, not on the picket line but in their studies, they are asked, What does it mean to say that something is good or that something is bad? they will offer either of the following answers: (a) Good and evil are culturally determined; there is no such thing as absolute good or evil (Moral Relativism or Contextual Ethics). (b) Good and evil are emotive terms; if you say that something is good you have given information about yourself (your tastes and likes), but you have told me nothing about the thing (Emotivism).

Rarely is there any realization that the ethical theory stands in direct opposition to the moral practise. No one risks his life, or even his future, for mere matters of taste. Yet on any of these ethical theories moral judgments are ultimately no different than matters of taste. One or the other must be wrong. Either the moral theory is inadequate in which case the behavior may be justified, or if the theory is correct the behavior is foolish. I personally find the behavior to be sound and the theory to be nonsense.

I am convinced that our concrete moral judgments are as founded in experience and hence as objectively justifiable as any other judgments that we make about experienced states of affairs. In this paper I will attempt to defend this conviction. What I propose to do is offer a conceptual model of what is involved in making the judgment, ". . . is good." Then I will use this model to examine briefly two dominant positions in contemporary ethical theory, viz., Kant's Deontology and Contextual Ethics.[1] Since I am committed to moral judgments being founded on experience, I will have to show in what ways these two positions are sound. Similarly, because of this presupposition, I must also show how it is possible for there to be errors in moral judgments. Finally, I will make some comments on how my model is relevant to Jewish religious thought in general and I will apply my model to a specific issue, viz., Emil Fackenheim's presentation of the dilemma of autonomous and revealed morality in his article "The Revealed Morality of Judaism and Modern Thought." [2]

I

Definition of Terms

A. Values

A1. The terms "good" and "evil" are used in many ways. Sometimes they are used as emotive expressions, e.g., "The chicken soup is good." More often they are used to express excellence or skills. For example, the judgment "this is a good knife" involves the following claims: (a) A knife has certain functions insofar as it is a knife, e.g., cutting. (b) To fulfill well these functions proper to a knife the knife must possess certain properties, e.g., to cut the knife must be sharp. (c) This knife possesses these properties.

A2. Neither of the above uses of the terms "good" and "evil" are moral uses. We will consider in this model only moral uses.

A3. The terms "good" and "evil" are value terms.

A4. There are different kinds of value terms. Four such kinds are, mathematical, aesthetic, truth, and moral values.

A5. Mathematical values:

A5a. Values cannot be defined. Rather they can be enumerated and it can be shown how they are used.

A5b. Mathematical values consist of an infinite list of natural numbers. For example, the value of 2^2 is 4; the value of 4^2 is 16, etc.

A5c. In the statement "2^2 is 4," "2" is the term or object which has the value, ". . .^{2}" is the context, and "4" is the value. Contexts are functions of terms. Only terms in context take specific values. Objects alone have no values. Functions alone have a range of values, i.e., a list of all of the possible values that may be assigned to a function depending on its term. (A term is an object in context.) For example, 2 alone has no value, but . . .^{2} can have any number of values (4 for 2^2, 16 for 4^2, 36 for 6^2, etc.).

A6. The description of what is a particular kind of value consists in the following: (a) Enumerating a list of these values. (b) Specifying their range. For example, mathematical values are natural numbers which range over mathematical propositions which consist of mathematical functions and natural numbers as their objects. (c) Providing criteria for the application of these values to that over which they range, i.e., enumerating rules by which applications can be judged to be correct or incorrect. For example, part of understanding what mathematical values are is to be able to say that "2^2 is 4" is correct whereas "2^2 is 5" is not correct.

A7. The aesthetic values are "beautiful" and "ugly." The truth values are "true" and "false." Neither aesthetic nor truth nor mathematical values should be confused with moral values.

A8. That the mathematical, truth, aesthetic, and even moral

values have no existence of their own outside of value judgments in no way means that these judgments are not objective.

B. Moral Values

B1. The moral values are "good" and "bad."

B2. The moral values range exclusively over (a) relations (b) between persons. In other words, if something is not a relation between persons it makes no sense to say that it is morally good or bad. However, sometimes by analogy the value terms are extended to apply to the persons themselves.

B2i. Persons are conscious beings.

B2ii. "Consciousness" may not be definable but its range in use is intelligible. Generally, humans fall into the class of conscious beings, whereas stones do not; whether or not animals do is problematic. More specifically the distinction between persons and non-persons or conscious and non-conscious beings can be characterized as follows: At one level we may say that a conscious being is able to be the immediate cause or agent of some of its actions. (Such acts are called "voluntary.") At another level, imagine two entities both self movers in the sense that each is the immediate agent of some of its actions where one of the entities is an automaton of the other. Imagine that the automaton is programmed so that its actions and the actions of that of which it is a copy are overtly the same. It still is conceivable that the original is in the class of conscious beings and its copy is not. So far as this distinction is intelligible the notion of "consciousness" is exact.

B2iii. Persons in relation have moral values. Persons alone have not. Relations whose terms are persons have a moral value range.

B3. Every relation between persons involves obligations, i.e., responsibilities arising out of the relation upon each participant in the relation. These responsibilities need not be symmetrical, i.e., given a relation between two persons the responsibilities of one of the participants in the relation may be very different from the responsibilities of the other. For example, consider the responsibilities of a student and a teacher in a student-teacher relation.

B4. Success and failure in fulfilling the obligations that arise in morally judged relations are the criteria by which particular moral values are determined. In this sense judgments of moral right and wrong are judgments about obligations.

B5. Actual success and failure are the criteria of judgment and not intended success and failure. Intention is a sign that an agent is conscious, and moral relations are limited to relations between conscious beings. Hence intention enters the moral situation only as a precondition for moral judgment.

B6. The obligations themselves are not morally judged. Rather these provide the criteria by which moral judgments are made. However not all obligations are admissible. Some obligations are morally self-contradictory.

B7. A self-contradictory moral obligation is an obligation whose fulfillment destroys the relationship. For example, if A demands that B kill him he makes a self-contradictory demand. If B fails to fulfill the demand the relation ends, i.e., it is unsuccessful. However if B fulfills the demand and kills A the relationship also ends. This is what it means to say that the obligation is morally self-contradictory. It is not logically self-contradictory.

B7a. Relations involving only self-contradictory obligations are morally neutral. In cases involving choice where the contrary choices are all morally bad, the relations themselves are morally neutral. Hence cases of mercy killing are not moral contexts.

B8. The terms or participants in moral relations are either individual persons or collective persons. Collective persons are simply classes of persons consisting of their members only. Nations are examples of collective persons.

B9. Moral relations involve a minimum of two persons. A person has relations to himself and obligations to himself. But these are not moral contexts. One consequence of this is that while I may be the source of your moral obligations and you may be the source of mine, neither of us can be the source of our own moral obligations. Hence whereas I may impose moral worth on you in your context and you may impose moral worth on me in my context, neither of us may impose any moral worth on ourselves. Alone we have no value. (The word *nachas* is an expression of this moral state-of-affairs where one may bestow value on another through his acts but not on himself.)

B10. The terms or participants in moral relations may be individuals with individuals, collectives with collectives (e.g., relations between nations), collectives with individuals, or individuals with collectives.

C. General Characteristics

C1. The statement "R is good" resembles the statement "P is true" where P is a proposition about some experienced state-of-affairs, e.g., "the table is blue." That P is true is not given in experience, but the judgment is nonetheless objective and based on experience. All that is needed to make the judgment is the experience of P. The same may be said for the proposition that R is good.

C2. The contexts discussed here are only simple in that they involve single relations between two or more terms. We have not considered complex contexts involving two or more relations between two or more terms. As there is a moral logic for simple contexts, so there is in principle a moral logic for complex contexts. However, the criteria for judgment in the latter logic may be radically different from the criteria in the former. An example of a question involving a logic of complex contexts is, "Am I morally responsible to be loyal to my country concerning matters in which I judge my country to be morally wrong?"

II

Kant's Deontology

A. Insights

1. Kant clearly recognized the different senses of the term "good," and he saw that in none of the senses in which "good"

was used to express excellence of function was the term being used morally (A1, 2)[3]. He offered the following proof: If good is reducible to any set of characteristics of a thing, then the statement, "X is good" and the statement, "X has such and such characteristics" would be equivalent. However, where the word "good" is used with moral significance this equivalence does not hold. The question "Ought X to have such and such characteristics?" is perfectly intelligible in a way that the question "Ought X to be good?" is not.

2. Good is not identical with anything in the world. The good may or may not exist. If it does it is something supremely good (whatever that means). However, even then that thing and good are not the same. Good functions only as a predicate term (A8).

3. The terms "good" and "evil" are simple terms and therefore not definable (A5b). All that can be shown is how to use them. Thus the major task of moral philosophy is not to provide definitions but to develop a logic of moral judgments (A6). Towards this end Kant developed his various formulations of the Categorical Imperative.[4] Unfortunately Kant thought that this one rule was sufficient to make all moral judgments.

4. If moral judgments are to be moral they must be objective (A8). Kant's Categorical Imperative provided a necessary condition for such objectivity. However, Kant thought that it was sufficient as well as necessary.

5. Kant recognized that moral value judgments are possible only when persons are involved in what is judged. This led Kant to assume that moral values reside in the will (B2).[5] However, what is a necessary condition for moral judgments, viz., the will, Kant judged to be a sufficient condition.

6. All moral judgments involve expressions of obligations. A sign of this fact is that the statement, "X is good" more resembles in its logical form the imperative "Do X!" than it does the explicative "X is F." This linguistic feature misled others (not Kant), such as C. L. Stevenson, to conclude that moral judgments are not statements about facts (C1). Kant himself was also misled by his insight in that he confused the criteria for moral judgments with the judgments themselves. It is an

easy "slip" to make. (For example, the behaviorist identification of color percepts with light waves.)

7. Kant recognized that not all obligations are morally admissable. His Generalization Argument[6] is a sufficient criterion to exclude such obligations. It is the sound insight of the Utilitarians that, at least within this context, arguments from consequences are morally admissible. However, this argument is not a sufficient criterion to make all moral judgments (B5).[7]

B. Mistakes

1. From Kant's recognition that moral values are neither things nor in things (B2), and that where persons are not involved moral judgments cannot be made, he concluded that moral values range over the intentions of acts rather than over the acts themselves (B5). As a consequence of this it follows that overt acts do not enter into moral judgments. But this is clearly false. To unintentionally kill someone is not as bad as intentionally killing someone, but manslaughter properly is as much a crime as is murder. The recognition of this moral fact is a strength of Utilitarianism over Kant's Deontology.

2. Since Kant thought that intentions alone are what is good and evil and that the will is a sufficient condition to determine moral judgments, he concluded that persons are the source of their moral values (B9). This is difficult to imagine. I certainly am the source of some of my obligations, but as I was free to originate them I remain free to end them. If this is so, such obligations differ radically from moral obligations. In his *Treatise of Human Nature* David Hume asks us to imagine a desert island on which a single person is living in a situation in which there is no chance that any other person will ever find the island. If we further exclude God from the imagined situation, is it the case that this unfortunate person has any moral obligations? Hume said that he could not imagine any. Neither can I. That moral obligation demands a social context is a sound insight of those who defend either Utilitarianism or Contextual Ethics.

3. A number of problems arise from Kant's claim that the Categorical Imperative and the Generalization Argument are sufficient rules for moral judgment. One problem is that it be-

comes impossible to identify morally neutral contexts in relations between persons. But certainly not all obligations are morally admissable (B7a). Equally important is that while these rules provide negative tests, i.e., ways by which we can decide that some maxims are bad, they do not provide a positive test, i.e., a way by which we can decide that some maxims are good. Of course this criticism presupposes that there are morally neutral obligations. Finally, these rules are not able themselves to account for exceptions to the rules which in fact there always are.[8]

C. Contextual Ethics

The soundness of Contextual Ethics is its realization that general formulae are not in themselves absolutely good or bad. Moral judgments depend on contexts. If nothing else the study of anthropology teaches us this (A5, B2). The problem with this position is that it concludes from the above fact that moral judgments are thus not absolute. But this is wrong. Squaring has no definite mathematical value, although it has a determinate range of values. But there is nothing indefinite about the judgment that two squared is four. Similarly, killing has no definite moral value for sometimes killing is at least morally neutral. But that in no way means that the killing of six million Jews by the Nazis is not an absolute moral judgment. One of the major insights of Thomas of Aquinas in his *Summa Theologica* is that all moral judgments contain circumstances as an essential aspect of what is being judged, but that this fact of moral judgment in no way relativizes the concrete decision. Moral judgments are relational but they are not relative.

III

Jewish Religious Thought

1. For those of us who understand Judaism primarily in religious terms Judaism is fundamentally a form of historical relation between God and a particular people, Israel. Following our model, this relationship, whose terms are an individual person (God) and a collective person (Israel), is characterized by the

obligations which arise in this relation. Insofar as these obligations are the obligations of Israel they may be called "Torah."
This understanding of Judaism is common to all religious group-
ings within the Jewish people. The issue between them involves
the determination of which obligations are not proper in this
relationship. The model outlined above both characterizes this
situation in Jewish religious thought and provides a framework
in which the differences between the various Jewish religious
groups, insofar as they are theoretical and not institutional, may
be discussed.

2. The model also sheds light on a particular puzzle that has
plagued the philosophy of religion since the days of Plato. There
is certainly a close and intimate relation between religious and
moral values, but the characterization of that relation has
always been considered perplexing. In the *Euthyphro* Plato's
Socrates asks, Is piety willed by the gods because it is pious or
is it pious because it is willed by the gods? Saadia Gaon in his
Beliefs and Opinions attempts to explain the difference between
rational and nonrational commandments. Many Jewish college
students ask, Am I concerned with moral issues because I am
Jewish or because I am a human being? All of these questions
are ultimately the same question, viz., How are religious and
moral values alike yet distinct? Our model suggests an answer
to this problem.

Religious values are a species of moral values. Moral values
are the values of relations between persons. Where one of those
persons is God they are called religious values. Religious values
are thus a subspecies of moral values whose range is personal
relations where one of the persons is God. They are determined
by the success or failure of persons in fulfilling the obligations
which arise in relationship with God.

On this model the mediaeval conception of good and evil
as accepting and rejecting respectively the commandments of
the will of God becomes intelligible. However, to say that God
is the source of these values is to speak metaphorically. Literally the values arise in the relationship of God and other persons.

3. Also on this model the peculiar notion of chosenness in
which a single God makes different demands upon different

people becomes intelligible. In any relation R the nature of that relation in the particular is determined by its terms. Hence the determination of the relation aRb and the relation aRc, where "a" and "R" remain constant, will be different because the second term of that relation is different. Thus it is quite intelligible that whereas eating pork may be morally neutral for a Christian, it may not be morally neutral for a Jew. The reason is that the source of the commandment is the relation with God and not simply God.

4. That this model fits the religious language of Martin Buber is obvious.

IV

Dilemma of Autonomous and Revealed Morality

1. Emil Fackenheim has raised the following dilemma for modern Jewish philosophy:[9] Kant argued that a duty is moral only if it is done for no reason other than itself and that this condition can be fulfilled only if the source of the duty is the moral agent himself and not someone else. Now if Kant is right then it follows that if a given duty has its source in someone other than the moral agent, even if that someone else is God, then the imposed duty is not moral; and if it is moral then it originates in the will of the moral agent himself, and the revelation of the particular duty by the other, even where that other is God, is superfluous. In Fackenheim's own words:

> Either he [Kant] concedes that the will can and must impose the God-given law upon itself; but then its God-givenness becomes irrelevant in the process of self-imposition and appropriation; or else he insists that the God-givenness of the law does not and cannot at any point become irrelevant; but then the will cannot impose the law on itself—it can only submit to it for such non-moral reasons as trust in divine promise or fear of divine threats.[10]

Thus one seems to be driven by the principle of autonomy, i.e., the doctrine that any moral duty if it is moral is self-imposed, into one of two alternatives both of which are inadmissible. Either divine law ought to be obeyed because God commanded it, in which case it is not moral, or because it is moral, in which case the commanding by God is superfluous. The problem is how to find a way to demonstrate that the commandments are moral and that their divine origin is a relevant feature of their being moral.

Fackenheim himself proposes the following solution to this problem:

> The freedom required in the pristine movement of the divine commanding Presence, then, is nothing less than the freedom to accept or reject the divine commanding Presence as a whole, and for its own sake—that is, for no other reason than that it is that Presence. . . . The divine commanding Presence may force the choice on a singled-out man. It does not force him to choose God, and the choice itself (as was seen) is not heteronomous; for it accepts or rejects the divine commanding Presence for no other reason than that it *is* that Presence. But this entails the momentous consequence that *if and when a man chooses to accept the divine commanding Presence, he does nothing less than accept the divine will as his own.*[11]

The duty that a man freely imposes upon himself is the duty to make God's will his will. In doing this those duties which originate in the will of God also have the force of originating in his own will. In this way the principle of autonomy is not violated in claiming that divine commandments are moral and the necessity of divine revelation to the moral situation is preserved. To will what God wills one must know what God would will. Revelation is the source of that knowledge.

2. The style of the above discussion, as Fackenheim explains in the introduction to that discussion,[12] is a style common to the Jewish Middle Ages. It consists, in Fackenheim's own words, in a "confrontation between philosophy and Judaism." Presupposed in this confrontation are two independent affirmed sources of truth, one religious and the other secular, which

appear to be in conflict with each other. In the Middle Ages the two sources were the Torah, as understood in the light of rabbinic interpretation, and a particular understanding of philosophy whose source was Plato and Aristotle. The areas of conflict centered around physics. (For example, is the universe created or eternal? The Torah seemed to say that it was created, whereas physics seemed to claim that it is eternal.) The two sources of conflict in this present case are the Torah[13] and Kant's ethics.

Given the apparent conflict of the two affirmed sources of truth one may resolve the conflict in one of three ways. (a) One may argue that the conflict is merely apparent but not real. This approach is characteristic of the greater part of Maimonides' *A Guide for the Perplexed,* and it is the approach that Fackenheim follows in this case. (b) One may argue that the conflict is real and in the light of that conflict one may modify the claim that originates in the religious authority. This is Gersonides' approach in Book III of *The Wars of God,* and I have followed it in my article "On Knowing God." [14] Or (c) one may argue that the conflict is real and in the light of that conflict one may modify the claim that originates in the secular authority. This approach is characteristic of Hasdai Crescas' *The Light of God* and it is the approach that I would propose in the present dilemma.

It must be noted that in following either of the latter two approaches the argument for modifying an authority must arise purely from within that authority itself and not from without. To propose a modification of religious authority solely because of its conflict with secular authority and conversely to propose a modification of secular authority solely because of its conflict with religious authority are illegitimate moves. To do so is to deny the authenticity and/or the independence of the two affirmed authorities. In this case the conflict would not be solved; it would be abandoned. In other words our goal is to avoid losing the game by winning, and not by quitting.

3. I object to Fackenheim's solution to the proposed dilemma on two grounds, one religious and the other philosophic. My religious objection is that if Fackenheim's characterization of

the moral situation involving divine commandments is correct then there ought not to be dissent from divine will. I believe that this is not the case and, what is more, I believe that it is not an accurate or satisfactory portrayal of the accounts that we read in Scripture about the situations in which man meets God. Let me briefly mention two of many Biblical cases that I have in mind in making this accusation: The first is the account given in Exodus, chapters 32 and 33, where God wills the destruction of the children of Israel because of the golden calf incident and Moses asserts his will against God's will on behalf of Israel. I would want to approve of Moses' action. But given Fackenheim's solution to the autonomy dilemma I believe that he would be required to disapprove. The second is the account given in I Samuel, chapter 15 in which God condemns Saul for not killing Agag, the king of the Amalekites. While I would agree that Saul's motives for his act of mercy may not have been the noblest, and that Agag himself was far from being the noblest of men, I believe that Saul did the morally right thing, even though in this case, unlike the former, he could not convince God that his dissent from God's command was morally justifiable.

4. My philosophic objection, which in this case is more important (for the reasons stated above in (2) of this section), is that I do not think that the principle of autonomy is correct. To refer specifically to my proposed model of what it means to say that ". . . is good," I deny the principle of autonomy for the following reasons:

(B2a) Moral values range over relations between persons and not over persons themselves, as Kant is here asserting.

(B7) A self-contradictory moral obligation is an obligation whose fulfillment destroys the relationship. For this reason to kill anyone, except in cases of self-defense or possibly in cases where the one to be killed is no longer a person (as someone might argue who defends mercy killing), is not morally justifiable no matter who wills it and no matter if the conditions under which the act is willed conform to Kant's Generalization Argument. This follows because the Generalization Argument is a necessary but not a sufficient condition for moral judgment. (Cf. Kant, Insight 7.) However, given the principle of autonomy there is no reason why the Generalization Argument would not be a sufficient test for moral judgment.

Finally (B9), moral relations involve a minimum of two persons, whereas if the principle of autonomy were admissible then there could be moral obligations where, both actually and in principle, one person is involved. (Cf. Kant, Mistake 2.)[15]

5. Furthermore, I can think of no good reason why Kant himself, given the premises on which he constructed his formulations of the Categorical Imperative, would have posited the principle of autonomy other than the following (which in my opinion is not a good reason): Kant's assertion of the principle of autonomy follows logically from his claim that the will is the only thing that is good in itself. This proposition is the first axiom of his moral theory as that theory is presented in his *Groundwork of the Metaphysic of Morals*.[16] Kant argues that the only candidates for what is good in itself are the will, what he calls "gifts of fortune," and what he calls "talents of the mind." The "gifts of fortune" consist of those things which, according to Aristotle, the undisciplined mind would call happiness, e.g., having fame and fortune. The "talents of the mind" consist in what traditionally one called virtues, e.g., intelligence and courage. Kant then argues that the latter two candidates do not qualify as being good in themselves because if they are combined with other factors their moral worth is either increased or decreased. For example, wealth, a gift of fortune, increases in moral value when it is used for desirable ends, e.g., eliminating poverty; but when that wealth is used for undesirable ends, e.g., oppressing the poor, its value decreases. Similarly, conscientiousness, a talent of the mind, is to be valued in a physician, but it does not have the same value when applied to a thief. Thus, since one of these three candidates must be good in itself and neither the talents of the mind nor the gifts of fortune qualify, the will must be good in itself.

I would like to raise two specific objections to Kant's argument in this case: (1) The objections raised against the other two candidates ⁼apply against the will as well. It is certainly desirable that a person should "act only on that maxim through which he can at the same time will that it should become a universal law." However, when that maxim is that all persons who are Jews should be sent to concentration camps the value of the agent's consistency diminishes (cf. footnote 7). Similarly it is desirable to have a governor of a state whose motives are to serve the people rather than to advance his own political future. However, given a governor who believes that universities ought to be suppressed but that to suppress them is not politically wise, I would prefer a governor whose motives were not so pure. (2) Given any three candidates for moral worth, "a," "b," and "c," "a" may have value in itself, whereas "b" and "c" do not. Yet it may further be the case that "a" combined with "b" and/or "c" is more valuable than "a" itself, or that the combination of "b" and "c" is more valuable than "a" alone.[17] Even if we overlook the first objection the force of this claim is that even if the will is the only thing that is good in itself it does not follow that there are not other things more valuable than the virtues of an isolated will. (3) Kant's argument shows that where no will is involved no moral judgment is possible. But it does not show that the will itself is what is good. (Cf. Kant, Mistakes 1.)

There are some who may object to this approach to moral issues on the grounds that it is too formal, and moral life, after all, is an emotional matter. To such a charge I can only say that moral life is certainly emotional but the evaluation of that life need not be. If it be replied that it is impossible to rationally conceive moral life, the answer is that a schema has been provided for doing just that. If the schema is inadequate, show how it is inadequate. However, that, too, is a rational assertion. And if it cannot be shown to be inadequate, then the objection seems to be unimportant.

NOTES

1 I will follow this approach because the proposed model largely expresses those features of these two ethical systems which I find to be cogent. Ideally the model should appear only at the end of a discussion of every factor that is involved in my positing the model. However, the demands of time force me to be selective in my discussion. Consequently I will follow this inherently less desirable method.

2 *Rediscovering Judaism,* Edited by A. J. Wolf, Quadrangle, Chicago: 1965, pp. 51–76.

3 The numbers that appear in parentheses in this section are references to the propositions in the model presented in Section I.

4 "Act only on that maxim through which you can at the same time will that it should become a universal law." This imperative was to be used to judge all moral acts in the following way: (a) Take the act and express it as a demand (maxim). (b) Universalize the maxim, i.e., make it generally applicable. "Shoot John" is generalized either to "Shoot everyone" or "Shoot anyone like John." (c) If it is possible to will this generalized maxim (universal law) then the act following from the maxim is good. Otherwise it is evil.

5 Kant's "will" is what we have called "consciousness," i.e., that which is the distinguishing mark of persons.

6 "If the consequences of everybody doing X are undesirable then nobody ought to do X."

7 For example, the case of the consistent Nazi in Hare's *Freedom and Reason.* You are speaking with a Nazi who says that all Jews ought to be sent to gas chambers. You then convince him that, unknown to him, he also is a Jew. By Kant's test alone if he is willing to send himself to a gas chamber—and some would have been willing—his position is not morally objectionable.

8 On this problem see G. M. Singer, *The Generalization Argument in Ethics.*

9 Fackenheim, *op. cit.*

10 *Ibid.,* p. 61.

11 *Ibid.,* p. 67.

12 *Ibid.,* pp. 52–53.

13 The Torah in this case is not understood by Fackenheim in precisely the same way that it was understood by the mediaeval Jewish philosophers, but nonetheless the resemblances between the two are sufficient to call both rabbinic interpretations.

14 *Judaism,* Winter 1969, pp. 64–83.

15 For current discussions of the question of whether or not there can be moral duties to oneself see the following:

George Marcus Singer, "On Duties to Oneself," *Ethics,* Vol. 69, 1959, pp. 202–5.

———, "Duties and Duties to Oneself," *Ethics,* Vol. 73, 1962–63.

Paul D. Eisenberg, "Duties to Oneself: A New Defense Sketched," *The Review of Metaphysics,* Vol. 20, 1967, pp. 602–34.

I call particular attention to the Eisenberg article. If his arguments are correct and there can, in fact, be moral duties to oneself, then I would be forced to modify my claim that (B9) morally judged relations involve a minimum of two persons, which in turn would force me to abandon most of the objections to the principle of autonomy that I am here considering. I do not believe that Mr. Eisenberg's argument is successful but the discussion of those arguments here would be too technical and too lengthy for the purposes of the present paper.

16 See the H. J. Paton translation entitled *The Moral Law,* Barnes and Noble, New York: 1950, pp. 17 and 61ff.

17 See G. E. Moore's discussion of what he calls "organic unities" in *Principia Ethica.*

THE JEWISH BACKGROUND

DOES TORAH MEAN LAW?

Jacob Neusner
Professor of Religious Studies
Brown University
Providence, Rhode Island

In mistranslating the word *torah,* which means "teaching," by the word *nomos,*[1] "law," the Alexandrian scholars who rendered the Bible into Greek opened the way for bad exegesis and excellent homily.

The meaning of Torah is not limited to law. Anyone who has read the Pentateuch knows that it embodies far more than purely legal matters. There are, to be sure, those who feel that the Torah's meaning is exhausted by its legislative aspect. R. Isaac, a Mishnaic sage cited by Rashi, commented that the Pentateuch should have begun with Chapter 12 in Exodus where the first actual laws appear, and not with the creation story and the genealogical tables. Others seize on the legal aspect of the Torah to erect a false parallel, maintaining that the *old* dispensation was of law, while the *new* is of love; the *old* consists of meaningless form—the *new,* of infinite meaning; the *old* is Apollonian —the *new,* Dionysian.

If Torah does not mean law, then these supposed antitheses collapse, and with them falls the weight of the theology they are forced to bear. In the end, these antitheses are important only to Christians who cease to believe in Christ. Lacking the old convictions, they are compelled to seek new justifications for what, to them, is a worn-out faith. Wanting desperately still to be Christians, they find a new rationale in the antithesis of priestly and prophetic Judaism, of law and inner sanctity. Not by faith, but by the synthesizing of Jesus do they find Christ.

Out of this apparent mistranslation of Torah into *nomos* may, nonetheless, come an insight into the grand perspective embodied

155

in this error. "Law" meant more then than it does to us. It is for us to penetrate the meaning of *nomos* as conceived by ancient men.

What, indeed, did *nomos* mean to the Hellenic mind? To be sure, it meant law. It meant also that which is in habitual practice and use. *Kata nomon,* in Hesiod's *Theogony,* means "according to custom or law." The dative means "conventionally." Significantly, in architecture the word has the meaning of "the course of the masonry." M. P. Nilsson, in his *History of Greek Religion,* says, ". . . . the word *nomos* involved for the Greeks the idea of an enactment which is the decree of someone, whether man or god, and is therefore not the result of physical necessity. This sense of the word is better expressed by 'convention,' but on the other hand, the latter translation does not convey the idea of compulsion and command which underlies *nomos.*" One dimension of the word is "the way things are" and, as applied to Torah, "the necessary convention of the universe."

A passage from *Oedipus the King* illuminates the inner sense of *nomos.* Jacosta says repeatedly that there is no inner order in the world, no habitual usage in the universe. The god may have something in mind, but we shall never know it. We as men confront a world of chaos.

> *No man possesses the secret of divination.*
> *And I have proof: an oracle was given to Laius . . .*
> *That he should die by the hands of his own child . . . .*
> > *What came of it? Laius*
> *It is common knowledge was killed by outland robbers . . . .*
> *There, then, Apollo did not so contrive it . . . .*
> > *What he intends,*
> *The god will show us in his own good time.*

And again:

> *Fear? What has a man to do with fear?*
> *Chance rules our lives, and the future is all unknown.*
> *Best live as best we may, from day to day . . . .*

Such things [as oracles]
Must be forgotten if life is to be endured.

The chorus answers Jacosta, pointing up the blasphemy:

I only ask to live, with pure faith keeping
In word and deed that Law which leaps the sky,
Made of no mortal mold, undimmed, unsleeping,
Whose living godhead does not age or die.

And again:

Zeus! If thou livest, all-ruling, all-pervading,
Awake! Old oracles are out of mind.
Apollo's name denied, his glory fading.
There is no godliness in all mankind.

Jacosta has asked: "Why should we fear oracles, when there is no such thing as foresight?" H. D. F. Kitto comments: "Best live at random, as one may—a doctrine which would deny the very basis of all serious Greek thought; for while Greek life was still healthy and stable, the Greek believed, as if by instinct, that the universe was not chaotic and irrational, but was based on an . . . obeyed law. . . . In the Oresteia we find moral laws which have the same sort of validity as physical and mathematical laws. . . . The problem there is to find a system of Justice that will fit into this framework without disastrously contravening these laws. To the mind of Sophocles, this *logos* shows itself as a balance, rhythm, or pattern in human affairs."

If human life seems to us chaotic, it is
Because we do not see the entire pattern.

How then shall we understand *nomos*, the Law, by which the Septuagint translates Torah? Apparently, the Alexandrian scholars chose the proper word for Torah. Torah is indeed law, but not just in the prescriptive, legal sense. The *nomos* of Torah is not merely legislation; rather is it the greatest gift revelation might have brought to man—the pattern, the description of the inner workings of the world; it is the customary usage that governs eternity. This truly comprehends the *nomos* both of Torah and of Alexandria. It is the law which describes the way man is, the way Israel came to be and needs to be identified. Israel, in this grand sense, is not commanded to keep the laws governing human relations, the Sabbath and other commandments of the Torah. Israel is Israel in that it does these things, in that the law which is set forth in the Pentateuch articulates the otherwise ineffable mystery of being.

This is, however, a Platonic and Hellenic idea. How does the Athenian notion of *nomos* survive the journey to Alexandria? In substance, very well; in form, not at all. Philo Judaeus, who best represents the thought of Hellenistic Jewry, uses what is, substantially, the ancient concept of *nomos*. In the words of H. A. Wolfson, "Sometimes Philo treats of . . . ideas . . . as a totality . . . as the pattern or the cause of the world as a whole." Further, Philo identifies the laws of the Jews with the practice of wisdom.

Professor Wolfson continues, "In Greek philosophy, according to Plato, Polema, Aristotle, and the Stoics, enacted laws, if they are enacted by wise legislators on the basis of reason, are in a certain sense also laws in accordance with nature. Philo says, if it is law in accordance with nature that is sought after, then philosophers might as well give up their effort to devise such a law by their own reason. Only a law which was revealed by God who is the creator of nature can be in accordance with nature in the true sense of the term."

Philo inquires in the spirit of Rabbi Isaac: Why did Moses preface his laws with the story of Creation? It is to show "that the world is in harmony with the Law, and the Law with the world, and that the man who observes the Law is constituted thereby a loyal citizen of the world, regulating his doings by the purpose and will of nature, in accordance with which the entire world itself is administered."

This, the design for the universe and for man, is, indeed, Torah in the profoundest sense. The only problem in Philo's definition is that for this idea he uses not *nomos*, which in

Hellenistic literature means mainly legislation and convention in the strictly legal sense, but *logos.*

Alas, one cannot claim that the original intent of the translators of the Bible into Greek was to intimate this more compelling meaning of *law.* I might argue that they could not properly call the Torah *logos,* and so chose the nearest possible equivalent, *nomos.* But even if this could be proved, it is a feeble argument indeed. Nothing, as the Talmud says, stands in the way of a man's will. When the scholars of Alexandria said *nomos,* they meant *nomos,* at least in the plain sense of the term.

This sense for the inner relevance of Torah in revealing an understanding of all existence was, however, common to the Jewish thought of this period. *Genesis Rabbah* (a source for ideas current in the Talmudic period, though edited rather late) teaches in its opening homily:

Scripture says:
"The Lord made me [the Torah] as the beginning of His
    way,
The first of His works of old.
I was set up from everlasting, from the beginning,
Or ever the earth was . . . .
When He appointed the foundations of the earth,
Then I was by Him, as a nurseling;
And I was daily all delight,
Playing always before Him." (Prov. 8.22, 23, 29-30.)

The Torah says, "I was God's instrument. According to the custom of the world, when a mortal king builds a palace, he does not build it by his own skill, but with the skill of an architect. And that architect does not build it out of his own head, but employs plans and diagrams in order to know how to arrange the chambers and the wicket doors. So too did the Holy One, blessed be He, look into the Torah and create the world." The above concept is cited by Philo himself. Professor Wolfson points out that Philo uses it for his own purposes, stating that the architect carries his plans in his "soul," that is, in his rational mind.

While the first level of meaning for *nomos* is not demonstrably this larger sense of divine design for the world, nonetheless, the rabbis understood the Torah to be that grand design. The earlier, Hellenic sense of *nomos,* now comprehended exclusively by the word *logos* is, notwithstanding, entirely relevant if we would understand what the Alexandrian scholars meant when they called the Torah *nomos* or "law."

In *Oedipus the King,* Jacosta demands: Why should we fear oracles when there is no such thing as foresight, and no order in the world?

The Alexandrian scholars would answer her: "It is true that we do not have the foresight of oracles. But we are, after all, men and Greeks, and do not see the universe naked and chaotic. The universe has its laws and its ways. There is such a thing as foresight, for there is Torah—a plan and a design for all existence. This Torah—this inner law of the universe—is what we mean by *nomos.*"

Here is the plain sense of what the authors of the Septuagint had in mind in translating Torah as *nomos*—and here is our homily.

NOTES

[1] For the use of *nomos* in Pauline theology, cf. R. Bultmann, *Theology of the New Testament* (N. Y., 1951), translated by Kendrick Grobel. Vol. I, pp. 259–269.

Dr. David Winston offers the following comment: "For a detailed analysis of the meaning of *nomos,* see Sties, "Nomos Basileus," in *Philologus,* 83 (1928), p. 251 ff. Cf. also Pindar, fr. 169; Hesiod, *Works and Days,* 276 ff.; Kerakleitus, fr. 114 (diels); Herodotus 3.38; Sophocles, *Antigo,* 450 ff., *Old. Tyn.* 863 ff. Stier shows by an analysis of these passages that *nomos* originally referred to the moral order of the universe. It took on, however, a very different meaning in the writings of the Ionian philosophers, who contrasted it with *phusis* (Pseudo-Hippoc., *Regimen,* i.ii, in vol. IV in Loeb ed. of Hippoc.)." *See also* Nahum N. Glatzer, *Hillel the Elder: The Emergence of Classical Judaism* (N. Y. 1956: Bnai Brith Hillel Foundation), pp. 51–53.

CONFRONTATION OF GREEK
AND JEWISH ETHICS:
PHILO *DE DECALOGO*

Samuel Sandmel
*Professor of Bible
and Hellenistic Literature*
*Hebrew Union College—Jewish Institute of Religion
Cincinnati, Ohio*

Since the topic is theology and ethics, the words I am about to speak are directed narrowly to the specific topic, rather than to a general exposition of Philo. I do not know what has gone on in the other sessions. Specifically, I do not know whether those assembled have ever come to any meeting of minds on a definition of theology. There are two usual definitions which, though related, are quite different, involving a distinction that goes back at least to the beginning of the nineteenth century. Let me put these as questions. Is theology merely a systematic inquiry into the tenets of religion? If yes, then theology, when it relates to the Bible or to the Rabbinic literature or to Philo or to the Church Fathers, is an antiquarian pursuit. Or is theology, on the other hand, a living system which is obligatory on (or commended to) the modern communicant? Antiquarian analysis is a much safer pursuit than is the provision of ongoing relevancy, for the latter is much more arduous.

Yet assuming that there could be some definition agreed on, so that there resulted some consensus about the premises, and assuming that it would be possible to collate the ethical mandates from the past and make them relevant for today, it would still be possible for wide differences of opinion to exist. This is so because the ancient ethical systems are partly attitude and partly programmatic, but necessarily they cannot remain programmatic for every age and every situation; the more complex society becomes, the less easy it is to adapt general ethical attitudes or ancient programs to specific modern needs.

The relevancy of raising the question of Jewish and Greek

ethics could possibly be merely antiquarian. On the other hand it can stem from this important consideration that, by and large, Jewish ethics historically was considered to be a divinely revealed mandate; normally, in our general thinking, we assume that Greek ethical theories are without a divine origin, and emerge, as it were, out of experience or out of speculative analysis. I think that I will be able to demonstrate that this latter is quite an oversimplification. But let me ask a question, just so that we have a background question to shape our discussion: In what way is Jewish ethics markedly different from the ethical mandate that comes out of the French Bill of Rights, the Declaration of the Rights of Man, the American Bill of Rights, or out of the series of ethical thinkers who cannot properly be allocated to any specific religious tradition but who are secular? The confrontation of Jewish and Greek ethics long ago is a kind of forerunner to the problem of religious versus secular ethics today. We have, in the person of Philo, the result of the confrontation of these two systems.

I have selected the treatise *Concerning the Decalogue* for a number of reasons. First, as Philo's treatises go, it is relatively short; second, I guess that we are all interested in the Ten Commandments; third, the treatise lends itself, I believe, to the best introduction to the special topic that we are looking at, as it is handled in Philo's thought.

The last thing that I think is necessary or desirable for us, unless you think otherwise, is for me to read certain portions which are beautifully homiletical. You can do this on your own and I do not think that there is any great need for us collectively to do so; there is good sermonic material here, especially when you come to Shabbas *Yisro*. But the extent of the confrontation of allegedly secular ethics with allegedly revealed ethics is, I think, better exemplified in *Concerning the Decalogue* than anywhere else.

With respect to the external format, there is a comment that has to be made. The essay is divisible into two parts, the first dealing with the first five Commandments and the second with the last five. This division is significant only because it is found elsewhere, in other treatises of Philo, and also in IV Maccabees.

This division sets into equilibrium, on the one hand, piety, which is man's obligation to God and, on the other hand, the virtues, which are the enumerations of man's obligations to his fellowman. Obviously, piety, man's relationship to God, must yield consequences, and these consequences are man's relationship to his fellowman. But if you divide the Ten Commandments in half, the fifth one would be, "Honor your father and mother"; then you could ask, "How does that relate to God?" This is the one commandment that I think it is worthwhile mentioning to you because, Philo, having decided to divide things into the typical two-part pattern, must strain a little bit to justify his allocation. Here Philo's ingenuity enters in. Parents, insofar as they are procreators, are like God, and insofar as they are mortal, they are like men; the honoring of parents is kindred to honoring God. The limitation of the mortal lives of parents is a good transition to enable Philo to move on to man's obligation to his fellowman. So, honoring one's parents is subsumed under piety to God.

Rather notably in this essay, when Philo comes to give an interpretation of the tenth Commandment, he interprets, "You shall not covet," in pretty much the same way that some modern scholars have rendered it, namely by the word "desire." I think in English there is quite a margin of difference between "desire" and "covet" in that "covet" is a stronger word, for it implies that aggressive action results from coveting, but that desire itself can be limited and contained. Philo moves from his use of "desire," into introducing the question, "What are the total passions of which desire is one?" In answer, there are four passions; in addition to desire, the other three are grief, pleasure and fear. I mention this item so as to lead us into the specific discussion of our topic: What was there in the way of ethics in the Greek world and what was there in the Jewish world, and how did these things come to be equated with each other?

I ask you to accept, at least tentatively, the following as true. All of Philo's religious sentiments are Jewish, and hence, he believes in revelation. He believes in God, and he does not feel that he has to prove His existence. So, too, he believes in prophecy. His explanation of his beliefs, of how things happen, is Grecian. When he wants to describe the phenomenon of prophecy, he gets this directly from Plato. I do not think that Plato ever contended that he himself had been a recipient of prophecy, for Plato was only describing how prophecy works. Philo will borrow the definition from Plato, but the contention in Philo that there *is* such a thing as prophecy is Jewish. (Only indirectly does Philo regard himself a prophet.)

As a consequence of this tendency to use Platonism and Stoicism to explain Jewish religious intuition, Philo's exposition of Jewish ethics is necessarily Stoic and Platonic; hence, the need to enumerate the passions as four. One thing you might notice is that he does not normally use the word *ethics*. Like the Stoics, he uses the word *virtue*. He speaks, in many places, of four cardinal virtues, as the Stoics did: justice, prudence, temperance, and bravery. Piety towards God wavers in his treatises between being a summary of the four cardinal virtues, and the impetus (the generic) out of which the others (the specific) ensue. (You can see, of course, that there is a great deal at stake, in the distinction as to whether piety and four virtues are a summary, or whether they are the source and subsequent derivation.) Philo accepts Stoic terms, Stoic mannerisms, and Stoic standards. In *Concerning the Decalogue,* he explains Jewish law in terms of Stoic requirements, and in the treatise which follows it, called *Concerning the Special Laws* (by "special laws" Philo means the specific Mosaic regulations which in the Bible come immediately after the Decalogue), Philo, still in Stoicism, regards these laws as only expansions of that which is adumbrated, already intimated, in the Decalogue. The Decalogue is, as it were, and to use an expression which Philo never uses, *roshay tayvot,* and the ensuing regulations are only the filled-in matter.

With respect to piety towards God, the substance of the first five Commandments, you can ask the question: If the exposition of what is involved in them is Grecian, in what way does Philo associate piety with divine revelation? The answer can get to be a little complicated but such an answer must be given to you or we will not meet the mandate of our topic. I should therefore fill in some things which are not in the treatise and this I now propose to do.

One of the principles that Philo holds with the Stoics is that man is able to learn both data, in the sense of information, and also to learn himself. Learning one's self means not only the ability to give the traditional Greek list of the five senses, graded as to quality with sight highest and touch lowest, and the four passions, but to perceive that beyond this knowledge lies the question of man's inner control of sense and passion. Moreover, one must infer from these terms that it is possible to move from the world of sense perception into the world of concept. Thus, if I see this table, if I touch this table, if I hear this table by moving it, then I am in the realm of perception; perception is that which is achieved by the five senses. If, having seen and heard and touched, I am able in my mind to fashion an image of a table, then I am now in the realm of concept. You say, does this not sound like Plato and the *World of Ideas?* Yes. An idea is that apprehension by the mind which is abstracted from the perceptions of the senses. Concept is the immaterial image, which arises after perception has done its work.

Let us imagine that there are two mathematicians who do not know each other but who have each decided to try to bisect an angle. If you remember this from your high school geometry, it can be done. If you get two competent and reasonable mathematicians, and set them on the problem, and if they use right logic and right method, they will come to the same end result. The fact that they come to the same conclusion implies that there is a body of universal knowledge which the mind can aspire to reach, if only the mind is able to work with true logic. If the mind does not work with true logic, then it cannot get to concept, and to such universal knowledge. The Stoics had spoken of this universal knowledge. Jews had spoken of Torah. When Jews ran into Greeks, probably as early as Ecclesiasticus, a grand equation was made wherein Greek wisdom, *sophia,* equaled *chochma;* and since *chochma* is found in the Book of Proverbs, which is in Scripture, *chochma* equals *torah.* The word which the Stoics preferred for the encompassing universal knowledge which a man could, by exercise and right reason, get to, is summarized in the word *logos.* The equation needs to be extended so that Torah equals logos, or vice versa.

There is no single, easy definition for *logos*. The only thing we can be certain about is that the translation of John, "In the beginning was the *logos* and the *logos* was with God and the *logos* was Divine/God," should not be, "In the beginning was the Word and the Word was with God and the Word was God/ Divine." *Logos* is not a word, nor *The Word*. Logos is not only reason; *logos*, indeed, is the whole complex of data that the reasoning mind can get to. Just as *chochma* has an implicit separate existence (hypostasis), in that *chochma* cries aloud in the streets, or builds a house in Proverbs, so *logos* has a separate existence. *Logos* then is not simply the capacity to reason, but is rather that goal of knowledge and the universal wisdom to which right reason can bring a person. On principle, any gifted person who learns data, who regiments his senses and his passions so that he avoids error, who uses right reason, can get to the pinnacle of living, which is to live simply by right reason. To live ethically implies both the comprehension of ethics as concepts, and also the resistance to the seductive or delusive capacities of the senses and the passions.

The religious question for Philo is: What is the relationship of a history of revelation to man's possible capacity to live by exalted right reason? The answer, which varies from time to time, would be found normally in two possibilities. One possibility, ignoring divine revelation, can suppose that certain men possess, as gifts from God, the traits by which these men, through learning, or practice (*askesis*), or intuition, or all of these, are enabled on their own to follow right reason to its ultimate destination of *logos*. But, on the other hand, God had pity on man and therefore made it easier for him, and revealed right reason in the pages of Scripture, with the result that man does not have to run the risk of relying on what might turn out to be faulty reason. Moreover, the second way implies there is a margin of difference between mere possibility and surety.

Consistent with these possibilities is Philo's allegorical explanation: Moses, the author of the Pentateuch, is the allegory for the *logos*. The *logos*, now in the sense of a body of wisdom, guides by means of its innate character. "Moses" does not command (this may shock you); he guides or exhorts, but he does not command, for "command" implies authority, but authority over a mind is irreconcilable with the freedom of the mind to learn.

Philo makes a distinction, which again is Stoic, between written *logos* and spoken *logos*. For the Stoics, speech is thought when it is uttered. Thought is speech when it is unuttered. Which is pure, thought or speech? We always manage not to say what we mean; hence thought is pure, whereas speech is impure thought. Moses is *logos* in the form of *thought*, and Aaron is *logos* in the form of *speech*, because Moses was tongue-tied and Aaron was his brother and was his mouth. The written requirements in the Pentateuch are on the level of Aaron, but he who knows allegory can penetrate into their profound meaning and get to the level of pure *logos*. Accordingly, if you observe the laws found in the *Chumash* on the literal level, without giving any thought to them, you are on the level of the mystery of Aaron, and while you are living by the *logos*, you do not *know* you are. But if you have become schooled, and inducted into philosophy and trained in it, then you live on the level of the mystery of Moses, because you know what you are doing. Philo has scorn for those who live only on the level of Aaron; they are the mere literalists. Philo, of course, lives on the level of the *logos*, of the mystery of Moses, as one might reasonably expect. Now, do you want to live by the *logos?* Then observe the particular laws, and thereby you will do so by coincidence. Do you want to live more deeply, indeed, deliberately, by the *logos?* Then study hard, and control your senses and passions, and learn, learn, learn. Learn to know not only the what of the Laws, but the profound why of them.

Shall we call this *logos* theory merely Stoic? No, it is partially Stoic, but it is more than Stoic. It is thoroughly saturated with a Jewish background. What makes this wisdom wise? That its source is God. On the other hand, in speaking *analytically* about the *logos*, Philo will often give it an overtone as though it is merely the Stoic body of immanent wisdom which permeates the universe. And when it comes to defining Jewish ethics, Philo inevitably gives definitions that can be paralleled in and buttressed by recourse to the Stoics. In Philo's use of the Stoic categories, he may have to put five Jewish items into four Stoic ones, that is, the last five commandments into the four cardinal virtues, but that is only because basically his enumeration is Stoic. One could put it this way, that in Philo the Jewish and the Stoic ethics are interchangeable in their substance, however they differ in origin.

But let us revert to our question. What is the mandate for man respecting the virtues?

It is necessary here to make some sort of correction, intimated above as necessary, of a prevailing view that Greek philosophy is simply a disinterested inquiry into the nature of things and that it was in some way an experiential matter. Now, obviously experience entered into Greek law. But for a good Stoic, what is law? Let me give you a definition. Law is that midpoint between tyranny and anarchy. Law is that which emerges when the monarch is a philosopher. It does not mean that he is a student of Philo or a student of Plato. What it does mean is that the king is able to regiment his senses and passions, to free his mind from the obstacles offered by the body, and to let his mind soar up into the *logos,* into the realm of ideas and there encounter what the Stoics called, inheriting the term from earlier times and developing it, the "unwritten law of nature." Now we have to pause and talk a little bit about this unwritten law of nature.

If you are a good Platonist, this table before us, which could be chopped up and could be burned up, was made by somebody who started with an idea of a table in his mind; that idea is not subject to decay or destruction. Now, the better your craftsman is, the more nearly your table, made of wood, is an imitation of the immaterial, ideal table. The worse the craftsman, the less correspondence there is. The ideal table is perfect. Putatively, there is a body of law which is perfect, and that is the law of nature. It is inherent in the very essence of things that it must be unwritten, because who ever tries to write down a law is like a carpenter who tries to make this table: there is a gap between his achievement and the ideal. The achievement is inevitably, in some degree, imperfect, and always inferior to that perfection which was in his mind when the artisan began. A philosopher king is able to let his mind range into the realm of ideas to encounter there the law of nature, unwritten, and then he turns the law of nature into the best possible written specific statutes. If he is not a philosopher, he does not have this ability. If he is not a philosopher, the laws come out of his caprice, or out of the whim of his personality, not out of nature. If he is a strong narcissistic person, the laws will be tyrannical, and not reflect nature. If he is a weakling who inherits the throne from his father, he will be a mollycoddle, and the end result will be anarchy, not true law. Hence, the true king is that philosopher who exceeds the rest of the populace in spiritual stature, as he often exceeds it in physical stature.

Now ask this question. Are the laws of Moses the unwritten law of nature, or are they the imitation of the law of nature? In answer, they are written, so that they must be the imitation. Where, then, do you find the law of nature in the Bible? In Genesis. Abraham, Isaac, and Jacob were philosopher kings who, by virtue of their ability to live by nature, were exponents of the law of nature, and all that Moses did in the laws of Exodus, Leviticus, Numbers, and Deuteronomy, was to write down there the record of the lives of Abraham, Isaac, and Jacob. If, therefore, you live by the laws of Moses, the particular laws, you will live like Abraham, Isaac, and Jacob, and you will be living by the law of nature. If you are a dumb literalist, you will be doing it coincidentally, on the level of Aaron. If you are a student, then you will be doing it with knowledge, and therefore you will know what you are doing, and be on the level of Moses.

The laws of Moses, according to Philo, are the best possible imitation of and substitute for the law of nature. They are that, as can be demonstrated by the circumstance that they are immutable and eternal. In Athens, the new king abrogates the laws of the preceding king, so the Athenian laws are never immutable. If you move from Athens to Sparta, the laws change, but the laws of Moses are everywhere the same. While, then, the laws of Moses belong in the category of written laws, they are the best possible approximation of the unwritten law of nature.

The Stoic, then, did not derive laws solely from experience, nor is the Stoic notion of an ideal king that of somebody who has tried X, Y, Z ways, and has said this one of them is the best. The ideal king is that person who has utilized philosophy as a discipline, so as to rise above appearance and to get to immaterial reality. The easy equation of philosophy as mere secularism emerging out of experience is a little bit unfair to the Greek tradition. If we make that corrective, that is enough for our present purposes.

Yet we want to press on to the question: Does Philo, equating Jewish ethics with the Stoic, really consider the Jewish mandates divine? To answer that we would have to give a resounding "yes." The fact that Philo can demonstrate their "validity" through the use of Plato or Stoicism, does not touch upon the issue, Does he consider them the products of revelation? He absolutely does. He can make more complicated the doctrine of *logos* by implying that God is so transcendent that God becomes immanent in the world only through *logos;* and he can thereby anticipate, and be parallel to that tradition among all philosophical mystics, that God in his essence is unknowable, and that it is only facets of God, such as the *logos,* that the mind can get to. In Philo, the mind cannot go beyond the *logos* to God. *Logos* is susceptible of synonyms, for it can be Moses or, elsewhere, the High Priest, also an allegory for the *logos.* The *logos* is the first-born of God; the *logos* is the only begotten, as the Christian has it, of God. You can use these synonyms; on the other hand, I do not know of any passage in which he gives a definition of *logos.* We give the definition when we see how he uses *logos:* The *logos* is the highest aspect of the godhead which the mind can get to.

Philo rejects the supposition that God is named *Elohim* (*theos* in Greek) or *Adonoi* (*kyrios* in Greek). God is nameless. For God, Philo usually uses the Greek expression *to on,* that which exists, a Platonic term. "That which exists" is, for Philo, an active idea. Philo at times tends to dissolve history, in that Moses is an omnipresent *logos,* transcending his allocation to that ancient period between the Egyptian enslavement and the settlement in Canaan, and thereby Moses becomes, instead, the existential experience of every man; nevertheless, Philo has the vivid belief in God, and in Scripture as a product of God. Oft-times, when you read a bit and piece here and there of Philo it sounds so excessively naturalistic that people who read Philo in excerpt are often betrayed by his naturalism. He, indeed, naturalizes every miracle that I can think of. He believes in miracles, but he always explains them in ways in which they are not miraculous, so that he sounds like a naturalist, but he has a firm belief in God. The Commandments, then, come from God, and the utility of philosophy is to explain how they come from God; only, Moses exhorts, he does not command.

To summarize at this point, Philo adopts the nomenclature of the Greeks respecting ethical formulation, and he makes equations, with the result that the Jewish ethics and the Greek tend to become virtually identical. But he insists on the superiority of the Jewish formulation; he concedes that gifted persons can conceivably get to goal without the formulation, but those who can are very few. Hence, you need Moses. But you need him so as to achieve the ethical goal, you do not need him to know the ethical content.

Since Philo was a Greek Jew and Paul was also a Greek Jew, I want to introduce something else for a contrast, because it may give a little more dimension to what we are talking about. In Paul, there is the contention, first, that righteousness cannot be achieved by abiding by the law; second, the law can be an obstacle to righteousness; third, there is a very curious passage (Gal. 3:19) that the Mosaic Laws were ordained by the angels, and angels is plural. Now what does this latter mean? There is destined to be a perpetual disagreement over the passage between secular students of the history of religion and most pious Christians. In another passage, in I Corinthians 11:10, Paul gives the mandate to women to keep the head covered "because of the angels." A reasonable explanation of "angels" is "demons"; the word is a euphemism. The law is the product of demons? Yes, as it is repeated by second-century gnostics. Fourth, the transition from sinfulness to righteousness is something that man cannot work out on his own. This is able to come about only through the action of God who can tranform man; it can come because the *logos,* Christ, died on the cross, and thereby atonement was made for man's sinful nature. The transition from sin to righteousness was made through this an act of grace on the part of God, and not because man did, or could do, anything to merit it. The supposition that man can merit righteousness supposes that man can observe laws and that there is something valid in their observance. This supposition tends to negate God's grace, for if grace is that which comes freely from God, then works implies that man can earn it, and hence grace is nullified. Paul raises the question, should sin increase in quantity so that God's grace can increase, and there Paul takes the stand of *me genoito, has v'halila.* If men do not earn righteousness, does grace come to everybody? No. It comes to those called, those predestined for it.

Is there in Philo any reflection of such suppositions that the laws are the product of a second-rate revelation, or the product of revelation by demons, or that man cannot observe the law, or that grace alone saves, and that grace is meted out through divine election? Almost none at all!

I have raised the issue about Paul for still another reason, because there is an implication which you can run into among your Christian colleagues from time to time, depending on how strongly Lutheran or Calvinistic they are. For some such Christians the whole realm of ethics is ruled out as a religious matter. In different ages, when vested interests began to arise, and various aspects of social problems emerged, there were reflections in Christian thought of different values invested in grace, predestination, and the like. Some distortion could arise. For example, if God decides whether you are to be rich or poor, and he picks you to be rich and he picks your neighbor to be poor, should you help out your neighbor? To do that, you are interfering with God's predestination. There are on record those who distort Calvin into a sanction for social unconcern, and argue against a state concern, because if God had intended "those people" to be well off, he would have made them well off. Or, if God had intended black men to be free and to have equal opportunity he would have created them that way, and for a preacher to get up and advocate equal rights is to usurp God's prerogative. Or, it could be used in behalf of special interests.

If a church owns a red light district, you as a minister must not speak out against it. Or, when you get the movement around the 1890's, the Social Gospel, which interpreted Christianity as a reform movement, then economic conservatives could cite Calvin or Luther or Augustine or Paul and say that social reform has nothing to do with religion.

There is often a dimension, then, in which Christians say that preachers should keep out of politics, which is different from that in which Jewish congregants say that rabbis should keep out of politics. What Jewish congregations mean is, "It is not good for us Jews to take the lead." That is, Christians can one-sidedly, but honestly, urge a traditional theological sanction for inaction, but Jews cannot.

Philo insists that a person can choose; he insists that a person can observe the law; he does not liquidate, as Paul does, repentance, this because in the Pauline system man can do nothing. There is no echo in Philo of the age-old Christian debate: does a man have the choice at least to qualify himself for grace? Augustine said no and Pelegius said yes and Pelegius was voted to be a heretic. There is nothing in Philo that frees the person from that moral responsibility which is implicit in choice. Man, according to Philo, can choose to observe the laws and can achieve the observance of them. And man can take those steps to advance to the *logos*. Grace is restricted to the mystic vision, as proved by *ophthe*, the Greek passive which renders the passive וירא of Gen. 17.1; man can prepare himself to receive the divine vision, but 17.1 uses the passive to teach that it is God's grace which determines who of the self-prepared receive it, and who do not.

Now what is it that we have encompassed? Philo's exposition of Jewish ethics is Grecian. His explanation of how the ethics is defined is Grecian. His bill of particulars is often Grecian. Yet he never abandons the Jewish assumption that the laws are literally the product of revelation. I concede that when he gets through rationalizing how revelation works, you may say that it is no longer revelation; that is why I find it necessary to emphasize that Philo does believe the laws are products of revelation.

There are a half-dozen passages in this treatise that I think you would be well advised to look at sometimes, if you do not feel like reading the whole thing. When Philo speaks about respect for father and mother, he is very eloquent. When he talks about idolatry, he lacks the uncharitableness of the *Epistle of Baruch* which is added to the book of Jeremiah in the Greek translation. When he talks about the *Shabbos,* it is really not in terms of those who worry about pressing an electric button, or something like that. For him, the *Shabbos* is that day in which you indulge in wisdom, and wisdom is where you separate the mind from the body, so that the mind can go up and commune with God. The Sabbath is really a spiritual essence in this most high-minded treatise.

You ask: Does Philo throw some light for us on our theological problems? That is why I began with the formulation, What are we looking for? Are we looking for an arrangement and analysis of what is in the ancient documents? That is only antiquarianism.

Are we looking for formulas? Even the ancient documents cannot give us specific programs. My two older sons and I are inevitably divided, completely divided, on what to do about Viet Nam, even though we talk from the same religious context. Honest people can interpret a common mandate in diverse ways. Respecting Jewish theology, I wonder whether we are not talking about a mandate for our people, based on a supposition of revelation which a naturalistic age has queries about. How good it would have been had Philo argued that Jewish ethics was different even in substance from the Stoic, and proved it. How good it would be if we could contend that Jewish ethics surpasses the secular, and prove it! I guess what characterizes the C.C.A.R. is that of its members 90% are naturalistic and 10% theistic, and it is searching for a mandatory theology which it desires should be 100% theistic, and no percent naturalistic. How one gets out of this dilemma I do not know. If I knew the way, I would tell you. Maybe to see the problem is in itself something of a virtue; maybe. I am not sure. It is a little too comforting to tell one's self that the answers are less cogent than are the questions.

REPROBATION, PROHIBITION, INVALIDITY

AN EXAMINATION OF THE HALAKHIC DEVELOPMENT CONCERNING INTERMARRIAGE

Lou H. Silberman
Hillel Professor of Jewish
Literature and Thought
Vanderbilt University
Nashville, Tennessee

In discussing the question of intermarriage[1] in Judaism one may begin with the unequivocal statement that the biblical tradition vigorously affirms tribal and national endogamy. Nahor, Abraham's brother, married his niece Milchah (Haran's daughter: Gen. 11.29); Abraham himself married his half-sister, Sarah; "she is indeed my sister, the daughter of my father but not the daughter of my mother" (Gen. 20.12). When a wife was sought for Isaac, Eliezer was sent to the land of Abraham's family to acquire a bride for his master's son, and did so from his immediate family, for Rebekah was the granddaughter of Abraham's brother and niece, hence his double first cousin once-removed (Gen. 24.15).

Esau, in addition to his Canaanite wives, married Mahalat, the daughter of his uncle Ishmael, thus his first cousin (Gen. 28.9). In the case of Jacob, too, Canaanite marriage was frowned upon, and he gained his wives Leah and Rachel from family stock, his first cousins, the daughters of his mother's brother (Gen. 29.12). If the tangle of tribal genealogy is to be believed in Numbers 26.59 , Amram, Moses' father, was married to his aunt Jochebed, daughter of Levi. In the book of Joshua, Caleb gives his daughter Achsah in marriage to her first cousin once-removed, Othniel. One cannot, of course, draw a conclusion that tribal endogamy was obligatory, indeed the narrative suggests that exogamous marriage was possible, but

179

endogamous was preferred. This is reinforced by the negative judgment upon the former. Abraham's insistence that Isaac not marry a Canaanite points in that direction, as does the side remark in Esau's case, who "saw that the daughters of Canaan did not please his father Isaac," they being "a bitterness of spirit unto Isaac and to Rebekah" (Gen. 28.8, 26.35).

The point is made on several occasions, that the offspring of exogamous marriage are the source of trouble and sorrow to the community. Thus in Lev. 24.10–23 the ancient narrative, used as a setting for the law concerning blasphemy, states that it was the son of an Israelite woman by an Egyptian father who was the original transgressor. In 2 Chron. 24.26 the conspirators who slew Joash are pointedly noted as Zabad the son of Shimeath the Ammonitess and Jehozabad the son of Shimrith the Moabitess. In the case of Rehoboam, Solomon's son and successor who did "that which was evil, because he set not his heart to seek the Lord," the fact that his mother was Naamah the Ammonitess is recorded by the Chronicler, too (2 Chron. 3.13–14). Setting these narrative materials together, one recognizes that what we are dealing with is social reprobation of exogamy but certainly not prohibition. It is not only a presupposed possibility, it is a recognized fact.

The full extent of the effectiveness of such social reprobation cannot of course be determined. Louis Epstein in his work *Marriage Laws in the Bible and Talmud* wrote that this general condemnation of foreign marriages probably accounts for the surprising fact that of the kings of Israel and Judah numbering thirty-nine and reigning for 393 years only two, and possibly three, married foreign wives. Unfortunately, several pages later he wrote, "One standard of life and ideals was set up by royalty; they favored foreign manners and alliances and therefore welcomed intermarriage." [2] Thus one is hard pressed to know what the real motivation here was. Perhaps the paucity of royal intermarriages stems from the fact pointed out by Rivers that "there is a definite tendency toward the association of endogamy and occupation in the cases of priesthood and royalty—and in some cases marriage within these classes is so strictly enjoined that it amounts to a form of endogamy." [3] If this be so, then it is, as I have suggested, unwise to draw any conclusions from the royal situation.

Instead, there are enough examples of marriage with foreigners to make it clear that no effective interdiction existed or was intended in the pre-exilic period. And further, in the elaborate legal formulation found in Lev. 18, not only does the core, reflecting an early *Grossfamilie* situation, but the later paranetic elaborations, pay no attention to the question. With, however, the Deuteronomic reformation, a new, more sharply formulated position was enunciated.

Epstein has pointed out, correctly I think, that the four occasions when negative attitudes toward intermarriage were developed were those connected with reformation movements following upon national crisis: the deuteronomic, the Ezranic, the Hasmonean, and the rabbinic after the two revolts against Rome. In the first case, the destruction of the Northern Kingdom, and the continuing threat, first of Assyria and then of Babylon, set in motion a movement that culminated in the program made concrete in Josiah's law book. Its concern was the cleansing of the land from foreign influences of every kind, political, social and religious; resistance to the surrounding nations; avoidance of contact with heathenism. Among the old themes revived to support this reformatory program were those of the Holy War, belonging to the days of the conquest when the six or seven nations who inhabited the land were to be utterly destroyed. Thus Exodus declares, "For mine angel shall go before thee and bring thee in unto the Amorite and Hittite and the Perizzite and the Canaanite and the Hivite and the Jebusite; and I will annihilate them." "I am about to dispossess them . . ." (Exod. 23.23; 34.11). In Deuteronomy the theme sounds again but with notable additions. Although the utter destruction language is used, it serves, it seems to me, primarily as a setting for the real intent of the passage, solemn interdiction of intermarriage: "You shall not intermarry with them; do not give your daughters to their sons or take their daughters for your sons," because of the dangerous result: "for they will turn your children away from me to worship other gods." This result is utterly reprehensible, "for you are a people consecrated עם קדוש to the

Lord your God: of all the peoples on earth the Lord your God
chose you to be his treasured people." (Deut. 7.1–11). Related
to this prohibition are these passages that deal with the community's relation with its neighbors. Once again older themes
related to the conquest were invoked to emphasize the need for
disengagement. Amalek is to be remembered as the vicious foe
with whom no peace is ever to be made (Deut. 25.17–19;
Ex. 17.14–16). The enmity of Ammon and Moab, too, is
recalled in order to justify their being placed in a position of
disadvantage. I use that phrase carefully because I am not really
sure what Deut. 23.4–7 intends. There are two possibilities: one
that connects it immediately with the subject at hand; the other,
remotely. The crucial clause in this section is לא יבא ... בקהל ה' .
A list is given of those who may not enter into קהל ה' : 1)
no one whose testes are crushed 2) no one whose member is
cut off 3) a ממזר 4) an Ammonite or 5) a Moabite. In the
latter two instances, this prohibition is extended to the tenth
generation; and what may be a final development עד עולם,
suggests perpetual exclusion. On the other hand, the same section discusses the situation of the Edomite and the Egyptian
and permits their entering into the קהל ה' of their descendants
in the third generation. This section may be understood to deal
with the problem of intermarriage and with the exclusion of such
groups as are mentioned even after conversion until the period
noted has passed; or it may be concerned with the period required by foreign settlers to obtain Israelite *Bürgerrecht*.[4] Talmudic exegesis took the former course and based its elaborate
discussion of marriage to proselytes from these several peoples
as well as the status of descendants of a ממזר *vis-à-vis* marriage
to pure Jews, upon this.[5]

Returning then to our question, it would seem certain that
the deuteronomic reformation sought to transform the social
reprobation of exogamy into a formal prohibition. However, it
is crucial to note at this point, as Epstein has underscored,
that the question of the validity of alien marriage was not
raised.[6] Löw, more than a century ago wrote in this connection:
"Das Gesetz spricht sich nämlich nun gegen die Zulässigkeit der
Mischehe aus, ohne sich über die jüridische Giltigkeit oder den

Rechtbestand einer solcher Ehe näher zu erklären." [7] Indeed the very nature of marriage at the time, he pointed out, placed the matter outside such a purview. It was a familial affair, dealt with outside any communal structures. It could be proscribed but it could not be made a nullity. The very term used in Deut. 7.3, תתחתן indicates that the marital relationship, although proscribed, was possible.

To proceed then: without attempting a description of the situation both in the land and in Babylon during the exilic period, one can conclude that the structures of communal life and personal relationship deteriorated or underwent change in one way or another in each of the centers. However this may have been, the period of the restoration in its several waves, saw once again a reformation movement gather strength and seek a sharper definition of the Judean community as a distinct entity—as the עם קדוש of Deuteronomy. Every level of life was touched by the reforming zeal of Ezra and Nehemiah, as the community, beleaguered from without and distraught within, sought its identity. The question of intermarriage was but one factor within the whole complex of ideas and attitudes that had to be dealt with in the period of the return. The kind of language, however, one uses to describe the reformation is often more revealing of contemporary attitudes and distinctions than helpful in understanding those of the past. Epstein, for example argues that unlike the earlier reform, this was motivated by "racial ideology." "The racial teaching was not altogether new . . . it was part of the original endogamous sentiment and of the national religion of the Hebrew people." [8] Now granting a highly emotional antipathy to the term racial, motivated by almost four decades of exposure to its demonic use in Europe, Africa, Asia and the Western Hemisphere, I nonetheless wonder if the term is at all helpful in understanding the past. That the ancient world, and the Jewish community within it, were possessors of exclusivist concepts goes without question; but whether they are susceptible of a simplicistic definition such as the word race offers is a matter of more than semantic logic chopping. The זרע הקדש of Ezra 9.2 is the עם קדוש of Deut. 7.6, expressed in a graphic simile drawn, as the juxtaposition of זרע and ארץ indicate, from agricultural, not sexual, life: a set-aside seed not to be mixed with other seed and scattered on the ground: והתערבו זרע הקדש בעמי הארצות . The closed society that the restorationist leaders sought to create was based upon a complex historico-politico-religio concept. Ezra's great petition in ch. 9 is a recasting of the credo narrative of Deut. 6.20–7.11 with an emphasis upon the prohibited covenant with the inhabitants of the land in terms of the marriage bond, already mentioned in Deut. 7.3. Marriage with the outside introduced a destructive element that would undermine the beleaguered society. Ezra's Judea, like its contemporary Athens, rejected the *barbaroi* as inimical to the very structure of the *kosmos,* the intricate and equipoised relationship of city and its inhabitants.

Ezra's reform added nothing new to the stock of ideas and attitudes toward the outside world; it merely reaffirmed them zealously and, using political authority, made them rigorously effective for a comparatively brief systolic period in Israel's history. And even here it is important to note that no question was yet raised about the validity of the marriage relationships with foreign wives. They are to be set aside, *i.e.,* divorced by the then prevailing procedure of which we have some examples from Aramaic papyri from Elephantine.

From this period as well there emerged an aristocratic caste system that once again emphasized priestly, noble, endogamy, but as well there appeared a proselytizing movement that sought to naturalize acceptable strangers into the religio-historico-politico community. One may surmise that more than one motive set this program going, but one thing is certain: only a self-conscious community, sure of its identity and secure in its position, thought itself capable of assimilating outsiders with impunity. The Ezranic systole was thus followed by a diastole in the later Persian and early Hellenistic periods whose success, however noteworthy, seems dearly to have been paid for.

It is only against such a background of relaxation and expansion that the Hellenistic crisis makes sense. In dealing with the Hasmonean revolt, it is important to recognize that the process of Hellenization, embarked upon by some segments of the Judaic community, was more than an act of religious apostasy. It sought an *Umwertung aller Werte,* the total transformation of the community into a "Greek" *polis, i.e.,* a transformation political, cultural, social, judicial, religious. With this Grecization, the reason for continuing in any way the prohibition against marriage with foreigners would, of course, vanish. Being of the same culture, the basis for distinctive existence would cease. Our trouble, the Hellenistic sympathizers argued, arose because *exoriothemen ap' auton,* "we separated ourselves from them." Our ethnic-cultural distinctiveness is the source of our difficulties, they claimed.

The Hasmonean triumph and the establishment of the Judean state meant that the community was now once again clearly defined as an historico-politico-religio entity. Once again, the lines of distinctiveness were more sharply drawn; yet there seems to be no evidence that the drive toward growth through proselytization came to an end. Indeed, later tradition suggests its continuation through reports of notable scholars who were descendants of proselytes. At the same time, however, the cultural destructiveness of the Hasmonean state underwent change. As Bickerman has pointed out, Hellenistic influence did not cease but made its impact less directly, no longer consciously attempting total transformation but touching social and personal life on many levels.[9] Yet at the beginning of the period, in the full flush of military and political triumph, there was an attempt once again to limit foreign influence. Thus the Talmud reports a restrictive decree with regard to intercourse with a heathen woman stemming from "the court of the Hasmoneans," [10] placed by Derenbourg during the reign of Simeon, 143–135, or the early years of John Hyrkan,[11] and there is other evidence pointing to exclusivist tendencies during the period. Yet it would be dangerous and unsound to claim too much for the period. There were undoubtedly, in keeping with the complicated situation, various attitudes and ideas. Thus the rigorous Book of Jubilees, 30.7, declares ". . . if there is any man who wishes in Israel to give his daughter or his sister to any man who is of the seed of the Gentiles he shall surely die, and they shall stone him with stones, for he hath wrought shame in Israel and they shall burn the woman with fire, because she has dishonored the name of

the house of our father and she shall be rooted out of Israel."
The same work interprets the prohibition against giving one's
seed to Moloch as referring to intermarriage: "And do thou
Moses command the children of Israel and exhort them not to
give their daughters to the Gentiles and not to take for their
sons any of the daughters of the Gentiles for it is abominable
before the Lord. And Israel will not be free from this unclean-
ness if it has a wife of the daughter of the Gentiles or has given
any of its daughters to a man who is any of the Gentiles." The
emphasis here suggests conflict and the reformation psychology
of the sectarians. It is difficult to know what the real situation
was in the late Hasmonean and Herodian-Roman period. One
of the problems is simply that the surviving party after the revolt
read its attitudes, positions and legal structures into the past,
beclouding the actual situation.

Once again it must be emphasized that we seem still to be
dealing with a situation in which interdiction and even violent
condemnation are the basic response to the fact of intermarriage. There seems to be no evidence that during the Hasmonean
and Roman-Herodian period there was more than a reaffirmation
of prohibition. Intermarriage took place and various groups
prescribed various punishments for such behavior. The party
that created the Book of Jubilees held that death was the proper
punishment and this seems also to have been the attitude of those
called "zealots" in *Abodah Zara* 36b. In other parts of the
society other forms of punishment may have been inflicted: exclusion, flogging, *etc.*, which were "private" acts—*i.e.*, they reflected party opinion. Those ordinances that have been described
as acts of the legislative council of the Hasmoneans were, according to the later reports, intended to discourage intermarriage which, of course, indicates that it was a possibility, *i.e.*,
it was a valid union although subject to punishment, depending
upon the part of the community from which the party involved
came. All we can determine is that there were important segments of the community for whom the traditional prohibition
was an effective means of preventing such marriage. However,
there seem to have been others who were more or less indifferent
to the prohibition and who were, therefore, willing to take their

chances. They may have assumed that loyalty to the temple cult was sufficient; that various atoning sacrifices overcame their guilt and they thus were unconcerned about the more vigorous opinions of others.

With the destruction of the temple and the state, and the passage of legal authority into the hands of a single party, the situation changed. The preservation of the community, in the form that party wished to construct it, meant that its ideas, attitudes, concepts, positions, interpretations, *etc.,* were now to govern the community. Insofar as the *Bet Din* at Jabneh and its successors dominated the scene as the source of law and authority, they were able to impose their ideas with some uniformity upon the community. Once again a beleaguered community emphasized those attitudes making for survival. Thus the strengthening of communal identity and resistance to any attitude that would diminish its life were of prime importance. Tannaitic Judaism once again closed ranks as did Ezranic Judaism, this time with more experience and a more inclusive platform on which to stand. Resistance to the heathen world became of basic concern. If one reads *Abodah Zara,* one sees at once that its desire was the total disengagement of the Jewish from the heathen communities at every point possible. Whatever legal material it inherited from the past, and from whatever source, was now put to the service of resistance, as it was enlarged and more carefully specified. The eighteen ordinances of the schools brought together from the sources all of the isolating measures and made them a bulwark against the world. The brash statement: "If Elijah and his court were to come and dissolve them, we would not heed," [12] suggests the uncompromising spirit of the time. Intimate contact between Jew and heathen, *i.e.,* marriage, was now viewed with the eyes of the author of Jubilees, and earlier zealotic punishment was accepted, if not encouraged, as the order of the day.

But such lynch law could not be the enduring condition. Thus all intermarriage was now deemed a transgression of a biblical commandment and, in keeping with the rabbinic rule, was punishable by thirty-nine strokes of the lash. That the biblical prohibition used to support the position that all intermarriage was forbidden, Deut. 7.2, referred only to the seven nations was perfectly obvious; thus further explanation and interpretation were required. The interpretation of the words כי יסיר "for he will turn [your son] away," was understood to include *all* who may turn him away, *i.e.*, all heathen, and was the way of solving the problem, according to those who interpreted "the reason of the scripture" (*i.e.*, since the reason is given for this case, we can apply the rule in all cases where the same reason applies). For the majority, however, who did not accept this hermeneutic principle, another basis was found. Deut. 21.13 with its permission to marry a captive woman was brought into play. The procedure there described was understood as an act of proselytism, and only after the captive had done what the text required of her could her captor marry her, which implies that previous to this, while she was yet a heathen, he could not.[13] Thus, through tannaitic exegesis the biblical text yielded a total prohibition against all marriage to heathen. More than that and of greater consequence was the second step. The purely private nature of the marriage contract was transformed and the question of validity was raised and determined. This distinction between prohibiton and invalidity, was, as I have intimated all along, the central change in the development of the Jewish position. Prohibition forbids the act but does not touch the act itself. Thus marriage as a private covenant—contract, home-taking, intercourse—lay beyond the scope of law. One may be punished for the act, but the act itself was not undone. Invalidity declares that the act is a nullity, a non-act. One cannot do it; one cannot enter into a marriage that is by legal definition a non-marriage.[14]

An examination of *M. Kid.* 3.12 (66a) will make this distinction clear: (1.) "Wherever this is *kiddushin* and there is no transgression," *i.e.*, where a valid and licit (permitted) relationship exists, "the issue follows the status of the male. Such is the case when the daughter of a priest, a levite or an Israelite is married to a priest, a levite or an Israelite." (2.) When there is *kiddushin* and there is transgression," *i.e.*, where a valid but illicit (interdicted) relationship exists, "the issue follows the status of the inferior—such is the case when a widow is married to a high priest, or a divorced woman or *haluzah* to an ordinary priest, or a *mamzeret* or *netinah* to an Israelite, or the daughter of an Israelite to a *mamzer* or *netin.*" These marriages are binding although interdicted. (3.) "When a woman cannot contract *kiddushin* with that particular person," *i.e.* that particular relationship is not valid, "but can contract *kiddushin*," *i.e.*, a valid relationship, "with another person, the issue is *mamzer*. This is the case when one has intercourse with any relation prohibited in the Torah." [15] (4.) "When a woman cannot contract *kiddushin* with that particular person or with others," *i.e.*, where no valid marriage relationship whatsoever is possible, "the issue follows her status. Such is the case with the issue of a bondmaid or a Gentile woman." There can be no *kiddushin* here, for a Gentile woman cannot be party to a marriage contract.

"An intermarriage is invalid," wrote Epstein, "not because it is prohibited, but because the heathen (like the slave) is incapable of contracting marriage within Jewish law, like the barbarian and slave in Roman law." This "'declaring a marriage invalid was a novel point in Jewish law." It has, wrote Epstein, "no logic in Jewish law. The tannaim learned this, evidently from Roman law . . ." [16] However, it is possible, as Boaz Cohen seems to suggest, that it was an indigenous development, an application of the principle of personality, *i.e.*, only Jews are subject to Jewish law of personal status. [17] Whatever the source, rabbinic Judaism, accepting the legal concept of validity-invalidity, made the marriage relationship with a non-Jew a legal nullity.

By the third century the stringency of anti-heathen laws in other areas of relationship seem to have been relaxed, [18] but with regard to intermarriage, the only discussions raised are those of R. Assi and Raba. The former suggested that, with the intermingling of the people, there was always the possibility that any Gentile may indeed be a descendant of the ten tribes, hence a marriage between Gentile and Jew could be of doubtful validity rather than absolute invalidity. No one took him up in this and the halakhah ignored it. [19] Raba, taking up the rejection of R. Simeon b. Yoḥai's interpretation of Deut. 7.3, argued that the prohibition here could not have been intended for Mosaic times since the seven nations were idolators and marriage with them would not have been valid, hence the text must refer to the period when they had become proselytes, and is intended even then to prohibit them.[20] This being the case, marriage with any of the nations is not biblically prohibited, although it is, of course, invalid: hence it is mere prostitution and is punishable not by thirty-nine stripes as a matter of law, but only on the basis of local custom. Rambam (*Issure Biah* 12.1) rejected the idea that such marriages are not biblically prohibited, but *Tur, Eban ha-Ezer,* 16 and *Semag,* neg. com. 112, accepted it. In no case, however, was the question of validity raised: all that was at stake was punishment for illicity.[21] Thus, the introduction into the *halakhah* of the legal concept of validity-non-validity of marital union: אין קדושין תופסין, קדושין תופסין had added to the entire previous development a new and transforming element. It was this structure that remained totally and unquestionably in force until the nineteenth century.

Before continuing with the last aspect of this development let me indicate why I have emphasized "totally and unquestionably." In *Semag,* neg. com. 112, Moses of Coucy reported that while in Spain, in 1236, he induced a number of Jews to put aside their Christian or Moslem "wives": הארכתי בדרשות כאלו בגלות ירושלם בספרד והוציאו נשים רבות בשנת תתקצ״ו לפרט.[22] This statement is quoted, often without comment, or is referred to as in Kohler's article on "Intermarriage" in *J.E.,* as though it were dealing with valid marriages, permitted by Jewish law. The unspoken argument lying behind the use of this passage seems to have run as follows: There must have been some reason why intermarriage between Jews and Christians was so frequently forbidden in the legal enactments of Christian Europe. The obvious explanation is that such marriages took place with frequency. The conclusion drawn is that such marriages were somehow valid from the Jewish standpoint, otherwise why would the church condemn them. Such reasoning, indeed, seems to be present in the arguments presented to the Assembly of Notables in Paris in 1806, as will be discussed below. The conclusion, however, completely ignores the halakhic enactments as found in the codes. Further, when one examines the enactments of the church councils and synods and their incorporation into national laws, it becomes evident that often, rather than responding to actual situations, they reflect the codification of the church's unrelenting enmity toward the Jewish community, whose very existence called forth a spate of enactments, whether or not they were relevant to the real situation. Thus, very early enactments, such as those of the Council of Elvira in Spain (c. 300),[23] at a time when the situation in the distant Diaspora may not yet have reflected the full halakhic development and marriages between Jews and Christians may indeed have occurred, became part of much later standard anti-Jewish legislation without reference to any actual problem. As for the statement in *Semag*, Löw suggested that it probably dealt with concubinage.[24]

Our concluding section is directed to a discussion of the point at which the rabbinic tradition and development, codified in the authoritative documents of Jewish law, was called into question. This is most generally assumed to have occurred during the meetings of the Assembly of Notables, called by Napoleon in 1806 to answer a series of questions about Jewish life and Jewish law, and the Great Sanhedrin of Paris, summoned in 1807 to confirm, as the highest Jewish authority in the realm, the replies given by the Assembly. Disregarding all of the other questions put, we turn our attention to that crucial to our discussion: can a Jewess marry a Christian or a Jew a Christian woman? Or has the law ordered that Jews should only intermarry among themselves?" [25]

Before examining the answers, it would be well to understand the situation. In the age of revolutions at the end of the eighteenth century, marriage became, in the eyes of the revolutionaries with their anti-clerical attitude, a matter regulated solely by the state. It was the state that was to determine what was permitted or forbidden, and while some restrictions emerging from older situations were continued, religion ceased to be a decisive factor in a multi-religious and, theoretically, secular state. What was involved in the question put to the Assembly of Notables was clearly the matter of recognizing the state's preemption of marriage law.[26] While this was the question and its intent, it threw the fat in the fire as far as the internal discussion within the Jewish community was concerned, for reform tendencies, not only of moderate but of extreme positions, were already present. Thus, although a commission was appointed to formulate an answer, two were forthcoming: one from the commission, dominated apparently by reformers, and another from a group of rabbis who, too, were part of the Assembly. From these two, a compromise answer was wrought.

The argument of the modernists had run something like this: 1) The Bible only prohibits marriage to idolators. 2) The Talmud declares that modern nations are not to be considered idolators. 3) Therefore, there is no prohibition against marriages with the modern nations.[27] The syllogistic logic of the argument seems unimpeachable but the propositions put together are not necessarily properly juxtaposed. Of course, the Bible prohibits intermarriage with idolators, according to R. Simeon b. Yohai's exegesis. Of course, for purposes of *dinē mamonot,* equity, certain severe restrictions against some groups, and particularly in the Middle Ages, as J. Katz has demonstrated, against Christians and Moslems, were relaxed, thus giving them legal standing and ensuring fair dealing by Jews with Christians and making certain Jewish-Christian relationships possible. But these were not intended to be applied in matters of *issurin,* ritual law, least of all marriage laws.[28] Thus, even though the logic be impeccable, the central question of invalidity is not really touched.

The rabbis, old-fashioned or otherwise, could not accept such a hybrid conclusion, hence, the compromise. The language of the Commission was accepted up to a point: the law (*loi* seems here to refer to the Pentateuch) does not say that a Jewess cannot marry a Christian nor a Jew a Christian woman; nor does it state that the Jews can only intermarry among themselves. The only marriages expressly forbidden by the law are those with the seven Canaanite nations, with Ammon and Moab and with the Egyptians (clearly *loi* means the passages in Deuteronomy). Thus, the prohibition, following R. Simeon b. Yohai's exegesis, applies only to nations in idolatry. Thus far, the first proposition of the reformers. Now the second: the

Talmud (notice the shift of subject from law to Talmud) declares formally that modern nations are not considered as such since they worship, like us, the God of heaven and earth; (but this concession was made, as noted above, in quite another context). However, the modernists' conclusion was not drawn. The apples and pears remained apart. Rather, the subject was changed to an historical disquisition: ". . . accordingly there have been in several periods intermarriages between Jews and Christians in France, in Spain and in Germany, these marriages were sometimes tolerated and sometimes forbidden by the laws of those sovereigns who had received Jews into their dominions." Here the responsibility for approving or disapproving these marriages is placed upon the rulers, and the impression seems to be left that no other authority was involved. The writers could certainly point to the overwhelming evidence of canon law to sustain their assertion, and thus the matter of Jewish law at this point could safely be ignored.[29] The answer then continued: "Unions of this kind are still found in France." (Made possible by civil marriage.) But now the moment of truth is at hand: "but we cannot dissemble that the opinion of the rabbis is against such marriages." The reason for this was, however, at once forthcoming. "According to their doctrines, although the religion of Moses has not forbidden the Jews from intermarrying with nations not of their religion, yet as marriage according to the Talmud requires religious ceremonies called *kiddushin* [advantage being here taken of the double meaning of *kiddushin*, the ritual ceremony and the legal relation] with benedictions used in such cases, no marriage can be *religiously* [emphasis in text] valid unless these ceremonies have been performed. This could not be done towards persons who would not both of them consider these ceremonies as sacred and in that case the married couple could separate without religious divorce. They would be considered as married civilly not religiously." [30] Here, of course, was the awaited answer. Civil marriage was affirmed, and as far as the state was concerned, the devil could carry off rabbis, priests and pastors with their religious ceremonies and benedictions. But this was not the end. The answer of the Assembly with its exquisite choreography of subtle side-steps had now to receive the halakhic sanction of the Great Sanhedrin where traditional rabbis would be faced with a far more difficult problem, the statement of the conclusion in halakhically acceptable terms. Its statement was clear and to the point: "The Great Sanhedrin declares further that marriages between Israelites and Christians, contracted according to the laws of the Code Civil are civilly binding and that, although they cannot be invested with religious forms, they shall not result in anathema." [31] The first part of the statement is of halakhic interest insofar as it applied the amoraic concept דיני דמלכותא דיני "civil law is law," to marriage. However, it was not a matter of abstract halakhah here at stake but the practical answer to the civil government's unspoken demand that civil marriage be recognized. The Sanhedrin was not ready to declare invalid what civil law validated civilly, so it merely used a traditional formula, applicable in quite a different situation, to deal with its present problem. What it was saying was, civil law is the law within its areas of competence.[32] The next phrase, however, indicated where it was not competent. The clause *"Bien qu'ils ne soient pas susceptible d'être revêtus des formes religieuses,"* [33] is ambiguous, for the phrase *formes religieuses* could refer merely to ritual procedure or it could touch the central problem of validity. The Hebrew text makes it unmistakably clear that the previous clause had given nothing away: "ואף על פי שהוא מן הנמנע שיהיו קדושין תופסין בהם כדת משה" "although it is impossible for *kiddushin* to be Jewishly valid in such cases" [34] In other words, the Paris Sanhedrin, far from sanctioning intermarriage, reaffirmed the existing halakhah, and sidestepped a dangerous confrontation with imperial power by applying a legal precept used in matters of equity to those of personal status.

On June 18, 1844, the Braunschweiger Rabbinerversammlung determined to affirm the decision of the Grand Sanhedrin, and appointed a Commission, composed of Holdheim, Solomon, Frankfurter, to formulate that determination. Unfortunately, no one present had a copy of the Sanhedrin's decision and depended upon remembered reports—so that the Commission's report read "Ehen zwischen Juden und Christen, Ehen zwischen Monotheisten überhapt, sind nicht verboten." [35] After it was submitted, one of the members of the Conference stated he recalled that the Sanhedrin's statement said that neither Christian nor Jewish clergy could be forced to officiate at such ceremonies.[36] Holdheim indicated he thought the original statement suggested that the problem revolved around the recitation of the benedictions.[37] After considerable debate, the Conference adopted what it believed to be the intent of the Sanhedrin: intermarriage of Jews and Christians, and in general the intermarriage of Jews with adherents of any of the monotheistic religions is not forbidden, provided that the parents are permitted by the laws of the state to bring up their offspring of such marriages in the Jewish faith." [38] That this is not what the Sanhedrin said or meant is evident from the discussion above. That this was, hardly intentionally on the part of the majority, a breach, or as Moses Mielziner wrote, "the entire abandonment of the Talmudic standpoint," is clear.[39] The reaction was sharp. The Augsburg Synod tabled a motion to endorse the resolution. Ludwig Philippson who had made the motion in Braunschweig to adopt the statement later repudiated it.[40] Geiger was satisfied to grant moral worth to marriage between a Jew and a Christian, concluded in a legal manner (by civil authorities only), and stated that "religion . . . cannot deny the validity [undoubtedly he meant civil] of such a marriage." [41] Einhorn, the radical reformer, was even more vehement. "Such marriages are to be strictly prohibited even from the standpoint of Reformed Judaism." His peroration rang out, "To lend a hand to the sanctification of mixed marriages is, according to my firm conviction, to furnish a nail to the coffin of the small Jewish race, with its sublime mission." [42] His opponent, I. M. Wise, was no less emphatic: "If any one does not believe in the living God of Israel and the Sinaic revelation, he has no reason whatever to believe in the sanctity of the marriage compact as being instituted by the law of God, and consequently has no cause to be married by a rabbi, who acts by that authority only." [43]

To conclude then, it need be noted only that outside of the action of the Braunschweiger Rabbinerversammlung, the halakhic position of the invalidity of the marriage relationship between Jews and non-Jews, no matter how it has been breached in practice, has remained theoretically unchanged in its binding force to this day.[44]

NOTES

[1] The two terms "mixed marriage" and "intermarriage" are used interchangeably, since no relevant distinction seems evident. At most "intermarriage" could be used to refer to marriage with a proselyte, but this presents no problem, although certain caste restrictions are found in the *halakhah*. It seems best to discard the terminological distinction.

[2] Louis M. Epstein, *Marriage Laws in the Bible and Talmud* (Cambridge, Mass.: Harvard University Press, 1942), pp. 150, 154.

[3] *Hastings Encyclopedia of Religion and Ethics*, VIII, 424b.

[4] This latter interpretation is that cited by Löw (see below) as the opinion of biblical scholars in the middle of the nineteenth century. Contemporary scholars understand the passage as referring to participation in "the cultic levy of the free men, whether for purposes of war or for the annual feasts, that is to say, for events at which the sacral union of the tribes appeared in full array." G. von Rad, *Deuteronomy* (Philadelphia: The Westminster Press, 1966), p. 146.

[5] *M. Yeb.* 8.3 and Gemara 76b-77a. In this connection the related question of the meaning of *mamzer* is of interest. It may refer, as Geiger derived its meaning: זר מעם to a child of a mixed marriage; or it may refer to a racial stock as in Zech. 9.6, וישב ממזר באשדוד "a mongrel people." See Epstein, *op. cit.*, p. 184. For our discussion, however, and particularly for the development of the halakhah dealing with marriage with foreigners in the strictest source of the term rather than the collateral question of marriage with certain classes of proselytes and disqualified Jews, the problem need not be solved.

[6] Epstein, *op. cit.*, p. 160.

[7] Leopold Löw, "Eherechtliche Studien," *Gesammelte Schriften* (Szegedin, 1893) III, p. 122: "The law only expresses its opposition to mixed marriage, without discussing the juridical validity or legal status of such."

[8] *Op. cit.*, p. 162.

[9] Elias Bickerman, *From Ezra to the Last of the Maccabees* (New York: Schocken Books, 1962) pp. 153-165.

[10] *Abodah Zara* 36b; *Sanhedrin* 82b.

[11] J. Derenbourg, *Essai sur l'Histoire et la Géographie de la Palestine*, p. 84, *apud* Soncino Talmud, *ad loc.*

[12] *A.Z.* 36a.

[13] *Kid.* 68b.

[14] Epstein, *op. cit.*, p. 174.

[15] In this connection the question may be raised concerning the child of a Jewish mother and a Gentile father, for according to the Mishnah quoted here, such a child would be *mamzer*. However, according to another rule, *Yeb.* 68b, "granted that he is not fit, he is not *mamzer* either." The discussion as to the status of such a child continued through the tannaitic and amoraic schools, some declaring it to be *mamzer*, others mitigating this status. The final halakhah designated it a legitimate Jew although unfit for priestly marriage (Rambam, *Issure Biah* 15.13). Epstein points out that in the earliest

rabbinic halakhah "no distinction was made between the child who had a heathen father and one who had a heathen mother (p. 194)." The status in either case was *mamzer* and, indeed, most of the authorities quoted by him (p. 196) follow this opinion; yet the final halakhah is lenient, despite the paucity of supporting positions. To the evidence supporting the strictest position Eugene Mihaly has suggested in a communication that *M. Bikk.* 1.4 be added for it seems to be speaking of a *ger* whose mother was an Israelite.

16 *Op. cit., loc. cit.*

17 Boaz Cohen, *Jewish and Roman Law* (New York: Jewish Theological Seminary, 1966) I, p. 339.

18 Epstein, *op. cit.*, pp. 174–175.

19 *Yeb.* 16b–17a.

20 *Yeb.* 76a, 78b.

21 Epstein, *op. cit., loc. cit.* The unnecessarily complicated discussion arose because the "sound exegesis" (Löw) of R. Simeon b. Yohai was rejected. It is clear that Rambam followed him and thus avoided the difficulty. See *Kesef Mishneh* to the citation from the *Yad.*

22 *Apud* Löw, p. 176.

23 See J. R. Marcus, *The Jew in the Medieval World* (Cincinnati: UAHC, 1938), pp. 101–102.

24 *Op. cit., loc. cit.* "R. Moses hat nämlich gewiss nur gegen das Concubinate geeifert, denn von Mischehe zwischen Juden und Christinnen . . . kann zu jener Zeit in Spanien nicht die Rede sein." See also, Katz (citation in the next note), pp. 102–103.

25 Jacob Katz, *Exclusiveness and Tolerance: Jewish-Gentile Relations in Medieval and Modern Times* (New York: Schocken Books, 1962), p. 191; Epstein, *op. cit.*, p. 178.

26 It would be valuable to see this matter in the general framework of the developing relationships between the French government and the Roman Catholic and Protestant Churches. Not only did the state preempt marriage law but other matters of personal status.

27 Katz, *loc. cit.;* Epstein, *op. cit.*, pp. 178–179.

28 Katz (*op. cit.*, p. 137) quotes Ha-Me'iri, the most lenient of the *posekim:* "concerning prohibitions of food and drink . . . other prohibitions of this sort [*issurin*] all the nations are alike." See in particular the chapter "Economic Intercourse and the Religious Factor," pp. 24–36.

29 Epstein, *op. cit.*, pp. 179–180. See above, the discussion of the unspoken argumentation behind the statement quoted.

30 Quoted by Katz, p. 193; Epstein, *loc. cit.*

31 Moses Mielziner, *The Jewish Law of Marriage and Divorce in Ancient and Modern Times* (Cincinnati: Bloch Publishing and Printing Co., 1884), p. 47; Löw, *op. cit.*, p. 189; Kohler, *J.E. s.v.*, Intermarriage.

32 See Katz, *op. cit.*, pp. 48, 49, 54, 62, 128.

33 Mielziner, *op. cit., loc. cit.*, note 1.

[34] Löw, *op. cit.*, p. 189.

[35] *Apud* Löw, *op. cit.*, p. 190; See also Kohler, *loc. cit.*

[36] *Ibid.;* See Katz, *op. cit.*, p. 192. "They went on to say that no Rabbi would officiate at the marriage of a Jew with a Christian." This refers to the statement of the Assembly of Notables.

[37] Löw, *loc. cit.*

[38] Mielziner, *op. cit.*, p. 48; Löw, *op. cit.*, p. 191.

[39] Mielziner, *op. cit.*, p. 48.

[40] Mielziner, *op. cit.*, pp. 48–49.

[41] Mielziner, *op. cit.*, p. 50.

[42] Mielziner, *op.cit.*, pp. 51–52.

[43] Mielziner, *op. cit.*, p. 54.

[44] *CCAR Yearbook*, LVII (1947), p. 161. In the light of the examination of the halakhic development, it must be concluded that it is still the position of American Reform Judaism that intermarriages, even when "performed" by a rabbi, have no validity from the standpoint of Jewish law, but are only valid as civil marriages civilly performed, since the rabbi does in fact act as an officer of the state. The use of "traditional" ritual language in no way touches the legal status of the marriage.

DEATH AND BURIAL
IN THE JEWISH TRADITION

Solomon B. Freehof
Rabbi Emeritus
Rodeph Shalom Temple
Pittsburgh, Pennsylvania

The modern metropolis is subject to extraordinary stress. At first it was inflated by a stream of immigration from the countryside. Then it was drained of wealth and ability by the counter-current of the flight to the suburbs. Now the core of the metropolis is a miserable and embittered ghetto. Who, then, can predict whether the modern metropolis will outlive its tensions? This question involves social engineering, but it is also a matter of individual character. The great cities will not surmount their present crisis unless there is enough hope and stamina in modern man.

In attempting to predict this segment of the future, one should not count too much upon history as a guide. Social situations never repeat themselves precisely. Nevertheless history may be an approximate guide. There were some situations in the past, there were certain personality-types in the older generations which, especially today, deserve our closer attention. For example, it might be helpful if modern social psychologists and historians gave new attention to the historic Jewish communities. These small enclaves of humanity were burdened with cruel, inequitable taxation and extortion, surrounded by hate, subject to fire and sword. They lived under relentless siege for centuries. Yet without any outside help, Jewish communities were able to maintain themselves century after century; and often when the communities were finally shattered by some invasion or expulsion, its survivors had enough vitality to move to a new land, to build new communities which, again, lasted for centuries. The fugitives from the communities of Mainz, Speyer and Worms built the enduring communities of Cracow,

Lemberg and Berlin. This vitality of the Jewish community, the stamina of its people, enabled human units to live through centuries of hate and enforced poverty and yet to come out of it all vital, confident, still believing in mankind and with strong faith in the future. No people in history went through more of the mud of human experience and came out cleaner than the children of the European ghettos. When we as moderns restudy the Jewish community and its children, we are dealing with a remarkable example of the unquenchable human spirit and the desire to build, build, and rebuild. It is hard to lose faith in all the inhabitants of the modern, threatened metropolis when one sees the unbreakable courage of the Jewish people.

What was the source of their inner strength? There are many answers and presumably each one contributes some element of the full explanation. There is certainly one important element and that is their long established social habit of mutual help. From the beginning the Jewish communities relied upon themselves. They organized voluntary associations for the support of study, for the visit to the sick, etc. One voluntary organization found in every community was the one devoted to the reverent burial of the dead. This organization had special status. It was given the reverent name of the Holy Society, *Chevra Kedisha*.

It is with some sentimental regret that we realize that this Holy Society which every Jewish community once loyally maintained has now virtually vanished from the Western world. There still are, indeed, many such societies, but their function is now limited and they are becoming fewer in number. The reason for this change is fairly evident. In the past the community and the congregation were identical. Now in America a Jewish community may have fifty separate congregations. These various congregations are often small, and with the constant change of American city neighborhoods their life tenure is often brief. Therefore the function of caring for the dead has moved into a new social phase and has created a new business or profession, namely the independent Jewish funeral director. Some Orthodox publicists regret this change and wish it were still possible for all funerals to be entirely in the hands of the congregational Holy Society. Yet the changes in city life have made the old way impossible, and now the historic tradition of laws and customs is in the hands of a professional business group.

The Jewish funeral directors have for many years organized themselves into an association. I know that it is central to the concern of this association to preserve such traditions as can be preserved, to modify those that need to be modified. This annual lectureship which begins today is in itself an evidence of the awareness of this association of the heavy responsibility which rests upon it. The purpose of these meetings will be to provide for those students who are near to their ordination an opportunity to learn the practical problems and to become acquainted with the established procedures involved in that human experience which they will need to confront, alas too often, in their rabbinical career. Since this purpose is a worthy one, continuing as it does the work of one of the worthy, self-help societies of the historic Jewish community, I am happy to give the first lecture in what I hope will be an ongoing series for many years.

The complex process of change which amounts to what we call the modern age and which has transformed the old self-help institutions of the Jewish community, has also created more than social change. It has penetrated into the mind and heart of man. Life has changed socially and also psychologically. The two, of course, are connected. Changes in social conditions create changes in individual moods and standards, and then changes in individual moods and standards create further changes in social conditions. It is evident that a significant part of modern change is the inward one. Not only is the Jewish community different, but Jews are different. Their attitude to Judaism has changed.

These changes in personal relationship to the religious tradition are evidenced by the very existence of a Reform and a Conservative movement, and by a large body of non-organized or half-organized avowedly nonreligious Jews. But there is a further evidence of drastic change to be noted in what calls itself Jewish Orthodoxy in the Western world. There is no doubt that there is a tremendous erosion in Jewish observance among the so-called modern Orthodox. All the civil laws, the business laws which occupy the last fourth of the *Shulchan Aruch,* are no longer observed. Very few businessmen will settle a contract dispute by a rabbinical Din Torah. The laws of *Kashrut* have been strangely modified. The home is still kept strictly kosher, but there are not more than two or three cities in the United States where there is an authentic kosher restaurant downtown in the business district. The laws of Sabbath have faded. Not many people who call themselves Orthodox will hesitate to drive on the Sabbath or to take an elevator. The laws of feminine hygiene, which occupy about a third of the *Yore Deah,* are neglected.

This growing erosion of Jewish tradition among those who call themselves Orthodox has not been adequately studied. It deserves to be. It would be superficial to dismiss it as a mere inconsistency or laxity and to ask by what right are certain commandments thrown aside and others held to. There is ground here for a serious and perhaps an important study in Jewish social psychology. What is the actual basis of this selectivity of observance? It clearly has a definite consistency and yet is unexplained. Why, for example, the tremendous emphasis on wearing the hat, when it is not even well based in Jewish law? Why the scrupulousness about breaking a glass at a wedding when that, too, is of doubtful origin? Why the great emphasis on Bar Mitzvah which, as a ceremony, is only medieval? And why, at the same time, the half-neglect of those foundations of Jewish religious observance, the Sabbath and *Kashrut?* There must be some social-psychological explanation of this remarkably widespread and consistent selectivity.

While this selectivity is being studied it should be noted that the least neglected and the most honored group of observances, maintained almost as in the past, are these groups of observances which concern us today, namely those dealing with death and burial. People who hardly go to synagogue for any Sabbath service will at the death of a parent go every single day for eleven months to say *Kaddish.* Hitherto they had neglected the holiday services, except the New Year and the Day of Atonement, but now they come to the last day of every Passover,

Shavuot and Succot to recite *Yizkor* for their parents. Even additional customs arise, added difficulties which have no roots in Jewish law but which people insist upon. There has grown up now a demand in two or three of the great cities, among pious people, that there must be not a bit of metal in the coffins, and special coffins are now made, held together by wooden pegs. People pay the extra expense. It has no basis in Jewish law (Greenwald's *Kol Bo,* p. 182; Freehof *Recent Reform Responsa,* p. 153 ff.), yet many people gladly pay the cost. They consider it proper and right.

Why should there be this extra scrupulousness with regard to death and burial, precisely at the time when there is less scrupulousness with regard to other areas of Jewish observance? Many explanations suggest themselves. Perhaps one explanation is that when some dear one dies, the survivor frequently has a sense either of guilt or, if not that, a sense of debt. We feel that there is perhaps something that we could have done and did not do. We feel we owe the departed something and, at least now at the funeral, we want to do everything possible. It is for some such reason that Jewish sentiment and, we might say, Jewish piety is strongest here. Since laws and customs in the area of death and burial are most reverently observed, it is frequently true that of all the areas of a rabbi's activities, his relationship to a bereaved family may make the deepest impression and give the most lasting help.

From only a few references in Scripture, laws and customs concerning death and burial have grown until they are now a large totality. Many of these observances are to be considered in the category of law, and many of them as customs not sufficiently established to have legal validity. In spite of the general mood of piety towards the laws and customs involved, modern living conditions have created a large area of variation between Orthodoxy, Conservatism and Reform. It would require a volume to describe adequately the entire spectrum of modern observance and, of course, it would therefore be absurd to attempt even a sketch of it in a lecture. At all events, as far as Reform observances are concerned, they can be found in the last chapter of Volume I and the last chapter of Volume II of

Reform Jewish Practice. In this lecture, in spite of the large
amount of material involved, it might be possible to give a
general impression of the field by attempting to elicit from the
various customs the basic moods which had created them. One
might say that all the variations of laws and customs spring
from certain attitudes and principles which have been deep-
rooted in the Jewish state of mind and which are likely to remain there, even though they may express themselves in still
different variations and even new customs. Let us therefore
see which are the basic attitudes of the tradition to this crucial
experience of death and burial.

I. *Life is Precious.* It is far from a commonplace to say that
in Jewish tradition life is precious. The very laws of capital
punishment, with careful restrictions limiting them, would indicate that life was never held cheaply. When we think of the
hundreds of crimes, including petty theft, that were capital
crimes in England almost in modern times, one can see the
difference in the attitude to the value of life. In Jewish tradition
the English proverb could never have arisen: "I might as well
be hanged for a sheep as for a lamb." So, too, the Biblical motive for social service is expressed in the words: "That your
brother may live by your side," *v'chay ochicho imoch* (Lev.
25:36). This reverence for life itself explains the laws which
surround and protect a dying man. His last hours are precious.
Nothing may be done to hasten his death, not even to change
his pillow and his position in bed. Yet while we may not hasten
death, it is permitted to risk those last few hours if there is a
chance to obtain a cure or, at least, a fair remission of the disease.
The Talmud in *Avodah Zara* 27b speaks of these last few
hours of life, *chaye sha'a,* and states that they may be risked if
there is a chance for healing and so, too, it is decided by
Jacob Reischer in *Shevus Yaacov,* III, 175. These laws against
hastening death are codified in the *Shulchan Aruch, Yore Deah*
339:1.

Yet the law also recognizes that when death is inevitable,
nothing should be done to prevent its coming (cf. Isserles,
ibid.). The famous story of Rabbi Judah's learned servant is
frequently cited. She stopped the prayers of the rabbis in his

behalf because these were delaying his death and thus were pro-
longing his suffering (*Ketuboth* 104a). Rabbenu Nissim in his
commentary to *Nedarim* 40a likewise says if a person is dying
and in pain, we should not pray too much for him to live
another hour. That is to say that just as a man has a right to
live, he has finally the right to the repose of death (see also
Sefer Chasidim #315–318). This balanced attitude of Judaism
to the last hours of life has a special bearing nowadays when,
with adrenalin and by other means, it is possible to keep the
hopeless patient dragging the chains of life for another miserable
hour and when, furthermore, the borderline between life and
death recently has suddenly grown vague. Doctors are now
beginning to debate the question as to when a patient is really
dead. Therefore the attitude of Jewish tradition is especially
significant. It declares that the last hours of life are precious and
a man must not be deprived of them by any action on our part.
They may however be risked if there is a fair prospect of healing.
Yet when there is no prospect of healing, then to force the
patient to live a few more hours is likewise wrong. As life is a
privilege, death is sometimes a blessing.

II. *The Body, Respected.* It is surprising how little reverence
was paid to the body of the dead in medieval times. Bodies
were often mutilated. Superstitious folk-medicine and witch-
craft regularly used parts of the dead body. The state itself
ordered the bodies of certain criminals to be mutilated. It is
horrible to us to visualize what was actually done to the body
of a criminal when he was "drawn and quartered," or how
regularly the hanged bodies of criminals stayed on the gibbet
for weeks and months until they either were decayed or were
consumed by predatory birds. As a matter of fact, the treatment
of the bodies of executed criminals is a basis of much of our
Jewish law on the care of the body of the dead. The Bible in
Deuteronomy 21:23 forbids keeping the hanged body of an
executed criminal overnight. It was considered, as it were, a
disgrace to God Himself callously to exhibit the body of even
a dead criminal. It is from this Biblical statement that the
Orthodox custom arose to bury all bodies on the day of death,
or as soon thereafter as possible.

This ancient Biblical requirement not to disgrace any dead body became or revealed a fixed attitude of Judaism, a general reverence for the body of the dead. Most of the specific laws with regard to the handling of the dead body are derived from a special case in the Talmud (*Baba Bathra* 154a-b). Certain relatives wished to have the body of a young man disinterred in order to determine his age at death and thus to decide whether a certain sale of property made by him was legally valid. Rabbi Akiba forbade the disinterment and said: "You may not look upon his ugliness." It was as if the dead would be shamed if the evidence of decay of the body were to be seen by the living. So strong were these feelings of respect that additional reasons to Rabbi Akiba's were later added, some of them indeed superstitious but nevertheless springing from folk feeling against uncovering the dead or even disturbing the grave.

It is upon the basis of this reverence for the body that most of the objections in Orthodox law arise against autopsy, which is permitted only under special restrictions. Also it is this reverence which is now finding its expression in new discussions in the law with regard to the most modern surgical techniques of transplanting parts of dead bodies into living bodies. The question involved here is not so much the permissibility of such drastic healing—almost anything is permitted if it will heal the sick. The question here is concerned with the almost inalienable right of the dead body to remain unmutilated. The decisions as to autopsy and the new transplant surgery are gradually being extended in the permissive direction, but the very fact that the discussion arises reveals the basic reverence in Jewish tradition for the body of the dead.

Of course this reverence was bolstered by the folk feeling that the dead have certain awarenesses, a certain modicum of life. One of the laws involves the rather pathetic idea that what the dead miss most is the privilege of fulfilling God's commandments. The dead are free from the commandments (Sabbath 30a) but somehow the folk feeling is that they wish they could still fulfill them. That is why the law forbade going into a cemetery with praying shawl and *tefillin* (*Ber.* 18a) because that would be mocking the dead, making them sad by their awareness that here is another *mitzvah* which they can no longer fulfill. Such folklore is the playful elaboration of a basic faith, going back to the Bible, that the dead are to be respected and protected.

III. *Holy Ground.* Since the bodies of the dead are to be respected, they must be put to rest in honor. Therefore almost every Jewish community except the smallest had a cemetery which was deemed sacred and kept in charge of the Holy Society. Originally burial in Palestine was in caves, usually family caves, and the dead placed in niches cut in the cave wall. Later in Babylon, where there were no rocky caves, ground burial, communal ground burial, became the custom. The fact that the original burial was in family caves explains the rather anomalous status of the communal cemetery. The law requires that members of a community should compel each other (*Kofin Zeh Es Zeh, Orah Hayyim* 150:1) to build a synagogue and to organize a school for the teaching of children, but nowhere does the law similarly require that the members of a community must compel each other to acquire a cemetery. Nevertheless, even lacking that legal basis, it became a universal custom for every community that could afford it to have its cemetery. This was deemed holy ground and the graves were deemed inviolate.

Once a body was buried it could not be disinterred except for certain specific reasons, as for example, to rebury it in the Holy Land, or to rebury in a family plot, or to move to a securer place (*Yore Deah* 363:1). To the legal objection against disinterment folklore again added further objections even against opening the grave. Of course in such medieval ancient burial grounds where it was necessary for the bodies to be buried three or four deep and where, therefore, the graves had to be opened, they were careful to see that each body was kept at least six handbreadths in all directions from the other. The body, as it were, owned its place (*Tefisas Kever*) and had the right to remain there undisturbed. Every now and then the lord of the manor or government officer commanded that a Jewish cemetery be cleared of all the remains of the dead. This was deemed a dire calamity, to be resisted in every possible way. When a body was disinterred, the family had to sit down in mourning for an hour. It happened once that a cemetery had to be cleared by order of the government. Moses Sofer (*Yore Deah* 353) formally forbade the relatives to be informed of the exact hour of the disinterment lest the entire community sit down and mourn for all their dead whose rest was now disturbed. When, alas, the living community itself was disturbed and the people were driven into exile, they went to the holy ground to bid their last farewell to their beloved and respected dead.

IV. *Sacred Sorrow.* All human beings weep for their dead, and so the folklore of the world records mourning customs in great variety. In Judaism this natural mourning was completely converted into a religious observance. The change served a double purpose. First, it gave a sure and regular outlet to sorrow and yet, simultaneously, it kept the emotion within bounds, for the intense grief at the time of death can often be terrible and dangerous. As far back as Scripture, the first laws of mourning were cautionary and negative. "Do not," says Scripture, "mutilate yourself in mourning for the dead" (Lev. 19:28). Since mourning for the dead became a religious ritual, it was inevitably elaborated into detailed laws as to the seven days, the thirty days, the year, etc. This complex legislation need not be discussed here. What is significant is the underlying intention to keep the wild torrent of sorrow confined to regular channels. It was to control excessive mourning that a special rule was established. When there was disagreement among the scholars as to whether additional mourning should be observed or less, then the principle we follow is to observe less mourning rather than more (*Halacha K'maykil B'avelus, Moed Katan* 26b). One of the various tests to indicate when the mourning was excessive and when it should cease was when a man's friends rebuked him (*Yore Deah* 389:5). In fact, the Talmud says that the man who does not moderate his sorrow is rebuked by God Himself, Who says: "Are you then more merciful than I?" (*Moed Katan* 27b).

Of course, as always, the creative imagination of the people added observances. Some of these observances were indeed superstitious and folkloristic, as for example, the covering of the mirrors, which is found among many European people. But most of the additions were religious additions. The saying of *Kaddish* for the dead, the annual custom of *Yahrzeit*, so correctly expressed the sacred feeling for the departed that it spread from Germany, the land of its origin, all over the Jewish world. The essential point is that mourning was not a wild torrent of emotions, but an organized, regularized stream of religious observances. Our mourning is not to be looked upon as our private business alone; it concerns our families, our communities and our relation to God Himself. Jewish mourning ritual, in all its variations, and except for a few superstitious expressions, was an integral part of our religious life. We converted our wild grief into a calm and sacred sorrow.

V. *Consolation.* One of the social changes that is occurring in our large cities concerns the custom of consolation of the mourners. Hitherto people visited the home of the bereaved during the seven days of mourning, but now the custom is increasing for them to go to the funeral parlor before the funeral service and there to greet the bereaved. Possibly this growing custom has its social basis. Perhaps it is because distances are greater, the community is no longer compact and families are not as mutually accessible as they were. Whatever it is, the new custom must be reckoned with and some adjustment is bound to occur in the Jewish methods of consolation. But whatever changes the growth of our cities brings about, the effort to console the mourner is deemed to be one of the great commandments. In fact, the Talmud (*Sanhedrin* 19a) considers it to be one of the noblest ways of *Imitatio Dei,* of walking in the ways of God. Just as God consoles the bereaved, says the Talmud, so, too, must you console the bereaved. This consolation of the sorrowing, being an honored religious duty, also, as is inevitable, became elaborated into many laws and restrictions. But nearly all of them reveal a certain basic mood, namely, to be patient and not to force words of consolation before people are ready to receive them. Thus it became an established law that when visiting the bereaved, the visitor must not say a single word of consolation until the bereaved speak first (*Yore Deah* 376:1). When they themselves are ready to discuss their sorrow, it is then that you may try to console them. In fact some scholars even say that in the first three days of mourning when the sorrow is deepest, you may not speak in consolation of the bereaved; they are not yet ready for it. This is not the established law, but even this minority opinion reveals the patient, sensitive understanding with which we must meet the bereaved. With whatever patient tact we can summon, we must console the bereaved; for that, in Judaism, is a religious duty, God-commanded and by God Himself exemplified.

The wholesomeness of Jewish tradition with regard to death and mourning must be counted among those social and psychological elements which kept the persecuted and harried Jews from becoming moribund and obsessed with death. The voluntary devotion which established the sacred society was in itself, aside from its specific functions, an example of the sturdy self-help of the embattled Jewish communities. The laws and customs which this sacred society jealously guarded expressed a certain fundamental mood, the sacredness of life itself, the revered status of the body of the dead, the holy ground where they rest, the sacred sorrow of disciplined mourning, and the gentle, understanding consolation of the bereaved.

It is in this final function that the modern rabbi may nobly serve. The people who come to him in their sorrow eagerly desire to honor their dead and to pay them such tribute as they feel they owe them and cannot otherwise give. Therefore the words that the rabbi speaks are listened to perhaps with more attention than many another address that he may give, because here the people are eagerly awaiting the tribute that he feels he can justly utter for the dead. In fact, if the rabbi omits mentioning certain weaknesses of the departed and mentions only his virtues, even this kindly selectivity is sanctioned by Jewish law (*Yore Deah* 344:1). The bereaved feel the need of doing honor to their departed and since that feeling is part of a noble tradition, it is amply justified. He who can effectively console reconciles the bereaved with God and brings him back to an allegiance to life itself. Those who can do that will fulfill the words of the Midrash: "Consoling the mourners brings happiness to the world." (*Aboth d'R. Nathan,* ed. Schechter, p. 89.)

GOD AND THE ETHICAL IMPULSE

W. Gunther Plaut
Rabbi, Holy Blossom Temple
Toronto, Canada

1. Why Love a Stranger?

Thirty-six times does Scripture warn us to treat the גר , the stranger,[1] in kindly, generous and loving fashion. R. Eliezer Hagadol, to whom the statement is attributed, knew his Bible thoroughly and the figure may be checked.[2] Our sages were already aware that this was an unusually high degree of repetition. Was it because of human weakness that one had to be so frequently warned about this matter? Or was there another reason?

The answer which R. Eliezer gives us is unfortunately rather cryptic, which caused a good many headaches to our sages who wrestled manfully with the great rabbi's explanation. The Torah, said R. Eliezer, warns us so often about the stranger, מפני שסורו רע

Now, if we would only know what this means! Alas, it is an almost oracular reply and it naturally elicited a flood of commentaries, some of them highly ingenious and others frankly emendatory.

Rashi, for instance, emends שסורו רע to שאורו רע , by which he means the swelling of the genitals (i.e., the evil inclination).[3] According to him, R. Eliezer's expression means: the Torah warns us so often about the גר because of his evil inclination— a rather prejudicial reference to the presumed unreliability of the stranger or proselyte. Elijah Mizrahi, in his commentary on Rashi, quotes Eleazar ben Samuel of Metz (the RAM), in reading שצורו רע , "because the stranger's god is evil," [4] and he defends his emendation on the grounds of euphemistic necessity, which hardly improves on Rashi.

215

Bertinoro does better, but only because he uses his imagination more freely.[5] He understands R. Eliezer to refer to the stranger's bad smell, for when you oppress him the odor of oppression will give him away and will make your ill treatment of him only too obvious. All of which is likely to leave the reader puzzled and unconvinced.

Whatever R. Eliezer's explanation, Scripture doubtlessly had its good reasons for repeating the injunction concerning the stranger so many times. It was not easy then, nor is it easy now, to withstand the temptation of exploiting the weak amongst whom the stranger, the widow, and orphan inevitably are found. And when it comes to loving the stranger who dwells in our midst—how much more difficult is this than loving one's neighbor, which is hard enough! (Some will of course assert that it is easier to love strangers than neighbors.)[6]

Actually, the frequency of repetition presents only a minor problem. A much more serious question arises from the fact that the Torah repeatedly tells us *why* we should respect and even love the stranger. Three of the best known passages will illustrate our dilemma:

> You shall not wrong a stranger or oppress him, for you were strangers in the land of Egypt. (Exod. 22:20)
> The stranger who resides with you shall be to you as one of your citizens; you shall love him as yourself, for you were strangers in the land of Egypt: I the Lord am your God. (Lev. 19:34)
> You shall not oppress a stranger, for you know the heart of the stranger, having yourselves been strangers in the land of Egypt. (Exod. 23:9)

The Torah apparently founds the mitzvah on two reasons: one is historical כי גרים הייתם בארץ מצרים and the other compassionate or, if you will, psychological ואתם ידעתם את נפש הגר . One needs to think but little about these stated reasons to appreciate that they do not really supply us with an effective motivation.

The psychological motivation occurs only once, although it

appears to be the more powerful. Jews of past and present have
indeed known "the heart of the stranger," having themselves
been strangers in many lands. This reminder of our past bitter
experience presumes that this remembrance makes us empa-
thetic with regard to others. Alas, while this is true for some, it
fails as a social and psychological device with all too many.
In fact, often men will revert to oppressive behavior in direct
proportion to their former depressed condition. Still, the argument is sound for some, and perhaps this is why it is given only
once.

But over and over we are told that the major reason for not
wronging the stranger is historical. We ourselves were strangers
once, therefore do not do to others what has been done to us.
All present-day homilies aside, Egypt and Exodus belong to the
far distant past. Will the rehearsal of this historic incident produce moral rectitude and even lead us to the well-nigh unreach-
able goal of loving a stranger? Should we not expect the Torah
to tell us that the real reason for treating the stranger decently
is that this is the right thing to do, since he is our brother?

The problem did not escape our ancient commentators. The
Mekhilta, in commenting on Exod. 22:20, say that the phrase
"You shall not wrong a stranger" לא תונה applies to wronging
him with words, while "nor oppress him" לא תלחצנו applies to
money matters. From this, R. Nathan deduces that the stated
reason "for you were strangers in the land of Egypt" applies to
verbal offenses only, for one should not reproach a fellow man
with a shortcoming which is one's own: מום שבך אל תאמרהו לחברך.

Having once been strangers themselves, Jews should not now
taunt others with being strangers. The Talmud further illustrates
this by quoting an earthy proverb: "Whoever has someone in
his family who was hanged should not say to the vendor: 'Hang
a little fish up for me.' " [7]

This solution—if it may be so called—apparently appealed to
Rashi who repeated it in various places,[8] but even his devoted
disciples who in turn elaborated on his commentary could not
see eye to eye with him in this matter. The argument was forced
and it did not say anything about the passage in Leviticus where
we are asked to love the stranger since we ourselves were stran-

gers once in Egypt. R. Nathan's pragmatic advice hardly
matches this exalted command.

Ibn Ezra also contributes little to the elucidation of our
problem, especially since he muddies the discussion by assuming
that גר means proselyte. The גר , he says, now accepts the
rejection of idols, hence do not oppress him just because you
have the power to do so. What makes Ibn Ezra's comment
invaluable, however, is his homiletical aside on the fact that in
v. 20 the Torah addresses us in the singular, in v. 21 in the
plural, and in v. 22 in the singular again. Says he: Everyone
who sees another person oppressing the weak and does not
help them, thereby is himself reckoned as an oppressor.[9] All of
which is splendid for sermons but does not explain the introduction of the historical reasons into the essentially moral command
to treat the stranger decently and lovingly.

The Ramban does not hesitate to reject Rashi's and Ibn
Ezra's explanations outright.   ואין בכל זה טעם בעקר   he says.
Why then the reminder that we were slaves in Egypt? Because
it draws your attention to the fact that God hears the cry of the
oppressed and saves them, as He saved Israel in Egypt. "For
you know the heart of the stranger" refers to the same central
point. You know what you did and felt when you were slaves,
you cried and redemption came (however, as Ramban is careful
to add, it came not because of your cry but because of God's
mercy).[10]

Abarbanel follows a similar line and explains the difficulty
as follows: "Just as you were strangers there (in Egypt) and I
made My name known to you and guarded you, so now for the
goyim who live amongst you, I am their God." [11]

Perhaps just because Rashi's commentary was in this instance
so obviously strained and, in fact, plainly unsatisfactory, it was
left to those who in turn commented on him to recognize the
textual difficulty most clearly. Of the major annotators of
Rashi, only Mordecai Jaffe fails to deal with the problem, but
Mizrahi and the two *gedolim* from Prague, the Maharal and
Shabbetai Bass expose the heart of the matter.

Mizrahi states flatly that   כי גרים הייתם   cannot be the reason for the command not to oppress the stranger, but is merely a historic reference,[12] and the Maharal with his usual perception simply says: The Torah commands us to love the stranger, and not to despise him—and that is it, no reasons need to be given.[13] Bass sums up his predecessors' insight in this fashion: Love itself is commanded, but not because we were strangers in Egypt. "For the fact that (Jews) once were strangers does not form the basis of their obligation to love the stranger." [14]

What then is the basis of the obligation? The key lies in Lev. 19:34. Just as the difficult command to love one's neighbor is rendered comprehensible only by the climactic ending אני ה so the command to love a stranger is climaxed by the reminder אני ה' . Without this, the command has no foundation; the fact that God is God is the final reason for human love. And conversely, "the esteem for and love of the stranger is the true touchstone of your fear and love of God," as Samson Raphael Hirsch remarked.[15] The expression, "for you were strangers in the land of Egypt," is designed to keep alive the awareness of God's role in Israel's history and thereby to re-emphasize that the foundation of our moral law is the existence of God.

Here, and here alone, lies the answer to our question. If Hermann Cohen says that the alien is to be protected because he is a human being, he is of course right. But when he goes on to say: "In the alien, therefore, man discovered the idea of humanity," [16] he tends to be misleading. For in the alien the Jew was first and foremost bidden to discover the presence of the redeeming God, and thereby he was to reinforce his bonds with all men.

The best summation of this solution is already found in the Torah itself, in Deut. 10:17-19:

> For the Lord your God is God supreme and Lord supreme, the great, the mighty, and the awesome God . . . [Who] loves the stranger, providing him with food and clothing. You too must love the stranger, for you were strangers in the land of Egypt.

2. Voluntary or Forced Giving?

It is no wonder that Jews are good fund raisers. Wasn't Moses the greatest of them all? Has he ever been equaled? He set out to gather funds for a building and, without committees or professional agencies (but with very precise architectural plans in hand), without fuss or bother he raised more than he needed!

The remarkable story which ought to be studied carefully by all fund raisers begins in Exod. 25 and reaches its climax in Exod. 36:4 ff:

> And all the wise men, that wrought all the work of the sanctuary, came every man from his work which they wrought. And they spoke unto Moses, saying: "The people bring much more than enough for the service of the work, which the Lord commanded to make." And Moses gave commandment, and they caused it to be proclaimed throughout the camp, saying: "Let neither man nor woman make any more work for the offering of the sanctuary." So the people were restrained from bringing. For the stuff they had was sufficient for all the work to make it, and too much.

"And too much . . . !" Was there ever anything like it before or after? No revision of plans was necessary because funds or materials were lacking. No follow-up drives, no quotas, no pledges to be paid off in five years, no mortgage and no mortgage burning. The whole thing was in hand right from the beginning.

We like to think, of course, that our forefathers had a special propensity for responding to religious needs. They were still a young congregation, filled with enthusiasm, and even their spiritual leader, though not precisely a fledgling youth, was still vigorous enough to last through forty further annual congregational meetings and reelections and to hold off some pestiferous trustees like Korah (a member of the anti-Canaanite Council who wanted to make the desert his permanent home and, in a manner of speaking, was granted his wish).

In fact, the three Sedras in question (*Terumah, Vayak'hel, Pekude*) put special emphasis on the voluntary nature of the Temple gifts. כל איש אשר ידבנו לבו "Let every man give whose heart makes him willing," this is the theme which runs through the entire description of the offerings. Despite their other short-comings the Israelites of the Exodus were a generous people, who set an example to all later generations. When it came to the building of God's house, greed and parsimony gave way to splendid liberality. O for the olden days!

But already the ancient rabbis were uneasy about this pat accolade, and students of the text have discovered serious problems beneath the shining surface. And they have come to the hesitant conclusion that even in the desert, fund raising was not quite so simple and not quite so spontaneous.

To begin with, after the initial statement in Exod. 25:2, which provides for a free-will offering, the Torah stresses the voluntary character of the contribution another four times (25:5, 21, 22, 29). Lo, he protesteth too much! The writer himself knew that the voluntary nature of the giving was somewhat in doubt, and the striking repetition seems intended to impress the reader.

Why was the "willing heart" of Israel at all in question? Because in ch. 25 the opportunity for giving is introduced by the usual peremptory address to Moses which precedes all out-right commands: "Speak to the children of Israel . . .," and in ch. 35: "This is the thing which the Lord commanded, saying . . ."

Moreover, in both places the term לקח (take) is used: ויקחו לי תרומה (25:2), and קחו מאתכם תרומה (35:5), which sounds suspiciously like some form of forceful suasion. And finally, to bring the problem to its ultimate confusion, in 38:26 we are unceremoniously informed that when it came to the collection of כסף for the Tabernacle, all suggestion of voluntarism was dropped and 603,550 men each contributed a levy of one *beka* or half-shekel.

So where are we? On the one hand the text speaks of con-tribution by voluntary subscription, but then there is also the divine command to give, of לקח as the method of collecting the funds, and finally we are told of an across-the-board assessment.

It almost sounds like modern times, except that the result was
better than the most up-to-date professionals usually can produce. Was it perchance that free-will offerings were tried first
and then abandoned for more rigorous means? In that case,
what happened to the vaunted spirit of ancient generosity? [1] But
we cannot really assume this succession of events because the
text starts with the command and ends with the free gift.

Our traditional commentators assumed that, if there was a
difficulty in interpretation, it had to be resolved in favor of
voluntarism. The sheer weight of the repetitions would give
emphasis to their conclusion. But what to make of the above-
stated objections?

The majority of the comments follow Rashi who says that
everything except the shekel was a free will offering. Ibn Ezra
puts it this way: 16 articles were required altogether of which
only one כסף was required of everyone, but nevertheless it
was included in the original statement although it is an exception.

What about the term לקח ? The Midrash sees it not as a
commanding term but as a veiled reference to לקח טוב in
Proverbs, i.e., to Torah, which is a good text for preaching
but does not elucidate our problem.[2] Ibn Ezra denies altogether
that לקח connotes more than an invitation to give, since the
word is followed by לי , and he cites as corroborating evidence
the use of this expression in I Kings 17:10. Similarly, he says,
the word סור (remove) is used peremptorily when followed
by מעל (as in Num. 16:26), but pleadingly when followed by
אל (as in Gen. 19:2).

Malbim follows this line of argument but refines it further.
He distinguishes between קח מאתו and קח ממנו . The former
is always invitational, he says, and the latter always commanding. He also draws our attention to the fact that if the text
were to say ויתנו לי (let them give Me) it would have constituted an obligation for everyone to give; but since it says
ויקחו לי (let them take unto Me) the only people commanded
are the gabba'im, i.e., the directors and the Building Committee.
They are bidden to institute and arrange for the collection
לקח ; the people are to give מנדבת לב ורצון חפשי . [3]

There are still other suggestions to resolve the dilemma, but already Saadia suspected that there could be no real solution to what was essentially a contradiction. He therefore claimed that there were in fact two collections, one compulsory and one voluntary. A neat answer, except that the text gives us no clue in this direction.

The answer, it seems to me, lies not in a forcible harmonization of the text or the Procrustean stretching of an essentially unambiguous term like לקח, but in a clear recognition that the Torah combines the command to give and the opportunity to be generous in the same story. Rather than press for an either-or we should recognize that both aspects are involved in every process of giving, whether תרומה or צדקה. At the foundation lies the divine command setting forth our responsibility; thereafter each man is invited to stretch his heart toward the highest goal. "Command the children of Israel," is the basis; "Let each one search his soul" is the way.

Of course, our modern fund raisers and Temple builders will object. "You can't do it this way anymore," they say. And, if they know a bit of text they may even point out that voluntarism is fine for weaving and other artistic contributions, but when it comes to money, should we not follow the Torah and make it an obligatory levy?

In reply I submit that lately we have not tried the true way of Torah. We only say: "Take contributions from them." But we do not stress: "This is the thing that the Lord has commanded." Either we are afraid to say this to our people, or we suspect that all too often, in our various collections and drives, the will of God may not readily be assumed as a foundation for the fund-raising effort.

NOTES

[1] In the Bible גֵּר is always a stranger, i.e., one from another place. Even Jews are in some instances referred to in this fashion. (Jud. 17:7-13; II Sam. 4:3). Rashi (ad Exod. 22:20) explains the term as "someone born in another place," but there are many who disagree with him and want גֵּר understood as proselyte גֵּר צֶדֶק . Mekhilta (Masekhta de-Nezikim, ch. 18) and Talmud (BM 59a et al.) intermingle the terms (cf. Lauterbach's notation in his ed. of the Mekhilta, vol. III, p. 138, and I. Goldschmidt's commentary on BM 59). Cf. also W. R. Smith, Lectures on the Religion of the Semites, pp. 75 ff.; A. Bertholet, Die Stellung der Israeliten und der Juden zu den Fremden (Freiburg, 1896); אינצ׳יקלופדיה מקראית under גֵּר ; Salo W. Baron, A Social and Religious History of the Jews, 2nd ed., vol. I, part 1 (Philadelphia, 1952), pp. 155–56; and J. D. Eisenstein's invaluable article in the Jewish Encyclopedia, sub "Gentile."

[2] BM 59b; Malbim ad Lev. 19:34.

[3] Rashi on Exod. 22:20. Lauterbach (loc. cit.) emends to סיורו the stranger "has a bad streak in him."

[4] Mizrahi on Lev. 19:34.

[5] Commentary on Mishnah BM IV, 10. See other references in Kasher, Torah Shelemah, vol. 19, p. 184, 130. See also commentaries on the parallel passages in Zohar II 99a, and Mas. Gerim IV, 1.

[6] The new JPS translation on occasion drops the command to "love" the stranger and instead speaks of the duty to "befriend" him (see, e.g., Deut. 10:18, 19). But in Lev. 19:34 it retains the command to "love" him. The reason for this variation in translation is not clear.

[7] BM 59b.

[8] E.g. on Deut. 10:19 and Lev. 19:34.

[9] See also the change of number in Lev. 19:33 and 34 and S. R. Hirsch's comment.

[10] Ramban ad Exod. 22:20. See the discussion of his viewpoint in Nehama Leibowitz, Studies in the Weekly Sidra (1st series), Mishpatim.

[11] Abarbanel, ad Lev. 19:34, actually uses the phrase: אני ה׳ אלהיכם In his comment on Exod. 22:20 he advances a slightly different argument: Don't oppress the stranger, for God may do to you what He did to the Egyptians.

[12] Ad Exod. 22:20.

[13] Ad Deut. 10:19.

[14] Ibidem.

[15] Ad Lev. 19:33-34.

[16] Quoted by Hertz in his commentary on Exod. 22:20.

[17] It should be stated that Shemot Rabba 33:3 and Tanhuma on Ex. 25:8 imply that what appeared to be generous free will was in effect an atonement for the sin of the Golden Calf, guilt rather than generosity. See also Nahmanides on 35:1.

18 Tanhuma *ad loc.;* Shemot Rabba 33:1.

19 Malbim on Ex. 25:2. His whole discussion is a delightful exercise in exegesis and homiletics. For instance: Why does it say: מאת כל איש? Because the offering was to be taken from rich and poor alike. Why does it say ידבנו לבו? Because the smallest donation was acceptable, even a single thread. And finally, he calls our attention to Haggai 2:8 where it says: "Mine is the silver, and Mine is the gold, saith the Lord." If that is so, did not the generation of the desert really give to the Tabernacle something that did not belong to them in the first place? True, says Malbim, but when a man gives for the sake of Heaven it is reckoned as if it were his, although he takes from the Lord and gives to Him!

SOCIAL ACTION

CIVIL DISOBEDIENCE
AND THE JEWISH TRADITION

Samuel G. Broude
Rabbi, Temple Sinai
Oakland, California

The problem of civil disobedience is very much with us. Events in the civil rights crisis—in the North as well as in the South—have sharpened critical attention on our own attitudes toward the law, government, and the state. More and more, rabbis have entered the struggle to attain racial freedom and equality of opportunity. In the course of participating in freedom rides, sit-ins, pray-ins, school boycotts and freedom schools, some have been arrested for breaking the law. Our involvement has raised questions by some congregants, not to mention questions raised by rabbis themselves.

When is it right to defy the laws of the state? Is it ever right to do so? On what basis? Who decides? What authority do we have for knowingly and consciously breaking a law? What makes our law-breaking "good" and that of our opponent "bad"? (A school boycott, as residents of the New York area well know, works both ways.) What rule of thumb do we have for determining what is, in fact, an act of civil disobedience? What is the basis, religiously, morally, of our moving into the area of illegality? Is the issue one of individual conscience, or does Jewish tradition impel us to take a stand?

The issue is one of ultimate loyalty. But there is more to it than this—at what point do I choose to demonstrate my choice of loyalties?

If I wish to express my dislike for a particular law, I may ignore the prohibition; or, I may refuse to pay the federal income tax because some of the income is used, say, for military expenditures. On the other hand, I might disobey civil law in order to secure minority rights, the right to equal treatment or full freedom of opportunity. Civil disobedience is a protest. I do not break the law simply for the sake of showing my independence, but in order to fulfill a higher law or to have enacted a more just law or to bring about a condition of greater freedom or justice.

Thoreau believed that the individual conscience must determine what is right. The law must conform to the right. An unjust government ought not be obeyed. "If the injustice is of such a nature that it requires you to be the agent of injustice to another, then, I say, break the law. Let your life be a counter friction to stop the machine . . . that I do not lend myself to the wrong which I condemn." [1]

The individual has a solemn responsibility. He must decide on the justice of his government, he must pass judgment on its actions (and not simply at election time), and he must make his right of consent to the government contingent upon the government's recognition of the individual as a "higher and independent power from which all its own power and authority are derived. . . ." Thoreau spoke from the principle of the given autonomy of the self rather than from a particular religious tradition.

Gandhi went further. When asked what it means to be a law-abiding nation, he responded, "We are passive resisters. When we do not like certain laws, we do not break the heads of law-givers but we suffer and do not submit to the laws. That we should obey laws whether good or bad is a new-fangled notion. . . . Such teaching is opposed to religion and means slavery." [2]

In any discussion of civil disobedience, the question of motivation, of ultimate purpose, is important. If civil disobedience is to have a moral basis, it must stem from moral concerns, from love of man and love of law. It must aim at greater rights (for a larger number) rather than fewer. The person involved in civil disobedience must be willing to accept the consequence of the law rather than attempt to defy the law and escape from penalty. He must be one who loves the law and loves mankind. Civil disobedience, then, is an action or inaction, motivated by love, in defiance of civil laws, which has as its aim the accomplishment of justice and righteousness.

Having defined civil disobedience, let us see what light our tradition can shed on these questions.

In the Bible we are taken by the sight and sound of the prophet confronting the king, again and again defying his authority in the name of a Higher Authority. We have before us what is still the ultimate issue in our contemporary dilemma: civil obedience as against Divine obedience. Whose law shall prevail? For whose law must we stand—for his whose power and authority are conceded by his human subjects, or His whose power and authority men assert, but whose will they may not always carry out.

Civil disobedience, in the Biblical context, means defiance of the political authority of the state for the sake of asserting the prior authority of God. The king must constantly be reminded that he is under God's rule, and that God's law must be administered by him, irrespective of the response of the people. Thus we find Saul, anointed by God's representative Samuel, and deposed by him, recognizing and admitting his failure in these words: "I have sinned, for I have transgressed the commandment of the Lord, and thy words; because I feared the people and hearkened to their voice." [3] The Biblical editor here asserts the primary claim of God's law on the king. There is no question as to whose law is the law of the land; since there can be no separation between the civil power and the Divine power, there is no question of divided authority or conflict of loyalty. There is one issue only: is God's agent in power, the king, living up to his commission or is he not? It is the prophet's task to decide and to act on his judgment. If this means opposing the king, then so be it.

Examples of this opposition are well known (Nathan reprimanding David, Elijah speaking against Ahab, etc.).[4] Elijah's activities involved more than verbal defiance. In an attempt to unseat Ahab and Jezebel, and at the risk of his life, he helped to foment a political-religious revolution. The king cannot be permitted to transgress human rights or property rights. If he does, he must be defied. When Amaziah told Amos to leave Beth-el, he argued that "it is the king's sanctuary, and a royal house." [5] He was asserting that Amos was "civilly disobedient." Amos replied, of course, that he was simply being "Divinely obedient," that his mandate came from God, and, therefore, he intends to go right on being disobedient to the king, as this is what the hour demands! ("Will two walk together," etc.) [6]

Our prophetic tradition in the actions of Jeremiah provides us vivid precedent for demonstration in behalf of God's moral demands. Jeremiah put bands and bars on his neck, and sent such bands to the kings of Edom, Moab, and Tyre, to dramatize their impending defeat by and subjugation to Nebuchadnezzar. [7] We may be certain that Jeremiah did not endear himself by such means to Zedekiah, king of Judah. When Hananiah broke the wooden bar from Jeremiah's neck, Jeremiah returned with an iron bar. [8] Nor had he made himself popular with Zedekiah's predecessor, Jehoiakim. He prophesied destruction and desolation. He was threatened with death for having spoken "against this city." [9] What had he said? Simply that "If you will not listen to Me, to walk in My law . . . then I will make this city a curse to all the nations. . . ." The issue is joined: *My* law against the king's, *My* law against the false prophets of peace and security. Is this civil disobedience? The "people" think so. But Jeremiah did not permit this to stand in the way of his task as prophet.

We are not discussing the question simply of speaking out against popular sentiment. This we may safely grant as being part of every rabbi's practice. We are concerned with actions taken against the legal and political authority of the land— disobedience to the express prohibition of the ruler or his agents. We cannot accept authority simply because it is couched in the cloak of the king or because it controls the legal machinery of the state. The religiously committed must judge whether or not their government follows the demands of God or its own expediencies.

The prophetic response is clear but there is a difficulty. In the days of Jeremiah, the king ruled by virtue of a Divine Constitution. How must we act now that civil acts and religious authority are distinct entities? For guidance, we turn to the Talmud and to the problem of *dina d'malchuta dina*.

The principle of *dina d'malchuta* is the far-reaching pronouncement of Samuel which enabled the Jewry of third-century Babylonia to accept the civil power as binding in all matters not directly in conflict with Jewish religious principles. There are those who cite this principle to argue that any deviation from "the law of the land" is not in consonance with Jewish tradition.

It should be obvious that as citizens of this country, and as adherents to Judaism, we have obligations to both. As long as these two claims on our loyalty do not pull in opposite directions, there is no problem. But when "the law of the land" outrages our Jewish conscience, when the law of the state permits discrimination against a group within the community or against a single individual, then it is our duty to protest even if we must break the law to do so. *Dina d'malchuta dina* was never intended to legitimatize the civil government under *any* circumstances, but only under conditions which do not undermine the proper expression of Judaism.[10] *Dina d'malchuta dina* permits us to participate in day-to-day citizenship, but not to deny God or His commandments.

Where do we draw the line?

A look at the four cases cited in the Talmud where the principle of Samuel is applied[11] indicates that rabbinic concern related to taxes collected by the (non-Jewish) government, as well as contractual obligations related to the purchase and possession of property of non-Jews. The refrain of *V'ha-amar Shmuel dina d'malchuta dina* insists that in every instance where the law of the kingdom is applied without prejudice, it is the law of the land.[12] However, where the tax is exorbitant for one person or arbitrarily levied against one group, or when the representative of the king is not authorized to raise the tax, or when the tax is not a fixed amount, the principle of *dina d'malchuta* does not apply. Such a tax is considered *gezel*, the collector an out-and-out *gazlan*, and, in the phrase used by R. Nissim, "extortion by the tax-collector is not the law." [13] Otherwise, so long as the people have voluntarily accepted the king's rule, they must accede to his regulations.[14]

This view is reflected also in the well-known phrase from the New Testament, "Render unto Caesar the things that are Caesar's, and to God the things that are God's." [15] This author implied more than "it's all right to pay the taxes." When the Herodians tried to trap Jesus with their question concerning paying the tax, Jesus is depicted as asking for a coin. Given one, he asked, "Whose picture is on it?" "Caesar's, of course." "Well, then, give him his coinage." We cannot keep from connecting to this the Midrash which compares a human king to God. "Look at a human king," say the Rabbis. "When he is proclaimed as king, he issues his coins. His image is stamped on every coin, and so all coins look alike. Not so with God. He, too, issues coins (human beings); on each is stamped His image, yet each one looks different." Jesus answered the question put by adding another dimension to it. "Yes, it's all right to pay the tax, since it's only giving to Caesar what ultimately belongs to him, but keep in mind to whom you ultimately belong." Render unto God what is His implies your ultimate commitment to the Divine. The terms of the question have been changed. The problem is no longer whether or not to pay taxes and thereby recognize the government. The important issue is: whose standards do you use for rendering judgment, who possesses you, whose image do you reflect, who is worthy of ultimate loyalty? This is more than a *d'rush,* it is our own question: where lies ultimate authority—in the State and its machinery, or in the ethical commandments of God which must be carried out by the State, and if not, then by those who will not settle for less?

Should we not use legal means to attain a moral end? Yes, if at all possible. But these are not "normal" times. In a time of social crisis it may be necessary, paradoxically, to break the law of the State in order to make it a true expression of God's law. Cannot the extremist use the same tactic? Yes, he can, but if he does, he is attempting to limit or deny rights, while we are attempting to assert greater human rights. Purpose makes all the difference. We are concerned with love of neighbor. He is con-

cerned with love of self. Does the end justify the means? No.
This question is inapplicable. We are here concerned with a
conflict between legal and moral. It is possible to be legal but
immoral (the Nazis passed laws), and it may be necessary, in
order to be moral, to be illegal. Certainly, we ought to conduct
ourselves legally as long as we can, but it isn't always possible
to be legal and moral at the same time. Then we must make
a choice. I am suggesting that for the religiously committed
person, there is no choice!

Dina d'malchuta dina is acceptable as long as law does not
conflict with ultimate Jewish loyalty, as long as it does not seek
to deny God. When law does, it must be defied. "God said to
Israel . . . 'do not rebel against the government, whatever it
decrees. But if it decrees that you shall nullify the Law and
the Commandments, do not listen to it.' " [16]

Not listening to the government may lead to the highest form
of civil disobedience—martyrdom. When our tradition counsels
us to die rather than commit idolatry, incest, or murder under
duress, it insists that there are limitations to the principle of
dina d'malchuta. Jewish tradition recognizes that men and
governments who seek to deny God or to deface His image are to
be defied. Surely we are not so parochial as to apply the idea
of sanctifying the Divine Name only to situations where Jews
are involved, or where Judaism is threatened. The obligation of
Kiddush haShem applies wherever God's image is not permitted
to be reflected clearly on the face of all His children. If we are to
stand with the Negro in this critical hour and crucial struggle,
can we permit any unjust man-made laws or man-made mis-
application of just laws, to stand in the way of sanctifying God?

The Talmud equates the sin of shaming one's neighbor in public with that of shedding blood.[17] Tosaphoth tells us that "shaming one's neighbor" should have been included with incest,
idolatry and murder as a condition in which death should be
chosen rather than compliance.[18] All of us are in daily danger
of publicly shaming our Negro neighbors by denying them full
equality of education, integrated neighborhoods, freedom of
movement, adequate employment opportunities. The only laws

which can properly claim our support are those which eliminate this shame, or at least do not permit it to prevail.

The only law that can lay claim to our ultimate loyalty is the law that we relate to as Commandment. Our problem is summed up in Rosenzweig's response to Buber: "For me, too, God is not a Law-giver. But He commands. It is only by the manner of his observance that man in his inertia changes the commandments into law, a legal system with paragraphs, without the realization that 'I am the Lord,' without 'fear and trembling,' without the awareness that man stands under God's commandments." [19]

This, then, is the issue. Do we stand under God's "commandment," or do we simply observe "laws"? Each of us must choose: do we obey man—or God? There is no neutral ground.

NOTES

1 Essay on *Civil Disobedience* (1849).

2 "On Passive Resistance" (from *Indian Home Rule,* 1909).

3 I Sam. 15:24.

4 II Sam. 11:1–12:15; I Kings 21:1–29; 22.

5 Amos 7:10–17.

6 Amos 3:3–8.

7 Jer. 27.

8 Jer. 26.

9 Jer. 28.

10 Moore, *Judaism,* Vol. II, p. 112; cf. Maimonides, *M.T., Hilchot Gezelah* 5:11–14; *Choshen Mishpat* 369:8, esp. the Mordecai and the Gaon there.

11 *Nedarim* 28a, *Gitin* 10b, *Baba Kama* 113a, *Baba Bathra* 54b–55a.

12 Commentary of R. Asher to *Nedarim* 28a.

13 *Nedarim* 28a.

14 Cf. Rashbam, *Baba Bathra* 54b.

15 Matt. 22:21; cf. Rom. 13.

16 Tanhuma on Gen. 8:16.

17 *Baba Metzia* 58a.

18 *Sotah* 10b.

19 Glatzer, ed., *On Jewish Learning,* N. Y., 1955, Schocken, p. 116.

RELIGIOUS RESPONSIBILITY
FOR THE SOCIAL ORDER:
A JEWISH VIEW

Emil L. Fackenheim
Professor of Philosophy
University of Toronto
Toronto, Canada

(Author's note)

The following article was part of a Protestant-Catholic-Jewish dialogue, held at the annual board meeting of the National Conference of Christians and Jews in Washington, D. C., on November 20, 1961. The other participants were Prof. J. Pelikan and Father G. Weigel, S.J. I have found the topic not only most important but also—if seriously tackled, and tackled in a brief statement—difficult and full of snares. Among the snares which I sought to avoid and expose are: (a) the mistaking of the separation of church and state for a dualism which makes religion otherworldly, and society either amoral or else morally concerned in a way which does not only not need religious inspiration but positively rejects it; (b) the belief (found in the various forms of "Biblicism" on the one hand, natural law positions on the other) that it is the business of religion to offer moral doctrines which are specific and concrete, and yet timelessly valid; (c) the opposite belief that, precisely because religion cannot offer such doctrines, it must confine itself to innocuous generalities, thus leaving the big decisions concerning war and peace, the implementation of social justice, etc., entirely in the hands of religiously and morally neutral "experts." In view of the current debate in the Reform movement on the issue of social action, the rejection of the last two of the above errors would seem especially timely. And the repudiation of the first is even more timely, in view of the increasing strains produced among us by the cold war.

I

If there is a single religious affirmation which, first coming with Judaism into the world, has remained basic to Jewish belief until today, it is that the God on high loves widows and orphans below; and that He commands men, from on high, to do His will in the social order below. Elsewhere, too, men have had an awareness of the Divine, and a sense of responsibility in the social realm. It was the distinctive contribution of the Hebrew prophets to proclaim that the two cannot be rent apart; that men ought to treat each other as created in the image of a God who challenges them to this task.

II

It is in the light of this basic affirmation that I must seek to answer the question concerning religious responsibility for the social order. And I must begin by opposing all attempts to tear asunder what the prophetic affirmation joins together; that is, on the one hand, a secularism which bids religion mind its business, of which responsibility for the social order is to be no part, and, on the other hand, an otherworldly religion which, accepting this advice, disclaims all responsibility for the social order. Forms of such divorce have existed in all ages. That they may exist in one and the same person has been terribly illustrated in our own time—by those Germans who thought it possible to be Nazis and Christians at once.

I must stress that opposing divorce between the religious and the social realm is by no means equivalent to rejecting the separation between church and state, of which more below. I must stress, too, that secularist social morality has often put to shame a social morality supposedly religiously inspired; that those rejecting or suspending belief in God have often done His will toward men more perfectly than those professing belief in Him. And this fact must give us pause. Even so, one may question whether secularist morality can, for long, treat men as created in the image of a God in Whom it does not believe; whether it can forever resist the temptation to reduce man, from an end in himself, to a mere means, thus degenerating either into a merely relativistic morality, or else—and worse—into one resting on pseudo-absolutes, such as the interests of a deified class, nation or state.

The dangers of divorce between the religious and the social may seem remote to North Americans, who tend to be practical in religion and religiously inspired in their social morality; and indeed, for the worst examples of divorce we must surely look elsewhere. Still, we are by no means exempt from danger. For a religious civilization such as ours invites a secularism assuming a pseudo-religious garb; and hence religion, meant to be openness to the divine imperative, may become a device for avoiding it. Thus, for example, those who begin by responding to the divine imperative, with a dedication to freedom and democracy, may end up deifying their dedication; and to the extent to which they in fact do so their actual dedication—as well as what it is dedicated to—is perverted. Of this danger, there are ominous indications in our time.

III

So much for the divorce between the religious and the social, which the prophetic imperative bids us oppose. What of their relation, which that imperative bids us affirm? This question, unlike the former, is fraught with great difficulty. And its essential cause is that, while the prophetic imperative is divine, the social world in which it is to find realization is human; and the human world has characteristics which render complex, not only any attempt to *realize* the prophetic imperative, but even any attempt—such as the present—merely to *state* it, in terms concrete enough to be applicable. Three characteristics must here be noted.

(1) All social organization involves power. But power is amoral before it can be made moral, and presumably it always retains aspects of amorality or even immorality. This fact confronts those who would heed the prophetic imperative with a dilemma. They may either forswear all use of power, in order to remain true to the prophetic imperative. But then they condemn their own efforts to ineffectiveness, at least beyond the most private relations and in the social order as a whole;

and thus they contribute either to total anarchy or else—more likely—to an amoral order based on naked power. Yet most forms of social order are better than anarchy, and a partly moralized order better than one not moralized at all. Alternatively, they may seek power, for the sake of the prophetic imperative which demands realization. But then they must recognize that they become compromised in its use; and their religious motivation is no protection against such compromise. Indeed, experience shows that power wielded in the name of God is subject to special perversions.

This is why those who are organized by commitment to the prophetic imperative cannot, on the one hand, escape their responsibility of moralizing power, while on the other hand they must resist all temptations to make a bid for direct power, confining themselves to indirect methods of pressure-by-exhortation. Here lies perhaps the deepest justification for the American principle of the separation of state and church.

(2) What must be the content of such exhortation? May religion advocate specific measures in the name of God, leaving to the state and society the task of their enactment? Here I come upon a second complexity of the human condition, which makes such a neat arrangement impossible. This is that concrete moral ends are, in the actual human situation, in conflict both with other ends and with the means required to enact them. I cannot think of a single moral and religious end, concrete enough to be directly applicable, and yet valid without exception. Thus believing all human life to be sacred I believe all wars to be evil; and yet I must admit that some wars had justly to be fought. But the concept of "just war" does not supply me with universally applicable criteria. Again, though believing in the Biblical injunction to be fruitful and multiply I cannot deduce from this belief the universal wrongness of artificial birth control. For I must measure the Biblical injunction against the dangers of overpopulation and mass starvation. In short, I find myself unable to subscribe to what has been called the natural law, supplying us with a knowledge of right and wrong sufficiently concrete to be directly applicable, and yet valid regardless of time and circumstances.

(3) Must religion, then, confine itself to the affirmation of abstract principles, leaving to other forces not merely the task of enactment but also that of specific application? Is religion confined to affirming in general the sacredness of life and liberty, and the evil of exploitation, but barred from taking a specific stand as to when life may be taken and liberty curtailed, and as to what constitutes a just minimum wage? Here we come upon this further characteristic of the human condition, that the moral and religious conscience of a society is manifest, not in an abstract affirmation of liberty or condemnation of exploitation, but in what it protests against, as constituting a case of curtailed liberty, or a case of exploitation. Relevancy lies in the particular. As for the general, this is apt to be invoked not only by the indifferent but even by the enemy; peace has been invoked by the mongers of war, freedom and democracy, by their worst foes. This tendency to hypocrisy is evident throughout human history. But, as George Orwell has shown with such depressing persuasiveness, not until the twentieth century have men made it into a system.

Another neat arrangement of the respective responsibilities of religion and society for the social order has thus collapsed. A religion which confines itself to general principles condemns itself to ineffectiveness and innocuousness. The Hebrew prophets, in contrast, were neither innocuous nor ineffective. And this was because they asserted the will of God, not in terms of abstract general principles, but in and for the here and now.

IV

In the light of these reflections, how, then, can I link, positively and concretely, prophetic religion to its responsibilities for the social order? The link is found, I think, not in rules or principles but in a believing attitude.

This believing attitude must, first, stubbornly insist that the will of God is to be done in the social world of man, and that we are responsible for our share in it. It must resist the temptation, born of the frustrations of all ages and especially of our own, of escaping into dualism, whether into a divine world above, unconcerned with man, or into a human world below, unconcerned with God and hence not really human.

This believing attitude must, secondly, face up to the will of God, not in general, or for some other place and time, but here and now. There is no situation which is morally and religiously neutral. There is no power struggle, however necessarily Machiavellian, which is not at the same time a situation in which the prophetic imperative speaks to us. And even the thunder of nuclear tests must not be allowed to drown its voice.

Thirdly, the prophetic imperative, being divine, must be taken with radical seriousness, not given mere half-hearted and niggardly concessions. It is one thing to be forced to compromise in the struggle against war, oppression, discrimination and poverty, and to accept such compromises temporarily and with an aching heart. It is another thing entirely to mistake what are at best incomplete achievements finally and self-righteously, as if they were perfect. This believing attitude can never forget that so long as the divine image is violated even in one single human being, the Kingdom of God on earth is incomplete.

Fourthly, this believing attitude knows that while the prophetic imperative is divine even our best efforts to respond to it are only human. And this is true not only of our organized forms of acting but also of our organized forms of belief, doctrine and preaching. Society and religion, even at their best, are under the judgment of God.

Finally and most importantly, this believing attitude knows that while we have our responsible share in the doing of God's will in the social world of man, the fate of that world is not in our hands alone. Throughout the ages, those committed to the prophetic imperative have always been threatened by despair when faced with the discrepancy between what ought to be and what is. This danger assumes unheard-of proportions in a world confronted with possibilities of total destruction. Today, more than ever, one can heed the prophetic imperative with any kind of confidence only if one heeds it with an ultimate confidence; with the confidence in a God who, while bidding us to work in His world, is also its absolute Sovereign.

TOWARD A THEOLOGY
FOR SOCIAL ACTION

Richard G. Hirsch
Rabbi, Director
UAHC Religious Action Center
Washington, D. C.

Were the title of this symposium "A Theology of Social Justice," this assignment would be fairly simple. I would take the fundamental concepts of Judaism—God, Torah, Israel, the Covenant —and show how each of these is related intrinsically to standards and goals of justice for men and society. Jewish history, values, and practices would corroborate the inherent Jewish stress on ethics.

But the title of this symposium is "Toward a Theology for Social Action," and that complicates our task considerably. The phrase "social justice" is general, abstract, and non-controversial. It is rather sobering to recall that even Father Coughlin named his reactionary, anti-Semitic, Fascist oriented newspaper "Social Justice."

"Social action" raises both the hackles and the hecklers. Social action implies collective action toward specific social objectives and, to define it even more narrowly, toward political objectives such as the passage of legislation. Social action is a means for achieving the end of social justice. So long as social justice remains a generalized theological imperative or a distant goal, there is general acceptance of the term, but when social action becomes the instrumentality for achieving social justice, then both the means and the end become controversial.

In a sense, history might be considered the process of redefining the general principles of justice. In 1776, "all men are created equal" meant that some men could live as slaves. In the 1860's, it was redefined to mean that no men should live as slaves and that Negroes were entitled to the rights of citizenship. In the 1960's, a new definition is evolving which recognizes that equal rights constitute a hollow justice without equal opportunities to secure those rights. We have come to realize that, under the guise of "separate but equal," Negroes are deprived of full equality. Within the last five years, our increased sensitivity to racial discrimination has awakened our sense of justice to other fundamental social and economic inequities.

Collective action is necessary in order to make the structures and practices of society conform to new definitions of social justice. This collective, or social, action invariably results in political conflict, but such conflict is an accepted part of the democratic process. What is not yet fully accepted as basic and proper to the political process is the fitness of social action by religious groups. Even though I am a "social actionik" I am not unaware of fundamental philosophic and institutional problems concerning the role of religion in society—and I am not uncritical of the methods and procedures followed either by our own movement or by other religious groups—but this is not the arena to discuss those questions.

The broadening scope of religious concern and the increased pace of religious participation in social issues necessitate both the development of expertise by religious activists and the reinterpretation and reapplication of moral values by religious thinkers. This in turn requires a process of constant interchange between practitioners and theoreticians, between activists and scholars.

In the contemporary ferment in the Church, there is a close relationship between Christian thought and Christian action. The new breed of Christian leaders are very much under the influence of the "new theology." It is no coincidence that the intellectual leadership for the new movements is to be found in schools of religion and theological seminaries. The encyclicals pouring forth from Rome, the statements of the World Council of Churches and the National Council of Churches, the spate of books such as *Christian Ethics and the Sit-in; Christianity and Power Politics; Non-violence and the Christian Conscience; War, Poverty, Freedom—The Great Christian Response;* and even *God is for Real, Man*—all attest to this process of rooting the Christian response to these revolutionary times in the Christian heritage.

With one or two exceptions, our Jewish seminaries and our theologians have been quiescent. Does not Judaism have something to say to our world? What distinguishes Jewish action from Christian social action? What distinguishes a synagogue social action committee from the local chapter of the American Civil Liberties Union, whose chairman is in all probability Jewish anyhow? If our social action program is not rooted in the Jewish heritage, then we act as Jews, but not in the spirit of Judaism. In the absence of scholarly creativity, (and I submit that there is almost a total absence of scholarly activity) one might conclude that our current social action programs are motivated more by חוקת הגוים than by חקוי לאלהים , more by imitation of Gentile patterns than by *imitatio Dei*. From a sociological perspective, a good case might be made for the validity of that statement. In our social endeavors, we have frequently converted מה יאמרו הגוים ("What will the Gentiles say?") into a positive force for action. There are many times when the most convincing reason given for engaging in a specific action is "The Catholics and the Protestants have already taken a position. . . ."

I therefore welcome this colloquium as an essential first step in formulating a Jewish theology of social action. The word "Toward" in the title of the symposium is extremely useful. We are not now at the point in our development where we could, in all honesty, eliminate that qualifying word. The plain truth is that among our scholars there is still too much blatant indifference and even outright opposition to the necessity for Jewish social action, to its purposes and its methods. I would therefore like to consider these remarks of mine as preliminary in the process of working "Toward a Theology of Social Action."

I offer three premises prerequisite to establishing the Jewish dimension in Jewish social action.

I. TRADITION IS RELEVANT TO CONTEMPORARY SOCIAL ISSUES

Some of our critics contend that we are what I call *"posuk* hunters," that first we formulate a position on a current social issue, which, because of our social stance, is invariably on the liberal side of the political spectrum. Then we hunt for a substantiation of our position in traditional sources. Such an approach, say they, is at best to engage in homiletics, and at worst, to violate tradition.

Let us examine this criticism. There is a certain scholarly virtue in emphasizing that when Hillel declared אל תפרוש מן הצבור, he did not mean "Do not separate from the community at large," but because of the context of his life, he really meant "Do not separate from the Jewish community." I suppose there is also justification for maintaining that the Tanach, despite its numerous passages of universalistic content and significance, is nevertheless primarily a Jewish response to Jewish problems in a specific period of Jewish history. And I suppose that there is validity in reminding the American Jew that both our status in society and the conditions of our society are radically different from the status of the Jew and the conditions of society when the halacha was in its flourishing developmental stages.

But since no situation today is identical with any situation in the past, does this mean that the halacha is of no relevance to the modern Jew? Was Samuel Holdheim correct when he said, "The Talmud speaks with the ideology of its own time, and for that time it was right. I speak from the higher ideology of my time, and for this age, I am right." Few of us today would accept the consequences of Holdheim's radical reform. Most of us would rather agree with Franz Rosenzweig, "I am opposed to the notion of 'all or nothing.' Neither 'everything' nor 'nothing' belong to us, but rather 'something.' "

Is not the search for "something" the dilemma for Reform Judaism in regard to all the *mitzvot,* the ethical as well as the ritual? What of Jewish tradition do we accept and what do we reject, and what are the criteria for our decisions? We know that in order to retain the spirit of Judaism, we need halacha, but we have not yet determined how to create a halacha consistent with the needs of persons and the demands for historic continuity of the people Israel. There is not as yet and, because we are Reform, will probably never be, any universally acceptable

path to the "something" of tradition. That is our real עול התורה ,
"the yoke of the Torah" which we have taken upon ourselves
as a movement. But that is also our promise.

How paradoxical it is, therefore, to find some Reform rabbis
who have rejected the "all or nothing" approach when it comes
to theology and ritual, but who do a complete about-face when
it comes to social issues. How paradoxical for those whose
movement is riddled with the uncertainties and inconsistencies
which are the inevitable consequences of the search for "something," to demand total certainty and consistency in the search
for relevance in the social arena. How paradoxical to hear some
leaders of the very movement which stresses the primacy of the
ethical declare that God's revelation permeates every aspect of
our lives—except the crucial issues tormenting our society. How
paradoxical that those who had to reject the traditional framework of halacha in order to try to save the essence of halacha,
who had to alter the *Siyag laTorah* in order to try to save the
Torah itself, now suddenly turn Orthodox in one area only and
feel compelled to consider the *Siyag* as an impregnable high
wall, preventing action in the one dimension which Reform
Judaism pioneered in revivifying. Shall we, as Reform rabbis,
restrict ourselves to offering guidance on matters of ritual and not
on matters of conscience? Shall we as a movement take a stand
on breaking the glass at a wedding and not on breaking the
pattern of racial discrimination?

There is another kind of criticism of social action which I
have found coming, curiously enough, from students at the Col-
lege-Institute. For example, during the course of lectures I gave
at the College, I described the social welfare practices of the
Jewish community throughout the ages and concluded that Jewish tradition maintains that the community must assume responsibility for the individual. This concept is one which has direct
applicability to current legislative proposals for increasing social
security benefits, expanding antipoverty programs, and establishing national standards of public welfare at a level and in a
manner to assure recipients dignity and self-respect. This
kind of statement, which to me was a rather simplistic generalization, would be challenged by some students on the grounds that

one should never state, "Jewish tradition says." There are Jewish traditions, but no tradition, there are Judaisms, but no Judaism.

I am critical of this approach to Judaism, but not only because I disagree with the theology. After all, we do believe that: כל מחלקת שהיא לשם שמים סופה להתקים. "Every controversy which is engaged in for the sake of heaven shall lead to salutary results." I am critical because of its consequences for the role of the rabbinate in society. To be sure, there are many streams within Judaism. One does not necessarily have to agree with what is considered to be the mainstream. But the rabbi is ordained to be a teacher of Judaism, to study tradition and teach tradition. As such, he is obligated to speak within the context of Judaism, as he sees it, whatever his interpretation may be, even if he has to discover his own stream. He may select, he may reinterpret, he may disagree, he may reject, but he has no right to ignore. Whatever potential influence a rabbi has, both within his congregation and the community at large, derives from the fact that he symbolizes Jewish tradition. He is not just another person. He is not just the head of another Jewish organization speaking in behalf of a specified number of Jews. He does not speak for Jews. He speaks for Judaism, for a 4,000-year-old tradition of morality, a tradition which has developed a unique sensitivity to issues of conscience. Therein lies his status in the eyes of both Jews and non-Jews. Therein lies his expertise. The rabbi may not have an advanced degree in the humanities, but he is supposed to have the most advanced degree in Humanity, in Humaneness. And this is supposed to come from his being a teacher of Judaism and from taking his stand within that framework. Otherwise, he has no right to call himself "rabbi."

I do not want to be a *"posuk* hunter." But I confess to you, my colleagues, that in our effort to be teachers of Judaism, there are times when we have engaged in *posuk* hunting. It would be far better were our stands on current social problems to issue forth from the wellsprings of the Jewish spirit. There are times when that is impossible because, stretch as we may, the issue has no counterpart in historical Jewish experience. Does that mean that we should not concern ourselves with the issue, that we have no conscience except that of the past, that when confronted by injustice, our teeth are set on edge only when our fathers have eaten sour grapes? There are other times when Judaism does have something to say, but its message lies buried because our scholars have not been aware of nor concerned with the relevance of the Jewish heritage for our time. What we need is a coordinated comprehensive effort to mine our treasure, to translate, collate, and apply our heritage—and this must necessarily come from נטורי קרתא , the "guardians of our city"—our scholars, and especially those who sit on the faculty of our seminaries.

II. ETHICS REQUIRES ACTION AND ACTION INVOLVES RISK

Ethics has meaning only when it is related to human experience. Were it not for the experience of slavery and the Exodus from Egypt, we would never have evolved the concept of freedom. Theology and life interact. Just as faith should motivate a man's actions, so actions shape a man's faith. "Practice what you preach" is made more, not less, significant by the knowledge that human beings tend to preach what they practice. That is the meaning of מצוה גוררת מצוה "one righteous deed produces another righteous deed." God's justice is an active agent in our lives. We become what we do. Social action nourishes itself, reinforcing our faith and establishing both a framework and a stimulus for further action. In Jewish tradition, salvation for the individual is inseparable from salvation for all mankind; personal ethics are inseparable from social ethics; and in our day social ethics are inseparable from social action.

But knowing when and how to engage in social action is not easy. Social issues are extremely complex. It is only בדיעבד (in retrospect) that the moral dimension becomes obvious to everyone. When today we look at the social action of Reform rabbis who, after World War I, stood on picket lines to support the rights of labor to organize, to improve working conditions, and to reduce the 72-hour work week, we can perceive the moral issue. Their critics at the time did not agree, and many of the rabbis themselves had doubts. When we look back on the

August 1963 March on Washington, there would be overwhelming support for the contention that the participation of so many of our rabbis and laymen was both moral and in consonance with Jewish tradition. A month before the March we were not so sure. There was great trepidation as to the political ramifications, as to whether or not it would be good for the cause. There was fear of violence, and potentially a situation in which we would have engaged in illegal acts.

In ethics, in contrast to physics, distance, whether chronological or geographical, sharpens the vision. The closer we are, the more we know, the more do we realize that the realistic options in today's decisions are never between extremes of good and evil, but between alternatives which, by virtue of the political process, are in themselves compromises.

If one looks for guidance only to the past, and expects to find an identical situation, one will look in vain, for no two situations are ever the same. That is why I find the "new morality" of "situation ethics" to be of so little consequence. When Joseph Fletcher contends that the codes of the past no longer are sufficient in themselves to solve the demands of morality in the present, he is saying no more than what Judaism has always maintained. That is why from the *taryag mitzvot* came the Mishna and Gemara, the *Shulchan Aruch* and the Responsa, the Reform movement and even this colloquium. Unfortunately, "situation ethics" exaggerates the demands of the "situation" and minimizes the demands of "ethics." When Fletcher posits love as the only principle, he is engaging in Aggadah and not halacha. As a matter of fact, his discussion is reminiscent of the debate in *Bereshit Rabba* (24:7) between Ben Azzai, Tanhuma and Akiba, concerning which is the greatest principle in the Torah.

But, if we look at the forces which have generated "situation ethics," there is a message for us. Fletcher's conclusions may be questioned, but he is well motivated. He does not want moral codes to obfuscate or prohibit the moral decisions so necessary to human welfare. And the truth is that there are many who are so overwhelmed by the complexities of every situation, that the general rules of tradition become a pretext for inaction and even for lack of concern in the present.

Those who are charged with responsibility in and for the social arena cannot afford the luxury of indecision. Whenever we engage in social action in Washington, we are torn between various alternative courses, none of which is ideal. There is always a risk that our action may be mistaken. There is always a risk in going from the general to the specific. No general rule remains general the minute it is applied to a specific situation, because no two situations are alike. Every general becomes a specific, and every specific becomes a general. For example, were we today to pass a resolution on behalf of the CCAR, endorsing the President's Civil Rights bill of 1967, that could be considered a specific application of צדק צדק תרדוף or some other general ethical rule. However, that specific in practice proves to be just another general. Let us say our resolution would be one page long. The bill consists of many pages. Between now and the time it is approved by the Congress, it will undergo hundreds of changes which are the result of hearings, debates, and political compromise. By the time it comes to a final vote, there will be only two options: that bill or no bill. Any decision we might make in regard to the final bill will be a far cry from the original resolution we passed. Action is a risk. We try to minimize the risk by acquiring knowledge. We seek information and counsel from every possible source. But after all is said and done, we must make a decision. To decide not to act is also a decision. It was Cato who said, "Never is one so active as when one does nothing." And it was our rabbis who said, הלומד שלא לעשות נוח לו אלו לא נברא . "He who learns without doing something about it, it would have been better if he had not been born." The fact is that on most issues, we do not take positions. In instances when we do engage in social action, we in effect declare that the risk of no action is greater than the risk of mistaken action. If theology has its leap of faith, social justice must have its leap of action.

III. SOCIAL ACTION SHOULD BE VIEWED AS A STIMULUS FOR THE RENEWAL OF TRADITION

In advance of this colloquium, selected responsa were distributed entitled "Ethical Attitudes in Medieval Jewry," dealing particularly with problems of informers, crime and punishment. The study of these responsa is a fascinating exploration into the ethical attitudes and practices of the past. But could it not be much more? These few responsa would be relevant to present concerns if our approach were oriented accordingly. Our nation is currently engaged in heated controversies over a number of civil liberties questions. What should be done about crime? Should our penal code and system be overhauled? What should be done with the House Un-American Activities Committee? Does government have the right to engage in wiretapping and other invasions of the privacy of the individual? These questions, or *Sheelot,* are presently framed in legislative proposals to which the Congress is going to give its *Teshuvah* in the form of laws, which in turn will both reflect and shape public opinion. Are these not real *Sheelot* for us and should not our study of tradition be motivated by the search for a Jewish response to them?

What I am calling for is a renewal of the traditional concept of Talmud Torah, from which no method is further removed than that employed in institutions which today bear the name Talmud Torah. Talmud Torah was not study for the sake of learning *Lishma,* for acquiring facts about the past, but rather study for the sake of guiding human conduct in the present. Talmud Torah did not begin with theoretical questions such as: what was the biblical attitude toward labor, or what was the medieval attitude toward informers, but with practical questions such as: when do we recite the *Shema* (significantly, the first statement in the Mishna)? How should the employer treat his employee? What are the obligations of the employee to the employer? The *teshuvot* are answers to contemporary questions by teachers who have selected and interpreted the relevant sources of tradition. Talmud Torah is a continuous responsum, a never ending process of renewing Judaism by reaching discriminatingly into the past to give counsel on current questions.

My criticism of our educational system, from the religious school level to our rabbinical seminaries, is that we are not asking the correct *Sheelot.* Social issues are not the only *Sheelot,* but they are major *Sheelot,* and in our day they confront all Jews, regardless of their Jewish knowledge, because they confront all men. Why not begin the process of Jewish education with these vital issues, in recognition that אין אדם לומד תורה אלא ממקום שלבו חפץ , "No one learns Torah except through the impetus of his immediate needs."

If social action is a fulfillment of Jewish ethics, then it is also an instrument for motivating study of Judaism. Jewish social action must become a vehicle for creating a *Torat Hayyim,* a Torah that lives because it addresses itself to life.

At the opening of the Freies Jüdisches Lehrhaus in Frankfort, Germany, Franz Rosenzweig delivered a remarkable address which states the challenge of our day:

> A new "learning" is about to be born—rather, it has been born. It is a learning in reverse order. A learning that no longer starts from the Torah and leads into life, but the other way round: from life, from a world that knows nothing of the Law, or pretends to know nothing, back to the Torah. That is the sign of the time . . . we all know that in being Jews we must not give up anything, not renounce anything, but lead everything back to Judaism. From the periphery back to the center; from the outside, in. . . . It is not a matter of apologetics, but rather of finding the way back into the heart of our life. And of being confident that this heart is a Jewish heart. For we are Jews.

THE MISSION OF ISRAEL
AND SOCIAL ACTION

Eugene Lipman
Rabbi, Temple Sinai
Washington, D. C.

In order to relate the concept of the mission of Israel to the theology of social action, certain words must be looked at carefully.

The first word is Covenant.

I do not know what happened at Mt. Sinai. I am relatively certain inside myself, however, that a direct line stretches from Sinai to my generation, an unbroken continuity of attempts on the part of our people to fulfill the covenant all of us entered into there with our God. I believe in that covenant, the Covenant of Sinai. I return to Sinai each Shavuot and relive the undertaking. My relationship with God, and for me, the relationship of Israel to God, begins with the covenant at Sinai.

Purpose is built into the covenant. This should be obvious: no covenant or contract can be purposeless, and no act of God can be purposeless. For these two reasons, then, the covenant has purpose. The fulfillment of that covenantal purpose is the mission of Israel.

The words Torah and *mitzvah* must be introduced.

Torah is God's revelation, His instructions to His covenant partner, Israel. *Mitzvah* is the specific response in action of the individual Jew and of the Israelite collectivity to the Divine command. Torah is God's expression of His requirements upon us in the fulfillment of our mission; *mitzvot* are our attempts in society and in our inner experiences to fulfill the mission.

A crucial word in this sequence is Israel.

Alternatives are available to us in our use of this word, and our choice among the alternatives can make a tremendous difference in our theology of social action.

265

1. Israel can be a physical entity, a collectivity, a real live community consisting of all Jews everywhere and the collective purpose which binds us. Traditionally this has been the view of Israel, the springboard for our concern about one another wherever we may live, the source of *kol Yisrael arevim zeh ba'zeh,* "All Israel is related each one to the other," the basis for the institutions created by Jewish communities over the centuries to aid and to rescue and to take care of their own people and of Jews everywhere. This physical entity, Israel, must reach out to all men both to teach Torah and to perform *mitzvot.*

2. Israel can mean any group of Jews committed at a given time to a deliberate course of action in fulfillment of covenant obligation. In this sense, conceptually an individual synagogue can be Israel, a B'nai B'rith lodge can be Israel, a Jewish Social Service Agency can be Israel, the UAHC or CCAR can be Israel. Whenever a group of Jews unites to perform a *mitzvah* collectively, in conscious fulfillment of covenant, that is Israel.

3. Israel can be a purely spiritual concept with no physical implications at all. It is the function of this spiritual concept to animate individual Jews to live their individual lives in congruence with the heritage of Israel, as they see it. This would probably be the view of the American Council for Judaism. This appears to be the view of some Reform rabbis and many Reform laymen, those who wish denominational status for Judaism, total sovereignty for the individual congregation and for the individual Jew within the congregation, no collectivity at all.

4. Israel can be a mystical concept, somehow uniting all adherents to it, whoever they are and wherever they are. Essentially, this is the thought behind the continuing—though decreasing—Christian use of the word.

If you choose to believe in Israel as a physical entity, a collectivity bound in our day to work collectively for the fulfillment of the covenant, for the bringing nearer of the messianic era, then the mission of Israel has one meaning. If you choose to believe in Israel as any group of Jews united at any given moment for a specific *mitzvah* or course of *mitzvot,* then the mission of Israel has a somewhat different meaning, though perhaps not a theological meaning different from the first.

But if you choose to believe in Israel as a noncorporeal concept or as a mystical bond among all who wish to accept it, then your concept of the mission of Israel is vastly different, and your theology must be so, too.

One more word in this sequence of definitions: Who is the partner in the covenant? Who shares the mission with Israel? What is His role in the enterprise? Your God concept matters, too.

For the theological naturalist, the concept of the mission of Israel, it seems to me, can have no *theological* implications at all. Our Reconstructionist friends inevitably had to give up the idea of the Chosen People, and if Israel means Jews to them (as appears to be the case), they cannot have a mission-of-Israel concept related to God, either. If God is process, He or It needs no partner, and Jewish civilization needs no theological purpose. National existence is its own purpose, and our judgments about what constitute proper social actions obviously must meet God's purposes when He or It is "our highest ideals magnified to perfection." (Roland Gittelsohn.)

For the finitists, Whiteheadian or otherwise, a theology of social action is not very important either, if at all. Having taken on a partnership with God, man's power is very great, his free intellect is decisive, and God leaves him alone. In this system, collectivities do not appear to operate of necessity and the idea of a people with a collective purpose is, I think, incongruent.

For the relatively pure Buberite, other problems arise. Buber's essay *The Spirit of Israel and the World of Today* confused me as it relates to our subject. I have no trouble with his concept of realization, with his continuing insistence that the Jew fulfills the spirit of Israel to the extent that he realizes his relationship with God and responds to the Divine command. I do have trouble when Buber moves to the collective, to the Jewish people, and limits himself to the fulfilling power of the Zionist dream, with the fulfilling meaning of the reestablishment of the State of Israel. For then he says nothing to us about *our* mission and the implications of *our* relationship with God as realization. I tend to share Berkovits' criticism of Buber for the incompleteness of his working out of the consequences of the I-Thou relationship with God. The God of Israel demands by His Torah; Israel responds via *mitzvot*. This is missing in Buber, and the Jew not resident in the State of Israel can so easily learn to be content with his individual self-realizing confrontations with God, content to remain unrelated to the collectivity and to any mission it may have as Israel.

There are various forms of theism among us, but I limit myself to mine. I live with a romantic, unintellectualized, Deutero-Isaianic concept of God. Between Isaiah 40-45, and in Job 38-39, I find almost everything I feel about God, almost all the words I need to try to express my experiences with Him, to the extent that I need to try at all. I believe simply in the covenant at Mt. Sinai. I believe simply in the Jewish people as a physical collectivity, with collective purpose—to do collective *mitzvot*. Both *mitzvot* "between man and God" *ben adam la'makom* (like worship), and *mitzvot* "between man and his fellow man," *ben adam l'chavero* (like social action) are intrinsic in my simple system. For me, the mission of Israel is not complicated— Messianic fulfillment—and I do not worry much about the distinction between "the days of the Messiah," *y'mot ha'mashiach* and the Messianic Era. Either way, I hold a rather mystico-psychological eschatological view.

Consequently, my own problems with a theology of social action center about which collective *mitzvot* God favors and which He opposes at any time, as I have to choose, and Israel has to choose, among the apparently infinite number of *mitzvot* our world needs to have done within it. Guidance is available to me, in three forms, and I feel obligated deliberately to use all three: I must consult recorded Torah maximally; I must consult the passionate, the compassionate and the learned maximally; and I must pray.

But this is no longer theology. This is response. This is the halachic process, the means I must use as a Jew to attack my uncertainties about all *mitzvot* and to come to action, despite all. My uncertainty in the area of *mitzvah* we call social action is no greater than my uncertainty about all other areas of *mitzvah* and the choices I must employ my free will to make regarding them.

In this framework, social action consists of pooling our uncertainties as Jews, then doing the job in the not firm but sincere conviction that it is a *mitzvah,* and using Yom Kippur for all it is worth if the action turns out to have been a sin. Fortunately, this traditional God of mine is a *salchan* possessed of infinite patience, and He does not abandon His people, His covenant people, His purposeful people.

SOME CAUTIONARY REMARKS

Julius Kravetz
Adjunct Professor of Rabbinics
HUC-JIR
New York City, New York

My purpose here is to address some words of academic caution in the direction of those who find that every movement proclaimed in the twentieth century as humane, progressive, and forward-looking has already been anticipated in the Jewish tradition and finds a congenial reception there.

The art of citation claims a long roll call of skillful and resourceful practitioners. As students of American history we recall the enthusiasm for the Old Testament of John Caldwell Calhoun, the doughty champion of states' rights, slavery, and nullification. For him the government of the twelve tribes in the wilderness came closer to perfection than any other devised on this earth, and was to be regarded as the model of what the American people ought to strive for.[1]

Our sources do not tell us how fashionable Calhoun's political thought was among the Jews of the ante-bellum South. We may assume that some of the rabbis who served Southern congregations before and during the War Between the States must have been encouraged by the example of their northern colleague Morris Raphall to rummage in the Biblical arsenal for scriptural armaments with which to support their region's course.[2] But let us not forget that those who have been moved by what they have regarded as nobler and more humane sentiments have also not been inhibited by scruples of academic fastidiousness in their own exploitation of the tradition. How many times has Malachi's plea "Have we not all one father? Hath not one God created us?" been wrenched from its particularistic context to serve the cause of good will between races and faiths? And what words have been pressed more frequently into the service of interracial amity than Amos' "Are ye not as the children of the Ethiopians unto me, O children of Israel"—hardly a compliment to the Ethiopians.

Perhaps the most scandalous example of such deliberately induced tunnel vision is the selective reading of the famous passage in Mishnah *Makkot* to support the position that Tannaitic Judaism has fixed the norm for the future halakhah by expressing unequivocal opposition to the death penalty. With what relish the advocates of penal reform quote the words "A Sanhedrin that puts one man to death in seven years is called a bloody Sanhedrin. Rabbi Eliezer says, 'Even once in seventy years.' Rabbi Tarfon and Rabbi Akiba say, 'Had we been in the Sanhedrin none would have been put to death.'" And here—well pleased with the sufficiency of their text—the latter-day abolitionists stop, just before the final retort of Rabbi Simeon b. Gamaliel who says in effect to his colleagues, "Such leniency would have made you responsible for the proliferation of murderers in Israel." [3] Evidently all sober and realistic references to the historical development of penal law in the halakhah and in the practice of the autonomous Jewish communities of the Middle Ages[4] count for nothing in the face of that badly scalloped Mishnah.

I

I have selected for discussion three embattled areas of contemporary concern. In each case the partisans of the so-called progressive position have sought to enlist the Jewish tradition as clearly supportive of their viewpoint. They are wrong.

In the past few years attempts have been made in a number of states to liberalize the laws of abortion. In most states the present law bars abortion except when it is necessary to save the life of the mother. Generally the proposed new measures would allow committees of qualified physicians to authorize feticide in those instances in which a pregnancy was created through rape or incest, in which there is a substantial risk to the mother's physical and mental health, and in order to prevent the birth of a child with mental or physical defects.

I certainly do not impugn the idealism of those who champion this liberalizing legislation, but I do question their ability to find unequivocal support "by looking to our religious laws and traditions for guidance," to quote the text of a typical resolution drawn up by a number of New York rabbis. A close reading of the material provided by our tradition obliges me to enter a respectful demurrer.[5]

Aside from the special instance dealing with the execution of a condemned adulteress who is pregnant,[6] the Talmud, and the Codes of Maimonides and Karo that derive from it, know of only one situation in which an embryo is to be destroyed before birth. The Mishnah teaches that if a pregnant woman is in such hard travail as to lead the observers to conclude that her life is being threatened in the process then the child inside her is to be cut up piece by piece, since the life of the mother has priority over the life of the child. Maimonides, followed by Karo, calls for the termination of the pregnancy by means of drugs or surgery, and makes the point that such summary action is mandatory. The fetus is not to be pitied but is to be regarded as one who pursues the mother and seeks to kill her (rodef).[7]

Now there are two schools of thought as to whether the destruction of a fetus under circumstances other than the one just mentioned is punishable as a capital crime.[8] The final halakhah rules that it is not. The killing of a human being is punishable only when the victim has been born and is capable of living.[9] The slaying of an unborn child is to be treated as an injury to the body of the mother. The permissibility of abortion, however, is hardly demonstrated by the fact that it is not punishable as murder. That which is excused as a fait accompli can also be forbidden ab initio.[10] For example, in strict Torah law as understood by the rabbis there is no capital punishment for the slaying of a child born before a full-time pregnancy, or of a person afflicted with a fatal organic disease.[11] Such acts, however, are strictly forbidden.[12]

An important question for us is whether the life of a human fetus is so precious as to come under the application of the law of saving a life in peril (pikkuah nefesh). Is Sabbath law to be violated for its sake? In the one relevant case mentioned in the Talmud the answer is affirmative. If a woman who has been sitting on a birthstool dies on the Sabbath one is to fetch a knife, even by way of the public thoroughfare, and cut open the womb to save the child. One Amora questions why it was necessary to specify this rescue in view of the accepted principle that in case of doubt (of peril to human life) one is to desecrate the Sabbath. The answer given is that without this ruling we might have thought that the law was to be violated only for the benefit of those who had at least the presumption of having been alive.[13]

On the grounds of "Desecrate one Sabbath for its sake so that it may live to observe many Sabbaths" a number of authorities apply this principle of rescue even to the fetus in earlier stages of pregnancy; and maintain, in effect, that a being for whom the Sabbath is to be desecrated is a being that is not to be destroyed deliberately except where it threatens the life of the mother.[14]

Regarding the potential *mamzer* the earliest judicial precedent appears to have been set by the prohibitory decision of Rabbi Jair Bachrach, who points out that the legal disabilities of the illegitimate offspring extend only to marriage with unblemished Jews, the holding of certain high offices, and dwelling within the sacred precincts of Jerusalem. In vast areas of ritual law and in the remedies and protections afforded by the civil and penal law the *mamzer* is the peer of his genetically impeccable fellow Jews.[15] As for the monstrous birth—a phenomenon that may be related to the "thalidomide baby" of our own time—the historic decision of Rabbi Eleazer Fleckeles states that its classification in the Talmud as "non-human" is limited in legal application to the laws of purification to be observed by the mother after its birth. A deformed child is not to be destroyed, for it comes under the protective laws applying to all men. Although he is dealing here with a child already born, the thrust of the author's reasoning, and his pointing to abortion as forbidden, though not punishable as murder, make clear his position that malformation during pregnancy does not compromise the embryo's claim to life.[16]

II

If the halakhic resources on abortion can be said to suffer from an embarrassment of riches, the source materials applicable to the conscientious objector suffer from an embarrassment of poverty. The Torah, of course, knows of a number of instances in which a man was to be excused from military duty: he who had not yet dedicated his house, he who had not yet enjoyed the fruit of his own vineyard, he who had not yet brought into his home the wife he had betrothed, and finally, he who was fearful and fainthearted. According to the rabbis the exempted individuals served in a kind of quartermaster auxiliary, supplying food and water to the fighting soldiers and repairing the roads.[17] We do not, however, find any category that would be the equivalent of the hodiernal conscientious objector unless we read into the words "fearful and fainthearted" the exegesis suggested in the Tosefta. To save the Biblical text from the charge of tautology it is suggested that "fainthearted" refers to a man of great physical courage whose usefulness as a warrior is nullified by the compassion he feels for all men.[18]

A much more realistic approach to the status of the conscientious objector begins with the principle of *dina d'malkhuta dina*—translated freely, that the law of the secular government is to be regarded as the law of the Torah. This principle is enunciated four times in the Babylonian Talmud, and is ascribed to the Amora Samuel.[19] It is not challenged in the Amoraic sources. There is no universal agreement as to its applicability, but generally it would be correct to say that where the government of the state is based upon a historic and stable legal tradition and is not the capricious expression of the ruler's will; and where the law does not discriminate against the Jewish inhabitants, then the principle of *dina d'malkhuta* is to be applied to the realms of civil law and public law, and to the power of the state to levy taxes and call up its citizens for civilian and military duty.

The drafting of subjects or citizens for military service did not become a serious problem for Jews until the end of the eighteenth century. The leading responsist of his age, Rabbi Moses

Sofer (1763-1839), treated the issue from the viewpoint of *dina d'malkhuta* and saw every justification for the Emperor to levy taxes upon his Jewish subjects and draft them into the armed forces of the Empire.[20] Remarkable also is the vigorous rebuke administered by Rabbi Moses Glasner of Klausenberg during the First World War to those of his fellow Jews who employed subterfuges to evade the draft, "for according to Torah law we are obligated to pay taxes, and the term *damim* has a double connotation—taxes in money and taxes in human form."[21]

In seeking to apply this principle to our own form of government, in which the citizens participate, through their chosen legislators, in the formulation of *dina d'malkhuta* we find that American military law recognizes the position of the conscientious objector, and a Supreme Court decision has extended the protection afforded by this status to those who hold no theistic beliefs. Of course it is the right of the individual American Jew, as it is of any other citizen, to press for legislation that will confirm or strengthen the position already attained. It is difficult, however, to discern any clearly defined norm in the Jewish tradition that commands conscientious objection to war on the part of the Jew.

III

My third illustration is drawn from the area of criminal law and police procedure. It is unnecessary today to expatiate upon the melancholy statistics pointing up the alarming growth of the crime rate in our country. Certainly the criminal is to be brought to book, but at what cost to the civil rights of the individual? In the past few years the Supreme Court has brought this question into sharp focus by handing down two decisions aimed at the most basic American police method utilized in solving crimes: questioning suspects and extracting confessions. Because it held, in the Escobedo case, that suspects have the right to counsel not only in the courtroom but even in the police station, and because it ruled in the Miranda case that a confession is not to be admitted unless the defendant had previously been apprised of all his rights, the Court has been accused of hobbling the police and indulging the criminal.

The Constitutional principle involved here is, of course, that section of the Fifth Amendment that states "nor shall he (any person) be compelled in any criminal case to be a witness against himself." Now it has been the practice in Jewish apologetics to tell us that the halakhah goes even further in its protective solicitude than the Fifth Amendment. The latter will not allow a forced confession: a man cannot be compelled to testify against himself. Torah law, however, will not admit even *voluntary* confessions in the realm of criminal or penal law.

In his rationale Maimonides suggests that many people are obsessed by the death wish. Their minds are sick, and they have suicidal tendencies. Such individuals might readily confess to crimes they did not commit. Then he adds, "But whatever the reason may be the principle of the matter is that it is a decree of the Divine King." When confronted with the instances of Akhan and the Amalekite who slew King Saul—both were executed on the basis of their own confessions—Maimonides seeks an explanation in the possibility that these were emergency decisions or applications of the King's law as exercised by Joshua and David.[22]

The Talmud, however, recognizes the need for creating safeguards against a law that rejects confessions in penal cases and that, if carried to the ultimate logical implications, might create dilemmas that would redound to the harm of vital social interests. For every Jew is under obligation to testify regarding a capital offense and to bear witness whenever his words might deliver a fellow Jew from a tragic plight.[23]

Think of a woman whose husband has disappeared. She is an *agunah,* and is not permitted to remarry until a witness appears to testify that he was present when her husband died, or that he had seen the corpse. Suppose that a witness comes forward with such information. How, we ask, is he certain? Well, he replies, he himself slew the deceased! Since, by definition, no man can incriminate himself he is therefore not to be established as the killer, and we operate with the legal fiction of *palginan dibburay,* that is, we split his statement down the middle, we accept his word as to the fact of the husband's death—thus liberating the *agunah*—yet we draw no conclusion as to his guilt.[24]

Is our tradition so clearly weighted on the side of the protection of the individual against that of society? I say respectfully that it is not. A conscientious examination of the source material will reveal that, on our theme, there is a storehouse of *halakhah l'maaseh,* halakhah for practical guidance. That is the product of a historical context in which the preservation of the Jewish community and the maintenance of public order were considerations of paramount importance. The guiding principle is laid down in a *baraita* found in two tractates:

> R. Eliezer b. Jacob said "I have heard that the Court may flog and pronounce the death sentence even when not warranted by the Torah yet not with the intention of disregarding the Torah but in order to safeguard it." [25]

No one who is unacquainted with the post-Talmudic responsa and other documents bearing upon the inner life of the Jewish communities can realize how critical a role this Tannaitic statement played in the thinking of the communal leadership. The most severe punishments, such as the death penalty, amputation of limbs, bodily mutilation, not to mention lashes, imprisonment, and heavy fines, were imposed on the basis of evidence that did not meet the strict requirements of Torah law, evidence obtained from solitary witnesses, from relatives of the suspect, by means of hearsay, from circumstantial indications, and from the mouth of the suspect himself.[26]

It is hard to stifle the temptation to indulge in academic "name dropping," but in this area one authority can speak for all—Rabbi Solomon ben Adret, known as Rashba, the leader of Spanish Jewry in the thirteenth century. He had received an inquiry from the leaders of a certain community who wanted to know whether their decision in a penal matter could be sustained in view of the fact that they had not complied with the rigors of the Biblical rules of evidence. His reply is memorable:

If the witnesses are regarded as reliable by the chosen communal leaders then they are empowered to impose fines and inflict punishment as they see fit. For we are dealing here with the preservation of society and if you base everything on the laws written in the Torah and are inhibited from meting out punishment except in accordance with Torah law the world will be destroyed, for we would require the procedure of witnesses and warning; and this is what the Sages meant when they said that Jerusalem was laid waste only because they gave judgment therein in strict compliance with Torah law.[27]

I should like to think that what I have been saying could be summed up in the words "Handle With Care." Before we hasten to put the Jewish stamp of approval on every movement of protest and reform we ought to engage in close study, in fasting, and in prayer. Are the Biblical supports we adduce in context, and are they pertinent? How are they reflected in the Aggadic literature and the Talmud? How has the idea fared at the hands of the rabbis who crystallized the halakhah, and what has happened to it in the crucible of history? To agonize over such questions is not an exhilarating experience but it is one way of restoring a measure of astringent skepticism to an area where it is badly needed.

NOTES

[1] Quoted in Parrington, Vernon Louis. *Main Curents in American Thought,* New York: 1927, Volume II, p. 170.

[2] Korn, Bertram Wallace. *American Jewry and the Civil War,* Philadelphia: 1951, Chapter II and III, *passim;* Schappes, Morris Urman. *A Documentary History of the Jews in the United States 1645–1875,* New York: 1950, pp. 405–418.

[3] Mishnah *Makkot* 1:10; 7a.

[4] R. Meir b. Gedalia of Lublin. *Responsa, Venice:* 1618, No. 138. Assaf, Simha. *Ha-Onshin Aharay Hatimat Ha-Talmud,* Jerusalem: 1922, pp. 18–20 and *passim.* Ginzberg, Jacob Meshullam. *Mishpatem le-Yisroel, A Study in Jewish Criminal Law,* Jerusalem: 1956, *passim.* Blidstein, Gerald. "Capital Punishment, the Classic Jewish Discussion, in Judaism, Vol. 14, no. 2, pp. 159–171.

[5] Three of the most comprehensive treatments of the subject in the recent halakhic literature are, to be found in the Israeli annual *NOAM,* by the Chief Rabbi of Israel, Issar Judah Untermann (Vol. 6 [1963] pp. 1–11); by the late Rabbi Moses Jonah Ha-Levi Zweig of Antwerp, Belgium (Vol. 7 [1964] pp. 37–56); and by the late Rabbi Jekiel Jacob Weinberg of Montreux, Switzerland (Vol. IX; [1966] pp. 193–215).

A more lenient position than that represented by these three authorities is stated by Rabbi Ben Zion Uziel, the late Chief Rabbi of the Sefardic community in Israel, in his responsa, *Mishpetai Uziel,* Tel Aviv: 1940, *Hoshen ha-Mishpat,* nos. 46 and 47.

For a treatment of the status of the human embryo in the Jewish Criminal Law of the Talmudic period see Aptowitzer, Avigdor, in *Jewish Quarterly Review, New Series,* Vol. 15 (1924–1925) pp. 85–118.

For a review and discussion of the post-Talmudic halakhic literature see Ginzberg, *op. cit.* pp. 223–236, 301–305; and Feldman, David, *Birth Control in Jewish Law,* New York: 1968, Chapters 14 and 15, *passim.*

[6] B. *Arakhin* 7a.

[7] Mishnah *Oholot* 7:6; *Mishnah Torah* (henceforth M.T.) Rozeah 1:9; *Shulhan Arukh* (henceforth S.A.) *Hoshen Ha-Mishpat* 425:2.

A threat to the mother that would warrant abortion could be psychological (*e.g.,* suicidal hysteria) as well as physical. See *Responsa Pri HaAretz* of R. Israel Meir Mizrahi, Constantinople: 1721, *Yore Deah* no. 2; also, Untermann, Rabbi Isser Judah, "Mizvat Pikkuah Nefesh Ugdarehah" in *HaTorah V'haMedinah,* Tel Aviv: Vol. 4, pp. 25, 29.

[8] Aptowitzer, *op. cit.,* pp. 85 ff. and *passim.*

[9] *M.T. Rozeah* 2:6–8.

[10] *Tosafot Hullin* 33a *s.v.*אחד נהי דפטור מכל מקום לא שרי. *Tosafot Sanhedrin* 59a *s.v.* אף על גב דפטור מכל מקום לא שרי ליכא. A careful reading of a third notation of *Tosafot* (*Niddah* 44b *s. v.* איהו), where we find the words, "we are to violate the Sabbath for its [the embryo's] sake *even though it is permitted to kill it*" shows that here, too, the *Tosafot* meant to say only that the killing is not punishable in human courts. For the glossator goes on to

liken this case to that of a man who was slain after he was in his death throes as the result of a beating by a previous aggressor; and then states that the slayer is excused from human punishment, yet we violate the Sabbath for the victim while he is still alive.   . . . דהא גוסס בידי אדם ההורגו פטור

ומחללין את השבת עליו

11 See note no. 9.

12 *Ibid.*

13 *B. Arakhin* 7a–b; *M.T. Shabbat* 2:15; *S.A. Orah Hayyim* 330:5; Regarding the negative ruling in *S.A. Orah Hayyim* 330:7 see Weinberg, *op. cit.* pp. 198, 199.

14 Among medieval jurists the author of the *Halakhot Gedolot*, quoted by R. Moses b. Nahman (Ramban) in "Torat Ha-Adam," Jerusalem: 1956, *Shaar Ha-Sakkanah* p. 11.

Among twentieth-century authorities, R. Hayyim Soloveitchik, in his *novellae* to the code of Maimonides, *Hiddushei R. Hayyim Ha Levi*, 1936, p. 95.

R. Asher b. Jehiel (Rosh) cannot imagine any danger to the fetus that isn't at the same time a danger to the living mother. See his commentary to *B. Yoma* Ch. 8, no. 13. The author of the *Korban N'tanel, ad locum* rises to this challenge by pointing out that there are women who miscarry often without harm to themselves. See also the example quoted by Rabbi Unterman, *NOAM*, Vol. 6, p. 3. In the realm of modern medicine there are situations in which it is necessary to administer intra-uterine treatment where a serious defect has been discovered in the blood system of the fetus, though the blood of the mother is not affected.

The Talmudic maxim is found in *B. Shabbat*, 151b, and in *B. Yoma* 85b. אמרה תורה חלל עליו שבת אחת שמא ישמור שבתות הרבה

15   . . . דדין ממזר לכל דבר כדין ישראל כשר וראוי להיות דיין גדול בחוץ

לארץ רק שאסור לבא בקהל ולישב בסנהדרין

R. Jair Hayyim Bachrach, *Responsa Havvot Jair, Lemberg*: 1894, no. 31.

See, however, the rationale of R. Jacob Emden, (*Responsa Sheilat Jabez*, Lemberg: 1884, I no. 43) for permitting an abortion in the case of an adulteress, because the mother deserved to be executed, though the Biblical law could not be enforced and because the fruit of her sin was accursed in the eyes of heaven.

R. Ben Zion Uziel, in a similar case submitted for his opinion, followed the rationale of Emden, and stated that the parents themselves are to perform the grim task (op. cit., p. 216).

16 *Responsa Teshubah MeAhabah*, Prague: 1809, Part I no. 53. See the summary by Rabbi Immanuel Jakobovits in "Jewish Law Faces Modern Problems" (*Studies in Torah Judaism*, no. 8) New York: 1965, pp. 74, 75.

17 Deuteronomy 20:5–8, M.T. Kings 7:3–15.

18 Tosefta (Zuckermandel Edition) 7:22. This interpretation is ascribed to Rabbi Akiba. In the Mishna (*Sotah* 8:5), however, Rabbi Akiba interprets the entire Biblical phrase in the literal sense, as referring to those who have no stomach for battle. R. Jose the Galilean interprets the passage as referring to one who is afraid because of the transgressions he has committed. The general opinion of the Biblical commentators and the final halakhah follow the Mishnaic position of Rabbi Akiba.

See also Landman, Jacob, "Law and Conscience," in *Judaism*, Vol. 18, no. 1, Winter, 1969, pp. 25, 26.

19 *B. Baba Batra* 54b; *B. Baba Kamma* 113a; *B. Nedarim* 28b; *B. Gittin* 10b; The statement is not found in the Palestinian Talmud.

For the most recent treatment of this concept see Landman, Leo, *Jewish Law in the Diaspora,* Philadelphia: 1968.

20 See his "Likkute Hatam Sofer," no. 29, printed as a supplement to his *Responsa, Eben HaEzer,* Vienna: 1896.

21 ... כי על פי דברי התורה הקדושה אנו מחייבין לשמע מצות המלך ולישא מס הדמים דמים תרתי משמע הן מס כספין והן מס הגוף שהוא הנפש כשאר אזרחי הארץ.

Printed in the Hungarian periodical *Tel Talpiot* 1916, no. 104.

22 *M.T. Sanhedrin* 18:6.

23 *M.T. Edut* 1:1, 2.

24 *B. Jebamot* 25a; *S.A. Eben Ha-Ezer* 17:7. For other examples of this accepted procedure see B. Sanhedrin 25a.

25 *B. Jebamot* 90b; *B. Sanhedrin* 46a; The translation follows Rashi's interpretation in the latter tractate, *s. v.* שבית דין.

26 Ginzberg, *op. cit.* pp. 22–41, 91–95.

27 Quoted in *Bet Joseph* to *Tur, Hoshen Ha-Mishpot* 2. The Talmudic reference is to *B. Baba Mezia* 30b.

THE MISSION OF ISRAEL

ON THE THEOLOGY OF
JEWISH SURVIVAL

Steven S. Schwarzschild
Rabbi, Professor of Philosophy
Washington University
St. Louis, Missouri

I. PHENOMENOLOGY OF THE JEWISH SPIRIT, 1945

When people think in 1968 about Jewish survival it can be assumed that the occasion for their consideration is the Six Day War of 1967 and its continuing consequences. We, too, will want to revert to that episode, but I wish to begin our exploration at another and more decisive point in contemporary Jewish history: the early summer of 1945—i.e., the hour when the Jewish people stood on both sides of the open doors of Bergen-Belsen, of Auschwitz, of Maidanek and Theresienstadt and the other camps of extermination, and when the full weight of what had happened to us there and throughout the Holocaust came bearing down on us.

The reality of the situation at that point was twofold: on the one hand, it was brutally clear that death and destruction, infinite pain and incurable physical and spiritual dislocations had reaped an abundant harvest in our midst. We were on the very verge of expiration; indeed, in some ways we had died, beyond revival. At the same time, we must remember, this condition prevailed, in varying ways and degrees, in all the countries and among all the peoples of the Old World, from the British Isles through the entire heartland of Eurasia to the islands of Japan and beyond. Slaughter and fire, the lie and the eraser had cut a wide swath not only through the peoples but also through the institutions and cultures of these continents. So we looked around us—we saw the scene—and, though with cracked voices and with bitter hearts, we first hummed softly and then sang in a swelling chorus the refrain of the Partisan song: *"Mir zennen do"*—"Never say we have walked our last road;" when all the roads will have been trod, and when all others will have fallen by the wayside, we—or at least a small remnant of Israel, the true שארית הפליטה—will yet present ourselves to proclaim: "We are still here—*mir zennen do.*" The greatest, the world-shaking and heaven-rending, the inexpungeably traumatic tragedy of Israel was accompanied, contrapuntally, as it were, by the increasing consciousness of the ineluctable, unextirpatable survival of the Jewish people throughout history—and if through that history then surely throughout eternity.[1]

It is relatively easy to trace the spreading and deepening realization of this truth among Jews over the last twenty-three years. Indisputably the establishment of the State of Israel, in the face of apparently insuperable hostilities and difficulties, was undergirded by the psychology of שארית הפליטה : "We've come through so much—we'll come through this, too"—together with the historical lesson: אם אין אני לי מי לי. (I remember, for example, the passengers of the "Exodus" speaking like this, and acting on it, the second time around on their itinerary between West Germany and the shores of Israel.) Again, when one talked with or read the expressions of many of the participants in the Six Day War,[2] almost a quarter of a century later, this immediately post-Holocaust posture was clearly noticeable, usually formulated in just these terms—and this was, in fact, true throughout world Jewry. Even theologically the appropriation of this consciousness, though more slow, can be observed: Eliezer Berkovits ended his notable polemic against "interfaith dialogues" with a rousing peroration to the effect that we, the eternal people, were present and witnesses when the Christian era began—we are still present and witnesses now that it has come to an end.[3] That was several years ago. Last fall this became, as we remember, virtually a stampede among rabbis, community leaders, and among the ranks of Jewry: "The Christian world has again stood by passively or even antagonistically. We're on our own. We're going to keep it that way."

II. The Classic Jewish View

If this is a correct phenomenology of the Jewish spirit after the Second World War, we do not need to stop long to prove that it stands in complete accord and direct line with the classic Biblical, Talmudic, mediaeval Jewish conception of the prospects of Jewish survival and its theology. I take it that the following is a legitimate summary of how our classic teachers envisaged the situation.

The model of the relationship between God and Israel in the Bible is, of course, the Covenant.[4] There are two ways of understanding that covenant—let them be called the ethical and the metaphysical. The ethical interpretation makes the religious, moral, and historical honor of Israel the prerequisite for God's fulfillment of His part of the Covenant, *i.e.*, the preservation and advance of the Jewish people: if they do not do their share He is relieved of His obligation and will let it lapse.[5] The advantage of this view is obviously the responsibility which it places upon the Jew and the ethical stimulus which it thus constitutes. Its corollary disadvantage is equally obvious: it is entirely too anthropocentric; it claims that history is determined by a large number of individual and collective subjective and irrational factors; it declares in effect that God's providence, or historical forces, can easily be detracked, rerouted, or even stopped cold by essentially trivial human incursions.[6] The metaphysical view, then, represents the other part of the polarity. It speaks of the ברית עולם ; it assures mankind that as long as the rainbow will be in the sky so long—which is to say eternally—will humanity persist, and it assures Israel that its survival is coeval with God's existence.[7] Here the emphasis is not on man but on metaphysical factors—God, the world or mankind as totalities, the over-arching purpose of history, etc. Ezekiel and others will thus let ethical considerations ride, at least for the time being, and announce redemption לא למענכם כי אם למען שמו. In this interpretation of the Covenant the advantages and disadvantages of the ethical interpretation are precisely reversed: it obviously possesses a view of history which is objective and rational, but correspondingly it tends to lower the status of human ethical responsibility.[8]

These two views are not mutually exclusive, and they are certainly not chronological or Bible-critical *realia*. Their relationship to one another is rather dialectical. The case of Ezekiel just adduced makes this point all by itself and in Biblical terms: ethics are by no means ejected from this historiographical scheme, anymore than historiosophy is absent from, let us say, Amos, for whom, nonetheless, history seems to be a function of ethics rather than vice versa. Certainly for the Bible as such both interpretations of the nature of the Covenant come together in an integral, dialectical unity. God's plan for history is unalterably determined, and man's ethical decisions are indispensable as well as constitutive. If you will, הכל צפוי והרשות נתונה. One Biblical formulation of this unity of opposites is the very doctrine of the שאר ישוב of which we·spoke at the outset as an historical reality. What the dialectical doctrine states at the very least is that, while Israel's actions are determinative of its survival, it is simultaneously true that this survival is divinely guaranteed in any case.

In classical Rabbinic Judaism this paradoxical view of the matter—empirically verified by Jewish history and doing justice both to the ethics as well as the metaphysics of the problem—becomes considerably more sophisticated and subtle. ישראל סבא, the eternity of Israel, founded on the eternity of God, נצח ישראל, is taken for granted by all.[9] This in itself is wondrous enough when we remember that Rabbinic Judaism is, after all, largely the product of the destruction of the Second Commonwealth and of the bimillenial fate of Israel in a tragic and always radically tenuous *galut*. The full sophistication of the belief in the divinely guaranteed eternity of Israel becomes clear, however, only when one tries to understand the extremely complex teachings of the Rabbis in which, again, they synthesize dialectically the polar demands of the ethics and the metaphysics of Jewish survival and destiny. In פרק חלק, *Sanh.* 96b-98a, the *locus classicus* is to be found of Jewish messianism and thus of the eternity of Jewish life. Especially the debate between Rabbi Eliezer ben Hyrcanus, who advocates the ethical interpretation,[10] and Rabbi Joshua ben Hananya, who advocates what we have called the metaphysical interpretation, is to be noted.[11] By superficial students their debate might be regarded as merely a Billy Graham-like verse-slinging match; the usual but equally superficial view is that the two represent mutually exclusive doctrines, and their debate is then taken as another illustration of the unsystematic nature of Talmudic theology. The fact of the case is that, by the time the debate is over, in this passage and in a great number of others the final result is precisely the dialectical unity of ethics and metaphysics of which we have spoken. Its lovely poetic metaphor is found in *Midr. Tehillim* 45:3: "Just as this rose grows with its heart toward heaven, so do you repent before Me and turn your hearts heavenward, and, like the dew, I will thereupon cause your redeemer to appear." [12] It takes the form, for example, of saying that Israel must conduct itself morally so that its destiny can be fulfilled (ethics) but that God will, if need be, constrain it so to act (metaphysics). Another frequent way of putting it is to say that God has determined the end but that Israel can, by pious deeds, hasten its advent. (Note the sophisticated nature of this formulation: human evil cannot delay, or frustrate, God's providence, though human good can accelerate it; *i.e.* God acts, as it were, in a limit-situation fashion.)[13] Perhaps the most highly developed stage of this particular formulation of the combination of the contingency-*cum*-necessity, what Ezekiel Kaufman has called רצון והכרח , of Israel's meaningful existence is to be encountered in the greatest of all Jewish eschatologists, Isaac Abarbanel, who schematizes it by distinguishing between the first period of אפשרות ביאתו , when, depending on human actions, the Messiah may come, and the subsequent period of חיוב והכרחיות ביאתו, when he will come regardless of human preparations, by divine fiat.

Of one thing there can, in any case, be no doubt: the Jewish consciousness of our generation that we and our children until the end-of-days will always proclaim *"mir zennen do"* is a simple perpetuation not only of the experience but also of the classic theology of Jewish history. Whatever the effect on it of the deeds of Jew and Gentile may or may not be, Jewish survival is guaranteed by God—subject, to be sure, to high costs and to qualifications in detail but not to fundamental anxiety. עם ישראל חי וקים.

III. PRACTICAL APPLICATIONS

Let us, at this juncture, try to indicate one sociologico-psychological and one "pastoral" practical application of our theological truism before we return to our main *heilsgeschichtlich* concern in the perspective of the last year.

The sensationalistic notion of "the vanishing Jew" has been widely circulated. With reference to the *galut*-Jew in general and the American Jew in particular it serves diverse purposes. Some Israelis and other שוללי גלות use it in order to strengthen their exhortations to *aliyah*.[14] I always suspect that certain Christian circles use it because their notion of the religious conquest of Judaism is still very much operative in their minds, if not always on their lips. American mass media use it in order to increase their circulation, which, like most reading matter in this country, depends in large measure on a Jewish suburbanite middle-class clientele. Furthermore, it would appear that there is a clinically sick streak in many American Jews who gratify their masochism by reading about their own imminent collective demise. (The fact that they are so interested in reading about it refutes their prediction.) At the same time the diagnosis of Jewry's mortal illness and the prognosis of the death of Judaism come in handy for those who want to justify their own defection from כלל ישראל : they can now point to the public confirmation that their course of action is in line with the *Zeitgeist,* and, indeed, with the inevitable course of history; furthermore, they can legitimately argue that no man can be expected to tie up his and his family's fate in a foredoomed venture.[15]

We will not bother to polemicize against that notion of "the vanishing Jew" at any length. This prediction has been made in literally every single generation of Jewish history.[16] One of the more frequently told such tales is that of Steinschneider who, under historically and culturally similar conditions to our own, is supposed to have asked a rabbinical student why he had come

late and, when told that the student had been detained at a
Zionist meeting, replied with some anger that, in our time, our
only task was to provide a decent funeral for the literary remains
of Jewish history. The facts of history—many facts of a very
long history—have empirically given the lie to all such predic-
tions, to the point where no reasonable man can, on purely empirical grounds, any longer take them seriously.

No one should mistake this attitude for a vapid or any other
kind of optimism: we referred at the outset to the symbiosis of
death and resurrection in the barracks of Auschwitz—surely no
one who proclaims: אני מאמין בביאת המשיח while he or his child is
walking into the gas-oven can be accused of liberalistic euphoria.
Furthermore, we are far from denying the sociological, cultural, and religious evisceration of the Jewish people anywhere,
much less in America; on the contrary, we watch its vulgarities
and mindlessnesses with horror. It is perfectly true: according
to all the natural laws of history, demography, and sociology
the people of Israel cannot much longer endure, and, certainly,
it cannot be expected further to be ethically creative. We have
no hope in *homo Judaeus.* All that we are saying is that to deduce from this condition the demise of the Jewish people and of
Judaism is itself a symptom of the sickness which the thesis
claims to be describing: it is to study the Jewish phenomenon
according to חוקות הגוים ; it is to leave God and His covenantal
promise out of account (as Laplace put it to Napoleon). One
need not subscribe either to R. Yehuda Halevy's metaphysical
biologicism or to Nachman Krochmal's Vicoism to accept the
truth with which we, too, have been concerning ourselves, that
there is a force at work in our history which overcomes and tran-
scends all these perfectly correct laws of general human history.
To put it epigrammatically: it is irrational not to believe in the
miraculousness of Jewish history.

The most immediately pragmatic form which the notion of
"the vanishing Jew" takes is the wide-spread worry about intermarriages. Statistics, analyses, papers, books, and conferences
on this subject proliferate. Parents and rabbis constantly warn
young people against its dangers—and the most flagrant of these
dangers is supposed to be to the survival of the Jewish people. I

always visualize God sitting in heaven, surrounded by myriads of His serving angels, with the instruments of His omnipotent providence at His side, going into a panicky conference with His counselors when news comes through that little Gilbert Shapiro from Scarsdale has, for his own socio-pathological reasons, decided to marry Christine Thomas from Dubuque on the campus of Omaha State Teachers College where they have met: the fate of the world and history, not to speak of the chosen people and its destiny, hangs in the balance! "He Who sits in heaven laughs—the Lord mocks them" (Ps. 2:4). There is, obviously, something ridiculous in this picture—even when it it is multiplied a thousandfold. The main point, however, is that Gilbert and Christine are obviously not going to make their decision—if decision it be—in terms of Jewish destiny; indeed, if that meant much to them they would not be very likely to have reached their present condition in the first place. What is more, by inveighing against their allegedly great and injurious treason to the ethnic and religious ties of their families and people one is doing exactly what they—like their academic, bohemian, artistic, and intellectual counterparts—are looking for: they are conducting a small-scale raid against their parents, *milieu,* and the God of their backgrounds—they require a father's disapproval so that they can rebel against it and affirm their independence; by imploring their loyalty one confirms to them that, in the first place, the objects of their resentment are very weak and vulnerable and that, in the second place, their attacks are hitting their targets.

I should think that we ought to deal with the problems of intermarriage in the full and confident consciousness of the theologoumen that nothing that anyone, Jew or Gentile, does can ultimately affect the fate of Israel as a whole. When a Jew and a non-Jew come to us with marital intentions—in a period, incidentally, when marriages constitute only a limited portion of connubial relationships—we present to them the full strictness of Jewish law. (I mention only in passing the Reform rabbis who, also in my community, violate conspicuously not only Jewish law but also the explicit consensus of historic and contemporary Reform Judaism and who continue to injure the unity of the people of Israel and the effectiveness of their colleagues by officiating wholesale at mock-Jewish intermarriages.) The inviolability of Jewish law and religious substance affirms their sanctity and viability beyond impertinent individual or collective amputation to the point of death. A Judaism that declares its reliance on God rather than on—never mind kings—effervescent small-fry is considerably more persuasive than a weak beggar going down on his knees to beg for consideration. "The Lord is with me; I shall not fear: what can man do to me? The Lord is for me as my self; thus shall I be witness to my enemies. It is better to rely on God than to rely on man. It is better to rely on God than to rely on princes. All peoples have surrounded me, but I have escaped them. The right hand of the Lord is upright; the right hand of the Lord acts mightily. I shall not die but live and tell of the deeds of God. He has much tried me, but to death He has not given me over" (Ps. 118). Especially in an age in which nothing succeeds as much as success I would hold that Jewish self-abnegation can be cured not with defeatism but only with—if you please—a divine, a messianic certainty of eventual triumph.

All of this does not, of course, mean that, relying on God's promise, we may lapse into human passivity. Jews have never done this: our metaphysics have always undergirded, not suspended, our ethics. Of course, we want to stop a Jew from defecting, in body or in spirit. But this is so because we hate to see any Jew—or any man—deprived of his share in the glory of Israel. We are worried about the incalculable deprivation which such a defection inflicts upon the defecting individual, not upon the people, faith and destiny from which he defects; we are anxious for the individual, not for God's providence.[16a] Of course, we want to do everything we can to strengthen, enrich, and disseminate *Yiddishkeit,* but this can be done not by begging unwilling—or, for that matter, even willing—individuals or groups, children, marriageable people, intellectuals, or what have you, to help us, the Jewish people, Judaism or God out of their respective troubles. What we must do is to externalize the resplendence of the spirit of God within them—to fan the sparks of the *schechinah* residing in the broken vessels

of the Jewish community—to plumb the sophistication of the
sod within the—usually misunderstood—*peshat* of Jewish reality.

IV. "NOT BY POWER . . ."

We now return to our main theme—the significance of Jewish
survival as we experienced it in 1945. The crucial question
which—consciously or unconsciously—has arisen for all who
have lived since is this: how did this survival, broken yet trium-
phant, tortured yet exultant, decimated yet fortified, come
about? What can we learn about how we are to survive from
how we did survive?

At the Eichmann trial the Israeli attorney-general Hausner
asked most European-Jewish survivors of the Holocaust who
gave testimony: Why did you not resist? Ben-Gurion, among
others, said that one of the major purposes of the trial was to
purge Jewish consciousness of a haunting guilt-feeling for not
having fought back against the Nazis but—as the Biblical
phrase, frighteningly transvalued, which is usually cited at this
point, goes—having "gone like sheep to the slaughter." Clearly,
the premise of the question is, in the first place, that it is better
to "fight back" than to die, without physical retaliation or defense, as martyrs, and, in the second place, that the survival of
the שארית הפליטה was due to those who, as heroes on the walls
of the Warsaw Ghetto, soldiers in the Jewish Brigade, members
of the roaming Partisan groups, or after the war as soldiers in
the Haganah or other military or quasi-military outfits, fought
against the Nazis and for the establishment of the State of
Israel. There can be little doubt that it is on the basis of essentially such premises that organized Jewry concentrates its memo-
rializations of the victims of the Holocaust on anniversaries of
the Warsaw Ghetto Revolt. Hence issues forth also a new
worldwide Jewish admiration for heroes of brawn—Israeli,
healthy, clear-eyed, wiry boys and girls with machine-guns under
their arms, Colonels Marcus, tanks and planes on Sunday-school
bulletin boards, etc.

This view of how Israel survived its most horrible threat has
undergone a rapid escalation. It began, shortly after the war,

with the glorification of the Jewish military and paramilitary fighters while the "passive" martyrs were lamented but, for the rest, relatively neglected. From this followed shortly two different but supplementary theses: the Hausner thesis we have mentioned, that there was something, perhaps something crucial, that was demeaning, immoral, possibly even traitorous about not having physically fought back, and the Hannah Arendt thesis that significant elements of the Jewish leadership and communities in Europe had actually collaborated with their people's exterminators. Mind you, even most of those who vehemently argued against the Arendt thesis accepted the premise that to die unresistingly is somehow shameful, and they, therefore, concentrated their attention on revolts in ghettoes and concentration camps and on Jewish leaders who were active in the war against the Nazis in order to try to refute Arendt's thesis.[17] The next step in the escalation was, of course, the resolution, in Israel and abroad, not to let ourselves be decoyed into such a situation again but rather, from the outset, to be ready to take to arms and other counter-aggressive measures against any actual or potential (and thus preemptive) enemy. This was certainly the underlying and usually proclaimed psychological posture immediately before and during the Six Day War; it was part of the *déja-vu,* the *déja-senti* atmosphere of those weeks when the beleaguered spirit of the Second World War was rife in the Jewish community—and it is the source of the predominant "hawkishness" in Jewish circles since then. The last and grotesquely Satanic degree of escalation which this interpretation of the Jewish history of our time has hitherto undergone is the doctrine enunciated in the current wave of Polish, neo-Stalinist Communist anti-semitism—that, by and large, it was the Poles—*mirabile dictu!*—who fought against the Nazis while the ranks of Jewry were shot through with traitors, collaborators, and cowards.

The subject is too painful, and I, therefore, want to try to summarize what is historically and morally wrong with this attitude as briefly as possible. In Israel and in this country a Jewish triumphalism has spread which is not lovely to behold. In the phrases תנועה למען ארץ ישראל השלמה are slung around which sound most ominous to anyone who has lived through the 'thirties of our century: "liberated territories," "the Greater Israel," "the call of the historic soil," "the metaphysical unity of the people and the land," "the irresistible destiny of the millenia," etc. Policy discussions are held about how to keep the numbers and the fertility of the Arabs (and sometimes even also of the Sephardim) in manageable proportion to those of the rest of Israel—satellite states are proposed as a more liberal way of dealing with the Near Eastern problem than wholesale removal of populations—the Israeli army is further enhanced as the chief tool of integration, education, and decision-making, where the Kibbutz had, surely, been originally cast in that role—generals become cabinet-members and ambassadors, together with previously proscribed terrorist leaders and right-wing chauvinists—let these examples stand for others as well.[18]

In a more technically theological sense the Israeli victory in the Six Day War has produced an immensely aggravated danger of pseudo-faith and pseudo-messianism. It is by now a cliché how Israeli as well as *galut* Jews without religious faith suddenly came to believe in miracles (performed by a non-existent God) and thought they were witnessing the אתחלתא דגאולה.[19] To which my teacher Prof. Akiba Ernst Simon replied epigrammatically: "I, too, would believe that it was a miracle—if I didn't believe in God so much." [20]

In March 1968 the "Newsletter on Religious and Cultural Affairs" put out by the Consulate General of Israel in New York[21] carried a rather stunning and worrisome summary of this pseudo-messianic mood in certain circles. The Israeli chief-rabbinate called for *hallel* on the anniversary of the conquest of Jerusalem—the laws of the restoration of the Temple were to be studied (in fact, of course, a great military parade was held)—the possibility of proclaiming Iyyar 28 a permanent holiday was discussed—"Chief Rabbi Untermann reiterated his considered view that 'the cardinal duty of פרסום הנס —publicizing the miracle, made the recital of Hallel on the anniversary of Israel's victory literally a Biblical ordinance דין דאורייתא גמור, and one was also authorized to say the Beracha accompanying it.' " (The Torah Education Department of the World Zionist Or-

ganization promised an early publication of Rabbi Untermann's
מצות פרסומא נסא וגודל השמעתא. Here one may ask: why do non-Ortho-
dox Jews hasten to protest against bureaucratic discriminations
against them in Israel but not about substantive matters, העומדים
ברומו של עולם, such as this? Rabbi M. Fogelman of Kiryat
Motzkin is quoted: "Is the miracle of our day less than that
of Hanukkah?" Rabbi Techorsh, member of the Chief Rabbinate
Council, advocated the recital of שהחיינו and על הנסים . Rabbi
Y. Abuhatzirach, also a member of the Council and spiritual
head of Israel's North African community, maintained (and,
perhaps, such views can be indulged depending on the history
of those who hold them) that last year's "recovery of ארץ ישראל
constituted the final step before the advent of the Messiah,"
warranting special readings from Torah and Prophets.[21a]

This is extremely dangerous talk. Theologically I would adduce at least three arguments against it, the first two cited from
—if you please—the Satmerer Rebbe's recent קונטרס על הגאולה,
וההמורה: 1) "Miracles" are miracles only when they are in
accord with the Torah and the *halachah;* otherwise, like the
miracles of the Egyptian magicians, they are deceptions of
Satan;[22] 2) Victories in wars, even those of the few over the
many, are always natural events, not miracles. Thus Hanukkah
celebrates the miracle of the oil, not the victory of the Hasmoneans.[23] Indeed, military victories are special opportunities for
the seductions of Satan.[24] I should like to add a third reason
for not regarding a victory in war a divine act, and I regret
that this kind of thinking is hard to come by nowadays in
Orthodox, Reform, or any other Jewish circles: R. Yochanan,
the central teacher in the eschatological discussion of פרק חלק ,
interpreting Jer. 30:6, asks why, in the messianic fulfillment,
"all faces will turn pale." [25] He answers that the angels and
Israel will turn pale because the salvation of Israel carries along
with it a comparative demotion of other peoples: "At that time
the Holy One, praised be He, will say: 'Those (Israel) are the
works of My hands, and the others (Gentiles) are the works
of My hands. How can I cause the ones to perish in favor of
the others!' " [26] And Rav Pappa (and Rashi *ad locum*) expatiate
further on this consideration. It might be argued that, despite

their misgivings, all the parties concerned nevertheless pray for
the messianic fulfillment and therefore the corollary derogation
of the Gentiles—but it must be remembered that R. Yochanan
makes the statement which we have quoted in order to explain
why he, like a number of others, exclaims: ייתי ולא איתמיניה—*i.e.*,
R. Yochanan prefers not to experience the messianic advent
rather than be an accessory to the plight of the non-Jews. Much
further genuine Jewish morality—or any other—cannot go! Can
we say less in the presence of Moslems and Arabs?

Turning to American Jewry, the triumphalism which we have
illustrated manifests itself here perhaps more flagrantly than in
Israel, perhaps precisely because it is at one remove. Hundreds
of rabbis sign full-page newspaper ads insisting that all of the
conquered land must be retained by Israel because—if you
please—otherwise the Soviet Union will have succeeded in
pushing the United States out of its strategic strongholds in
the Near East. Liberal Jewish professors, who had been in the
vanguard of the movement against the Vietnam War, demand
full American political and military commitment on the side
of Israel, and, though their dissenting voices are heard on every
other subject, a strange silence prevails toward the Israeli government on the delicate but crucial question of Arab-Jewish relations; the center of Jewish attention in this country has now
become "Negro anti-Semitism" and campus anarchism where
previously it had been equality and peace, etc.[27] I confess,
with great sadness, that I see a dominant note of rampant self-
assertiveness and self-righteousness in world Jewry, which may
be compared with the ideology of those against whom Jeremiah
prophesied, who thought that their strength lay in their own
arms and in alliances with foreign, pagan powers.

One is sorely tempted, at this point, to want to assert one's
Jewish "patriotism" against the inevitable accusations which
will be leveled. But let us, instead, go back to the original thesis
about the nature of Jewish survival as we witnessed it in 1945,
and let us see what happens to the real interests of the Jewish
people when that fragmented survival is looked at in another
light.

Certainly the Jews in the Warsaw Ghetto had every human

right to defend themselves and to fight back. The same is true
of all the other military or paramilitary expressions of resistance
and counter-attack. Rightly do we honor their memories. But
let us remember: in the first place, we lament to say that they,
too, died—if survival is to be the yardstick of tactical or ethical
worth, then we mourn to have to conclude that neither military
resistance nor martyrdom availed. In the second place, it has
been and is a terrible defamation of the third of the Jewish
people who went to their deaths to claim or to imply that because they did not fight back they either did not resist or—
חס וחלילה —collaborated. To be *mentshen* in the midst of inhumanity, to sanctify the name of God while surrounded by a
flood of heathenism, to study, teach, and pray in a world in
which only murder, rape, and brutality reigned, to squeeze a
precious drop of life through the sieve of all-consuming death,
and finally to go to one's death in ranks of thousands because
the world had turned into hell and no longer had a place for
decent human beings—who will rise and have the frowardness
to claim that this was not, in its way, the greatest, the most
admirable, the most heroic form of resistance,[28]—that the more
than five million who did not, as it happens, resort to guns,
knives, stones, and fire did not plant the banner of Israel, God,
and humanity fluttering high on the battlefield of history?[29]

Two thousand years of Jewish exilic history had taught the
Jewish people that the tree planted by the waters could bend
its branches to the storm and afterwards rise up again and grow
its fruit for the coming season. One has to be an assimilated,
Westernized secularist to see something dishonorable—as Bialik
did in עיר ההרגה and as so many Jews do today—in crouching
in cellars until, it is hoped, the beasts have passed by, in order
to save one's own and one's family's lives. To be sure, the gentle-
manly thing to do is to stand up straight, meet the badman in
the open street and get the first draw on him, but then, as
Maurice Samuel has put it, we choose to be Jews, not gentlemen.
And, when all was said and done, in 1945 a small but viable
remnant from the Holocaust had in fact survived. They stumbled
out of the camps, they raised their heads from the floor, they
walked blinkingly into the light, they came out of hiding and

disguise, and whispered: *"Mir zennen do."* And this was not a very small minority of our surviving people—it was the overwhelming majority of those who had, by God's unfathomable and cruel grace, somehow or other come through. They *were,* indeed, the Jewish people. They own our unqualified piety and love—as do all those who, to the end and into horrible deaths, exemplified what it is to be Jews, human beings, citizens of "the lands of the living."

It is almost universally said that the Holocaust is an irrefutable blemish on—if not denial of—God. This is true. It is equally true that the survival of the Jewish people—at all times and especially through the Holocaust—is an inexplicable handiwork of His. (It is, incidentally, little less cruel than the slaughter, as Elie Wiesel and others make clear.) We are entitled to put it blasphemously: God was so vicious as to kill us, and He was so vicious as to preserve us; to Him go all blame and all glory. The Jew came out of this furnace—dead or alive—pure as the driven snow. Under the Law הרוגי מלכות are, regardless of their personal merits or previous conditions, martyrs על קדוש השם.[30] Again we conclude: we survive by God's harsh decree, and those who survive testify, willingly or no, knowingly or no, gladly or sadly, to His majesty and sovereignty.[31]

Now we can once more jump forward to the Jewish history of the decades since 1945. We presented ourselves—"a brand plucked from the fire"—to the world in 1945, we pressed against the shores of the Holy Land and the doors of governments, and in 1948 the United Nations established the State of Israel. We ought to recall that at that time and for a while thereafter there were no more eloquent protagonists of the United Nations than we Jews. It is one of the sorrier consequences of the superciliousness and arrogancy of the last few years that now in most Jewish circles "the United Nations" is a term of deprecation. One need not have any exaggerated notions of its present capacities or wisdom to perceive the fundamental dangers and immoralities of this attitude. With respect to all three wars that Israel has had to wage since 1948 it is perfectly obvious that the idea that "with the strength of my hand have I acted and

with my wisdom, for I am smart—and I remove the boundaries
of nations" (Is. 10:13) is foolish even in purely political terms:
but for the support that literally all the great powers of our age,
the U.S.S.R., the U.S. and their satellites in 1948, Britain and
France in 1956, and America in 1967, provided, disaster could
easily have overtaken us. How long do we think we can live
in the Near East surrounded, indeed interpenetrated, by hundreds of millions of Moslems and Arabs in the middle of millions
of square miles of hostile territory and, in each blood-letting
round, come out victors? (Unlike the Arab countries, we cannot
afford a single defeat!) The Jew who is really committed to the
survival of Israel not just for another generation but לעולמי עולמים
will contemplate the needs of the hour in such a *specie aeternit-
atis,* however unpopular he may be among his fellows at the
moment. And even if it were conceivable that in the longest
run the Jewish people could maintain itself in the midst of such
a sea of enmity, what human, spiritual and moral price would
we have to pay for it? I always remember that when my son
was less than ten years old he came home from a summer in an
Israeli children's camp and said that his chief impression was
of barbed wire all over the country. The transvaluation of all
Jewish values which has already seriously set in in Israeli
and world Jewry would soon completely overwhelm us.[32] The
problem of our Jewish generation and of our children is whether
we can live with the ethics and politics of the נרדפים , having,
in some ways, ceased to be נרדפים .[33] I implore you and me and
all of us not to prove Nietzsche to have been right—that morality
is the rationalization of the weak.

At this point, finally, I can articulate my own form of Jewish
super-chauvinism. What we have been saying is simply that the
survival of the Jewish people is guaranteed by God—that we
need not really concern ourselves with it—that to preoccupy
oneself with it is a form of sickness, as health-faddists are invariably sick people[33a]—that to attribute our survival to human
instrumentalities including and primarily our own, inevitably
leads to the acts of *hybris,* גאוה , which victimize other human
beings and result in unending conflict and eventual defeat—and
that, on the contrary, the God Who has brought us this far will

also redeem His other promises to Israel. Like the תנועה למען א״י השלמה I, too, am unable to surrender—לעתיד לבא—one inch of the sacred soil of ארץ ישראל . We may implicitly believe that in the Redemption not only will the historic land revert to its divinely designated occupants but that, as Rabbinic literature amply proclaims,[34] it will be vastly expanded—yes, Hebron and Jericho, the cedars of Lebanon and the great river: "And He said to me: 'These waters go out into the eastern Galilee, descend into the Arabah, and end in the sea'" (Ez. 47:8). The late Chayim Weizman was asked about this messianic claim by a member of the Peel Commission when, back in 1936, he was ready to accept the first partition plan for Palestine, and he answered, not facetiously: God made the promise—God, not we, will redeem it. Our task is to be *mentshen* and thus— and thus only—to hasten the Messiah's coming, not by force or by magic or by superarrogation.

The kind of pseudo-messianism which we have previously had occasion to consider[35] is not limited to the "old-fashioned" circles of the Israeli chief-rabbinate.[36] The pop song that became the hymn of the Six Day War is suffused with messianic connota- tions: "The *Shofar* sounds on the Temple Mount, in the Old City,/ And within the caves in the rock rays of the Light shine. . . .", etc. Nothing less than the glossy official maga- zine of French Jewry, *L'Arche,* for Oct.–Nov. 1967 (No. 128) appeared under the red headline: *Jerusalem 5728—Le Méssie, va-t-il Arriver?"* Inside there is an article by Alex Derczansky still moderately entitled: *"Le Royaume de Dieu Reste à Con- struire . . . Mais on Sait Maintenant que Godot Doit Arriver,"* whereas Arnold Mandel, one of the intellectual mentors of con- temporary French Jewry and presumably a sensitive and so- phisticated man, the title of whose article graces the front cover, is quite sure that, at the least, the Messiah son of Joseph, "the political and national Messiah," has arrived *hic et nunc* "on our territory in the Jewish year 5728."

We cannot here analyze the whole complex and profound sub- ject of Jewish messianology. The least that must be said, how- ever,[37] is that this kind of thinking is grist for the mills of all the "realists," anti-utopians, and neo-conservative thinkers of our time—Reinhold Niebuhr, Jakob Talmon, Norman Cohn, Hannah Arendt, etc. Their argument invariably boils down to this—that utopianism and Jewish messianism are forms of *hybris,* עבודה זרה , which claim to be able to accomplish humanly what in truth only God can accomplish and, what is worse, which will always play havoc with human beings who do not completely fall in line with the messianic claims, on the grounds that they are not only political dissenters but blasphemers who want to undermine the reign of God Himself. This is, of course, a willful and purposeful distortion of the messianic belief. This belief in fact dictates that men must exert themselves as much as and more than they are capable of doing toward the messianic goal, in the hope—*nota bene:* not in the arrogantly sure expectation—that God will—in His own good time and for His own good reasons, not in any proportionality to these human efforts: "Not on our righteous acts do we make our petitions dependent"—bring about Redemption. It thus self-evidently subsumes the human part in bringing about the consummation to the onus of human fallibility, inadequacy, and sinfulness and to the divine prerogative of grace. Nonetheless, the "anti-utopians" have enough evidence, of course, with which to support their case, by the simple device of procuring it from the rich arsenal of pseudo-messianisms, which they proceed to identify with authentic messianism: their evidence of fanaticism, *hybris,* ruthlessness and inhumanity invariably stems from those who violate the fundamental Jewish messianic dictates: "Do not press the End!" [38] and "May those be devastated who calculate the End." [39]

An apparent contradiction might be pointed to in our argumentation: on the one hand, we reject the view of the anti-utopian neo-conservatives who advocate, at best, slow, small steps of melioration within the established structures of society—yet, on the other hand, we now raise the old Jewish motto "Do not press the End!"

Here we turn, for the last time, to the dialectical polarity of the ethics and the metaphysics of the Covenant. The ethics of the Covenant do, indeed, require us to act in such a way as to hasten the coming of the Messiah, *i.e.* to endeavor to establish the radical reign of peace, justice, and goodness on earth. But ethics are concerned with other men, not ourselves. Therefore, with respect to the peace movement, the Black movement, the social movement in our time (movements, that is to say, which are primarily concerned with men other than ourselves) our motto must be theirs: "All of it—here and now!" and on this motto we must act. This must apply, too, to the genuine problems of Palestinian Arabs: no reasonable Zionist has denied the at least partial justice of their case, and the plight of many of their people has lasted much, much too long. The metaphysics of the Covenant, on the other hand, are concerned, as we have seen, with the persistence of the people of Israel throughout history, *i.e.* primarily with ourselves. This God has assumed as His responsibility. Elie Wiesel quotes a midrash[40] that explains why the Jews opposed to Haman's attempt to exterminate them physically the spiritual resistance of repentance, fasting, and prayer: "When our physical existence was threatened we simply reminded God of His duties and the promises deriving from the Covenant." In short, the Torah is our business, Israel's survival is God's.[41]

It all comes down to the simple formula of the Levitical and Deuteronomic blessings-and-curses: if we fulfill the commandments of His will He will bless and keep us—it is not the other way around, that, if we maintain ourselves, He or we will be able to act as He desires us to: "If you walk in My statutes and keep My commandments and do them . . ., then will I walk Myself in your midst: I will become your God for you, and you will become a people for Me. I am the Lord your God, Who brought you out of the land of Egypt, so that you would no more be their slaves; I will break the bands of your yoke, and I will lead you integrally" (Lev. 26:1-13).

NOTES

[1] Cf. Emil Fackenheim on what he calls "the *mitzvah* of surviving," *Judaism*, XVI/3, Summer '67, p. 272.—One might make a comparison with the famous wisecrack attributed to the Abbé Sieyès: when asked what he had done during the French Revolution, he is supposed to have said: *"J'ai vécu."* Jewishly one might say that not to have lived but to have "lived above" and thus to have "sur-vived" is at issue.

[2] Cf. שיח לוחמים ed. A. Shapira, Tel Aviv 5728; cp. M. Rosenak, "Moments of the Heart," *Judaism*, XVII/2, Spring '68, pp. 211-224.

[3] "Judaism in the Post-Christian Era," *Judaism*, XV/1, Winter '66, p. 84: "No one can foretell what this new era holds in store for mankind. But we are here at the threshold of the new age. We who were there when the Christian era began; in whose martyrdom Christianity suffered its worst moral debacle; we in whose blood the Christian era found its end—we are here as this new era opens. And we shall be here when this new era reaches its close—we, the *edim*, God's own witnesses, the *am olam*, the eternal witness of history."

[4] Cf. e.g., Deut. 26:17, et. al.

[5] Lev. 26:23f.: "If you walk with Me cavalierly, then also I will walk with you cavalierly." Cf. Ex. 19:5f., Deut. 11:17, 28:24, Joshua 23:16, I Kings 9:7, Jer. 7, especially vv. 4f., 11, 15, 33f., Amos 9:7 and Rashi *ad locum*, Micah 3:11f., etc.

[6] Goethe said that "no one is a hero to his butler." To which Hegel replied, "That is so not because he is not a hero but because the butler is a butler." *I.e.*, the personal idiosyncrasies, even the ethical failures of a man, cannot ultimately be believed to be history-shaping forces. Otherwise, instead of studying the laws of economics we would have to investigate how a corporation executive liked his eggs on any given morning. *Cf. Phaenomenologie des Geistes*, ed. Lasson, pp. 81, 93, *et. al.*

[7] E.g. Ps. 105:7–10: "He is the Lord our God. His statutes are valid in all the earth. He remembers His covenant forever, the word of His commandment unto the thousandth generation, which He made with Abraham and His oath unto Isaac. He has established it as a statute for Jacob, an everlasting covenant for Israel." Cf. I Chron. 16:16; also Deut. 4:29ff., Is. 49:14–26, Jer. 31–34f.: "Thus says the Lord, Who sets the sun as light by day and the laws of the moon and stars as light by night, Who stirs up the sea so that its waves billow, Whose name is Lord of hosts: If these statutes vanish from before Me, says the Lord, then only will the seed of Israel cease being a people before Me forever." Cf. Gen. 17:7f., Ex. 13:16, Deut. 7:9, 33:27, Is. 54:9f., 59:21, Jer. 30:11, 33:25f., Hosea 2:21f., etc.

[8] Thus one arrives at the immoralism—either the reaction of a Hegel or the mechanism of a Marxism.

[9] Cf., e.g., "ישראל קימים לעולם„ ,ביאליק ורבניצקי, ספר האגדה, Cf. *Men.* 53b:11, 24–26. "R. Joshua b. Levi said: 'Israel will not experience complete extinction either in this world or in the text.' " Cf. also A. Marmorstein, *Studies in Jewish Theology*, Oxf. 1950,

"האמונה בנצח ישראל בדרשות התנאים והאמוראים„, א—ט"ז

10 In this passage as well as throughout Rabbinic literature, תשובה is usually mistranslated as "repentance," whereas in fact, of course, it means "moral conduct" in such instances.

11 For a good beginning of the kind of ethico-conceptual analysis to which this kind of literature ought to be subjected, see Emmanuel Lévinas, "Temps Messianiques et Temps Historiques dans le Chapitre XI du Traité 'Sanhedrin,'" La Conscience Juive, eds. E. A. Lévy-Valensi and J. Halperin, Paris 1963. For the theological dialectics of the Talmud, cf. also e.g. J. Petuchowski, "The Concept of 'Teshuvah' in the Bible and Talmud," Judaism, XVII/2, Spring '68, esp. p. 184f.

12 Cf. also Deut. R. 5:6.

13 Cf. Saadia Gaon, Emunot ve'Deot III/7: "Our nation is a nation only by virtue of its torot, and since the Creator has declared that the nation will persist as long as the heavens and the earth do it follows necessarily that its torot will persist as long as the heavens and the earth. See Jer. 31: 34f. . . ." Cf. Kuzari, II/34: "Do not believe that I, though agreeing with you, admit that we are dead. We still hold connection with that divine influence through the laws which He has placed as a link between us and Him. There is circumcision, of which it is said: 'My covenant shall be in your flesh for an everlasting covenant.' (Gen. 17:13) There is further the Sabbath: 'It is a sign between Me and you throughout your generations' (Ex. 31:13). Besides this there is the 'covenant of the Fathers,' and the covenant of the Law first granted on Horeb and then in the plains of Moab in connection with the promises and warnings laid down in the section 'When you will beget children and grandchildren' (Deut. 4:25). Compare further the antithesis 'If any of yours be driven out to the utmost parts of heaven' (ib., 30:10)—'You shall return unto the Lord your God' (ib., v. 2); finally the song, 'Give ear . . .' (ib., 32:1), etc. We are not like dead but rather like a sick and weakened person who has been given up by the physicians and yet awaits a miracle or an extraordinary recovery, as it is said: 'Can these bones live?' " (Ezek. 37:3)—Ib., III/10f.: "I have discovered that God has a secret purpose in keeping you in existence. . . . If an evil thought makes a man despair, saying: 'Can these bones live?' (ib.)—our greatness having been negated and our history having been forgotten, as it is said: 'Our bones are dried up and our hope lost; we have been condemned' (ib., v. 11)—let him think of the nature of the exodus from Egypt and all that is said in the section 'For how many beneficences unto us do we owe gratitude unto God!' (Passover Haggadah). Then he will have no difficulty in imagining how we will be restored to our estate even if all but one of us will disappear. For it is written: 'Fear not, oh worm Jacob (Is. 41:14), i.e., what remains of a man when he returns to be a worm in his grave!"—Cf. also Maimonides, Epistle to Yemen, ed. A. S. Halkin, N. Y. 1952, p. 25: "God has long ago given us the guarantee through His prophets that we will not perish and that we will not cease to be a significant people. As the existence of God cannot be terminated so our disappearance from the world is impossible. It is said (Mal. 3:6): 'For I, the Lord, do not change, and you, the children of Jacob, will not perish' (Cf. Sotah 9a). Furthermore, God has informed and promised us that He cannot possibly reject us completely and, though we may disobey Him and turn back His commandments, it is said (Jer. 31:37): 'For God has said: "As much as the heavens above can be measured and the foundations of the earth beneath can be plumbed, so will I reject all of

the seed of Israel because of all that they have done"—says the Lord.' This very point was even earlier made known to us by Moses our teacher, peace be upon him (Lev. 26:44): 'Yet for all that, when they are in the land of their enemies I will not reject them, nor will I abhor them, to destroy them utterly and to break My covenant with them—for I am the Lord their God.' " *Ib.,* p. 35: "It has been explained to us by Isaiah, the messenger of the nation, that the sign between us and God and the proof that teaches us that we will not perish is the persistence of God's Torah and His word among us. He said (Is. 59:21): 'As for Me, this is My covenant with them, says the Lord—My spirit which is upon you.' . . . And it is written (Is. 44:23): 'For You have we been killed at all times and treated as sheep suitable for slaughter.' " *Cf.* also *Yalkut Shimeoni,* 27b, beginning, to Ex. 19:2, where God's "eternal salvation of Israel" is counterposed to Israel's previsioned "offensiveness and blasphemy," on the basis of its function of "purloining worlds for Him."

14 Cf. the classic writings of Jacob Klatzkin—*Cf. The Zionist Idea,* A. Hertzberg, N. Y. 1960, pp. 314–328, esp. p. 320ff.

15 Arthur Koestler's *Thieves in the Night* was an anticipation of this attitude in our time, and his "Letter to a Parent of a British Soldier in Palestine" (*cf. Under Fire,* ed. D. Robinson, N. Y. 1968) is a proterrorist corollary.

16 *E.g.* Arthur Ruppin's classic *Die Juden der Gegenwart,* Berlin 1920.

16a Cf. H. Slonimsky, *Essays,* N. Y. 1967, p. 62: "The individual Jew may drop away, but Israel as a whole is held inexorably fast. Thus Johanan, the prince of the Agada, has the following to say in explanation of God's ontological definition of himself as אהיה אשר אהיה 'I can be whatever I may be to individuals, but as for the mass I rule over them even against their desires and will, even though they break their teeth' (referring to Ez. 20:33) אהיה לאשר אהיה ביחידים, אבל במרובים על כורחם שלא בטובתם כשהם משוברות שניהם (Ex. R., Romn 11b, col. 2)."

17 I wish I had kept count of the young Jews with whom I have spoken who, validly or no, are, as a result, finding themselves in the most serious of ethical perplexities now when they have to try to buttress their universal conscientious objections to waging war with Jewish reasoning.

18 There is by now much literature that can be adduced on this score. Cf., *e.g.,* C. Potok's review of a cluster of recent books on the Six Day War in the *N. Y. Times,* June 9, 1968, which ends: ". . . a new kind of Jew has been in the making during these past decades, the concept of the exile, with its picture of the cringing, long-suffering Jew (whose picture ?!), is now coming to an end . . ." *Cf.* D. Lang, "After the Sixth Day," *The New Yorker,* May 18, 1968, p. 104. The most frightening religio-political chauvinism comes from Prof. Harold Fisch of Bar-Ilan University: see "Land of Israel Movement," *Congress Bi-Weekly,* 35/3, Febr. 5, 1968, and *Niv HaMidrashiya,* Winter-Spring 1968, pp. 44–49, where he even rather likes Arab intransigence since it leads to Israeli expansion.

19 Mandel, "Le Méssie, va-t-il Arriver?" *L'Arche,* Oct.–Nov. 1967, no. 128, quotes an Israeli: "I don't believe in God, but of one thing I'm sure: this time He was with us."

20 Cf. Maimonides' striking position on miracles, which we cannot here rehearse but which can fairly be summarized as maintaining the possibility of miracles while denying in virtually every single case that one has occurred..

[21] Why does this publication always carry the front-page notation: "This publication is for your information and use, in any way you deem fit—therefore, please do not give any credit to the publisher"?

[21a] See further relevant halachic discussions summarized in I. Jakobovits, "Survey of Recent Halakhic Periodical Literature—The Occupied Territories," *Tradition*, IX/4, Spring 1968, pp. 101–104. Rabbi J. B. Soloveitchik's position represents a humane and wise bright spot in the spectrum. Cf. also *Or Ha-Mizrach*, XVII/3, July 1968, Y. Gershoni, "Is it Halachically Permitted to Surrender Palestinian Territories?" and I. Y. Untermann, "The Commandment to Publicize the Miracle" (Hebrew).

[22] *Op. cit.*, p. 69, *et al.*

[23] This argument occurs, of course, throughout Jewish history but especially in 19th-century liberalism. I have been sorely tempted to write a review of the Satmerer Rebbe's book to be entitled, for the reason here mentioned as well as others, "The Reform Judaism of Satmer."

[24] *Op. cit.*, pp. 34f., *et al.*

[25] *Sanh.* 98b.

[26] Cf. the famous midrash about God rebuking the angels while Egypt drowns in the Red Sea.

[27] Cf. *e.g.* R. J. Isaac, "Good Guys (Arabs), Bad Guys (Israel): The View from the Left," *Congress Bi-Weekly*, *loc. cit.*; A. S. Maller, "The New Politics," *The Jewish Spectator*, June 1968; J. L. Teller, "The New Populism and the Jews," *Conservative Judaism*, XXII/3, Spring 1968; M. Wyshograd, "The Jewish Interest in Vietnam," *Tradition*, IX/4, Winter 1966. Quite an interesting bibliography of this new American-Jewish turn away from "the Left" could be compiled—although, on the whole, it is not so much the writers who would make the point, since they almost always were conservatives all along and are merely making use of the new situation for their purposes (like the latter two mentioned here), as rather the obviously increased receptivity to and respectability of their views among the Jewish community.

[28] See Ernst Simon, the very title of whose book tells part of this story: *Creation in the Midst of Destruction—Jewish Adult Education in Nazi Germany as Spiritual Resistance* (German), Tuebingen 1959.

[29] Dr. Nathan Eck, of Yad VaShem in Jerusalem, reports the doctrine of Rabbi Nissenbaum of Warsaw that in the past, in order to save one's soul, one had to sacrifice one's life, *i.e.*, in the face of the Inquisition one had to perform קדוש השם whereas now the Nazis want to exterminate Jewish life, and, therefore, in order to save the Jewish mind one has to perform, above all, קדוש החיים *i.e.*, preserve Jewish life. (These questions were discussed at a Conference on Problems of the Resistance held at Yad VaShem the week before Passover 1968.)

[30] *Kuzari*, I/113ff.: "Rabbi: 'I see that you are reproaching us with our degradation and poverty. But the best of other religions boast of both . . .' The Kuzari: 'This might be so if your humiliation were voluntary. But it is involuntary, and if you had the power you would kill.' Rabbi: '. . . Yet the majority may expect reward, because they bear their degradation partly

from necessity, partly of their own free will. For whoever wishes to do so can become the friend and equal of his oppressor by uttering one word (*"credo"*) and without any difficulty. . . . If we bear our exile and degradation for God's sake, as is proper, we shall be the pride of the generation which will come with the Messiah and accelerate the day of the deliverance for which we hope. . . .' " Cf. also H. Cohen, *Religion der Vernunft*, Frankfurt am Main 1929, ch. XII, last paragr., Engl. transl., *Judaism*, XVII/3, Summer 1968, "From the Classics."—This is, all together, one of the most distressing *heilsgeschichtlich* points brought to the fore by the experience of the Holocaust. (Some of the following points have crystallized in my mind as a result of a long and searching conversation on this subject with Dr. Erich Fromm.) It is often argued that "the six million" are not מקדשי השם because many of them were not, of course, practicing religious Jews or even believers in God. The answer of *pietas*, theology, *halachah*, and historiosophy must be and is that anyone slain as a Jew—on whom the name of God was thus called, whether he knew or liked it or no—is a martyr. If a "martyr" is, etymologically, a witness, then witnesses witness regardless of their own subjective attitude to the content of their testimony. *I.e.*, we are dealing with an objective, rational postulate (cf. footnote 6): it is not that one deduces a martyr's status from the fact that he was a Jew but rather the reverse, the Jew's status from the fact that he was a martyr. (Cf., *Protest: Pacifism and Politics*, ed. J. Finn, N. Y. 1967, pp. 126ff.) See *Encyclopedia Talmudit*, "Haruge Malchut," vol. X, pp. 622–627: "Those slain by a government attain to atonement even though they had been wicked men—see Ps. 79:1f.: 'Thy servants' refers to such as were deserving of death but who, by virtue of the fact that they were killed, are called 'Thy servants.' . . . The atonement of those slain by a government is immediate . . ., as, for example, those who were killed in the destruction of the Temple, who had done all the evils which God hates, as is expounded by the Prophets, and yet Scripture says about them: 'They gave the bodies of Thy servants as food for the fowl of heaven.' . . . Those slain by a government attain to atonement even though they have not done repentance, *i.e.*, even though they were 'killed in the midst of their wickedness.' (See *Sanh.* 47). . . . Those slain by a government are to be properly mourned, and they are not to be deprived of any form of mourning. . . . Referring to those slain by a government that refuses permission to bury them, since it is thus impossible to count the seven and the thirty days of mourning from the time that that the grave is closed, one begins to count the period of mourning at the time that hope is abandoned for asking the return of the bodies. . . ." Cf. also the moving words written in 1912 by Rav Kook regarding the HaShomer socialists who lost their lives in defense of the *Yishuv, Zichron*, ed. R. Y. L. HaCohen Fishman, Jerus. 1945, pp. 5–9: he cites *Yoreh Deah*, 340-*Pess.* 50a: "No one can be compared to Jews killed by alien sovereignties," and says: "We are fortune's children when it comes to tears. . . . It is our happiness-*cum*-catastrophe that we may mourn these beloved victims according to our heart's desires, not only out of the emotions of our heart but also by virtue of the *halachah*. . . . But woe unto us that we are forced to make use of this good fortune."— Another aspect of the current Polish episode into which we cannot, unfortunately, enter is the astounding reconfirmation, which Nazi Germany first supplied in our century on a grand scale, of the eschatological thesis of Isaac Abarbanel (see B. Netanyahu, *Don Isaac Abarvanel*— . . ., Phil. 1956, pp. 202f., 315f.) and of others that the God of Israel and of universal history stamps His indelible will for the Jewishness of His chosen even on those who most actively deny it, Marranos, communists, etc. Adam Schaff, perhaps the best-known Polish academic philosopher, who, in his debate with Sartre, went so far in his self-de-Judaization that he made vulgar anti-Semitic wise-cracks, has now—as one example out of many—been removed from official and public life on the ground that he is a Jewish nationalist and—of all things—a Stalinist! I would go so far as to be prepared to argue that the Six Day War lies significantly at the root of the current Czech and French quasi-revolutions and the Polish quasi-counter-revolution. (Cf. *Jews in Eastern Europe*, III/9, May 1968: "World Communist Disunity over Jews and the Middle East.")

[31] Let anyone still wishing to quarrel with this thesis look at the case of Richard Rubenstein. Without going into his psychopathology, the least that can be said about his doctrine is that he thinks he has decided to divorce himself from this cruel God—thus he declares Him to be Nothing and teaches a revived religion of paganism, a return to the mother-goddess earth and her Canaanitish ways.

[32] Compare what was said in this country during the weeks after the assassination of Senator Kennedy about the psychological relationship between the Vietnam War and the predilection for violence at home.

[33] Cf. *B. K.* 93a, *Lev. R.* 27:5, *Pesikta deRav Kahana* (ed. Mandelbaum), p. 153; cf. generally and importantly, R. Kimmelman, "Non-Violence in the Talmud," *Judaism*, XVII/3, Summer 1968, esp. sect. III. Cf. the very title *The Religions of the Oppressed* (*A Study of Modern Messianic Cults*), V. Lanternari, N. Y. 1963. Cf. S. H. Bergman's lovely statement, quoted in D. Lang, *loc. cit.*, about being a minority as a majority, p. 92.

[33a] Freud said to Marie Bonaparte: anyone who asks about the meaning of life is already sick.

[34] Cf. *Sabb.* 30b, *Ket.* 111b, etc.; also my forthcoming "A Note on the Nature of Ideal Society—A Rabbinic Study," *Curt Silberman Festschrift*, N. Y. 1969.

[35] See p. 254, *supra*.

[36] *E.g.*, Chayim Shevili, חשבונות הגאולה Jerusalem 1967.

[37] See also *supra*, p. 254f.

[38] *Sanh.* 97a.

[39] *Ib.*, 97b.

[40] *Judaism*, XVI/3, Summer 1967, p. 281.

[41] In G. B. Shaw's *Joan of Arc*, Joan says: "Minding your own business is like minding your own body; it's the shortest way to make yourself sick. . . . I tell thee it is God's business we are here to do; not our own."

MEANING AND PURPOSE
OF JEWISH SURVIVAL

Arthur Gilbert
Rabbi, Assistant to the President
Jewish Reconstructionist Foundation
New York City, New York

With a skill rare in human culture, the Jewish people self-consciously found meaning and purpose in the events of their history—in both events of triumph and defeat, humiliation and glory. In turn religion—the self-consciousness with which we celebrate and communicate the values and insights gained from that history—has enabled us to endure, and with wisdom to shape our lives and contribute to man's salvation.

In a former period, the geography of the Jewish spiritual world was bounded by creation, emancipation from slavery, the revelation of the law at Sinai, and the establishment of the Davidic kingdom.

In their account of creation, the Jewish people revolutionized man's conception of his gods and himself. The Hebrews taught that Yahweh alone was to be worshipped as God. He was the Supernatural Being who created the forces of nature, who formed the things of the cosmos, in whom the Babylonian and then the Graeco-Roman world believed divinity to reside. Thus the Hebrew God of creation ruled over the world, providing it with order and reason, offering purpose and meaning to natural and human events. Man no longer was at the mercy of undependable amoral gods. Man could hope to find such spiritual purpose and power in life as to overcome dependency on the blind forces of fate.

Man was not the after-thought creation of his gods nor the servant attendant of tyrannical gods and despotic monarchies, as the Mesopotamian cosmologies insisted. Man, according to the biblical reconstruction, became the highest order of creation. Man was endowed with worth and dignity.

Through the exodus, a slave people who were no people, found redemptive purpose and became a people, self-consciously aware of the divine in human events. Man had the right to freedom. The Hebrews felt themselves charged with a collective responsibility to shape a social order in which justice would be achieved. The slave people saw the power of God in the miracle of humanity redeemed from bondage.

The law codified at Sinai also radically transformed the moral quality of the law codes of that period. Not a human master king but a faithful, powerful God, Himself, entered the covenant with His people. And under God's law, all of human society, the king and his servants, was placed in judgment. Jewish law was made equalitarian. Class distinctions were abolished. The law was made less harsh, although the punishment to be meted out to corrupt judges was made more severe. Slaves were to be treated as people not as inanimate property. The worship of nature gods through the magical misuse of man's sexuality was condemned.

The Jewish people understood that righteousness could be achieved only through corporate effort and that a people dedicated to a law of righteousness was unique. They defined the purpose and meaning of their existence to be the proclamation to the world that Yahweh is creator and law-giver, author of history. He is God alone.

The Davidic kingdom was the human apparatus for fulfilling the redemptive purposes of the Divine kingdom. Then tragedy struck our people: Exile. After restoration from that first exile, the Second Isaiah brilliantly dramatized the Hebraic conviction that God's authority over history was revealed in His unspoken graciousness to His people. His faithfulness to Israel would enable that people to be a light to nations. Our suffering in history disclosed man's corruption but it also revealed God's power to save the weak and oppressed. We had become the servants of God.

The Hebrew religion embraced—though in purified form—the sacrificial rites and ceremonies and the pageantry of the pagan world; yet quickly enough, our prophets taught the priority of righteousness over piety.

The first revolution in theology effected by the Jewish people was the affirmation of the existence of One God. The insistence that God demanded social righteousness as the highest expression of man's humanity was the second revolution.

From the Proclamation of God to a Concern for Human Salvation

Exile, restoration and then dispersion provided another set of historic circumstances for which the Jewish people had to provide explanation, and, in finding meaning for those events, to survive. Under the influence of the Persian and then the Greek world and through the leadership of the Pharisees, the Jews solved the problem with concepts of reward and punishment in life after death and a salvation not of this world: *olom habah* and *t'hiyas hamesim*. They created a law system that enabled the Jew to achieve salvation wherever he lived in the dispersion. They revolutionized, for a third time, the concept of God and religion by making God available to the individual through prayer and obedience to the Law, thus creating a link to God unrelated to place or possession.

In truth, the end-time, this-worldly hope of a universe filled with the knowledge of God remained. The role of Israel in heralding the Messianic kingdom endured. But the impatience of men was reconciled by the promise of the glory of immortality.

In response to Greek philosophy—which was concerned more with the whatness of the divine than with who he was—the biblical Yahweh became the Eternal. But a God whose essence is unknowable, whose characteristics are so unique that they cannot be defined or described, a God beyond historic function, is not a God to whom one can easily pray. So the God of philosophers remained the God of philosophy. Whereas the common folk turned still to the Supernatural Being who governed history, and intervened in human events, and answered prayers and assured man of just reward and punishment in the life-to-come.

A weak people exiled from their land, with no efficient power to establish corporate structures of social righteousness or to control their destiny, maintained their unity by strengthening their commitment to the ecclesiastical as against the national functions of their existence. Churchhood rather than statehood became the predominant characteristic of our people in dispersion. Through the ceremonies of religion and by obedience to rabbinical law, we maintained our assurance in God's salvation. Thus other-worldly rewards were added to our function as the witness to a Supreme Being.

The Crisis of Emancipation

With the French Revolution, Emancipation, and the Industrial Revolution, Jews were once again confronted by a profound crisis. Reform Judaism enabled us to accept meaningfully the opportunities of citizenship in the world. It renewed our faith in Israel's this-worldly mission as a witness people; but Reform Judaism repressed Judaism's physical and particularistic manifestations. The founders of Reform failed to realize that universal ideas need a functioning people to make them real. And that people must have about it distinctive characteristics if it is to endure as a people. It must also possess a land.

Furthermore, the best of Jewish ideals had become part of the emerging humanistic secular world. Democratic government, in fact, generated more spiritual dynamism than Sunday services in a Jewish Temple, even with the organ full blast. In addition, enlightened men found it increasingly impossible to believe in a Supernatural Being, even though His power was now proclaimed in aesthetically-ordered revised prayer services. Nor was there much concern for salvation in the next world.

The harsh truth we must now face, therefore, is that Jews in large numbers no longer believe in the Yahweh of biblical Judaism nor in the halachic salvation system of rabbinic Judaism.

Were it not that the Christian world, through discrimination and hostility, made our integration into it so difficult, there might not have been a Jewish people to have survived the emancipation.

The Zionist movement, a necessary antidote to the inadequacies of Reform's ecclesiastical Judaism and the world's anti-Semitism, carries with it its own distortion of Judaism. Nationhood without religious self-consciousness is pagan not Jewish. As Mordecai Kaplan has put it: "The possession of a land can easily be forfeited unless a people looks upon that possession as affording the opportunity for social life of supreme value to them because of the ideals it incorporates. . . ." [1]

Furthermore, Zionism seemed, to many, to be a movement subversive of the required battle to win freedom among men wherever Jews lived. We have not yet worked out conceptually our understanding of the relation between the state and the dispersion, the vision of Zion and the possession of Eretz.

Not Religionhood or Statehood but Peoplehood Defines our Existence

In approaching such issues, Mordecai Kaplan brilliantly suggested that we no longer define ourselves in terms of religionhood or statehood but as a *people*. That which unites Jews is not our participation in one fixed prayer service or agreement upon the laws of Torah, nor the possession of a land and the ingathering of exiles but, rather, our sense of ourselves as a people linked together by historic memory and experience and many shared values. The Jewish people celebrate their value system in religion and they act upon it among the family of nations through the State of Israel. But the concept of peoplehood encompasses the fragmented disparate elements that have resulted from emancipation.

This concept of peoplehood has been another revolutionary idea in Western thought. Jews have insisted on identifying themselves in unique and particularistic categories. Kaplan's formulation merely describes a condition that prevails. Functionally the result of our insistence on the value of peoplehood has been that we now contribute to the Christian world's recently-achieved awareness that man's salvation must also be linked to and achieved within a community, and that men are capable of multiple loyalties. Enlightened particularism makes possible universalism. Thus, a lesson in the value of both particularism and universalism has been the achievement of Jewish peoplehood and our stiff-necked no-saying role toward Western civilization's effort to standardize all persons.

The Holocaust and the Emergence of Israel

Within one generation, we have plumbed the depths of hell and witnessed the birth of a Jewish State. For some of our people, God was strangled to death in a concentration camp, and for others He was resurrected in a Six Day War. We are challenged to reevaluate the meaning and purpose of our survival.

For me, these new boundaries of the Jewish spiritual world—gas ovens and the possession of the Temple Wall—exclude from consideration completely the concept of God as an omnipotent omniscient Supernatural Being. These events, coupled as they are in one lifetime, affirm for me Mordecai Kaplan's insight. God is neither to be blamed for Auschwitz nor praised for recent Israeli military victories. No logic can account for God's impotence or hiddenness in one event and His power and graciousness in another without provoking me to abhor such a God. We can no longer speak of God in traditional terms.

Mordecai Kaplan is correct when he warns us that we must talk about God as a functional *quality* rather than as a "being" as we do in the Bible and in most of our prayer service, or as an "entity"—as we do in philosophical speculation.

"We have to identify as Godhood . . . all the relationships, tendencies and agencies which in their totality go to make life worthwhile in the deepest and most abiding sense. . . . Godhood can have no meaning for us apart from human ideals of truth, goodness, and beauty interwoven in a pattern of holiness. . . . When we believe in God, we believe that reality—the world of inner and outer being, the world of society and nature—is so constituted as to enable men to achieve salvation. If human beings are frustrated, it is not because there is no God, but because they do not deal with reality as it is actually and potentially constituted." [2]

The holocaust was the work of men who misused technological power and were permitted by our civilization to distort reality. Auschwitz was not the work of God nor the result of His hiddenness; nor was it evidence of a diabolical force within the structures of creation; nor is there a divine purpose in such horror. Evil is the consequence of man's failure to live according to those divine qualities within human creation that are manifest in the experience of dignity and holiness. Evil is not a power or a force. I reject Freud's concept of Thanatos, and Lorenz's instinct of aggression, and believe still in the essential correctness of Freud's earlier views and the rabbinic psychology of *yetzer ha-ra*. Violence and evil are the reaction to our misuse of human creativity. It is that which happens when we abdicate social responsibility. It is the consequence of injustice. It is the flowering of insensitivity to the divine quality possible in all human and social relationships. The fantastic magnitude and pervasiveness of evil should convince us too that we are right to reject concepts of other-worldly salvation. With the urgency of ultimate and final desperation, we must make our salvation in this world.

Some religious Jews speak as though the Six Day War was a victory. It was not. It was only an episode. The outcome of that encounter was the inevitable result of an Israeli cultural, educational and political heritage that has so far outdistanced the structures of Arab civilization in marshalling resources of spiritual strength and technological competence. It was our people's response to the experience and memory of mass murder. But skills in warfare are ultimately available to the Arabs. Their acquisition of technological competence and the will to victory, or military assistance from others and a subsequent defeat of Israel—may we never allow it to happen—bears no relationship to the divine potency or impotency or to the righteousness of the Arab cause.

If our religion is to enable us to cope realistically with the world, we must demythologize it of supernaturalistic tendencies. We must recognize as divine that which, in the human arena, enables us to make choices in life, and organize social structures of power for man's good not his death, for his blessing not his curse.

This is not to say that I can easily define those qualities that are Godhood. Certainly the mystic sense of the divine Thou is possible in individual human relationships. It is an indispensable ingredient of vital religion and an aspect of my personal conviction in the divine. But the God realized in the quality of personal and corporate human relationships must be sought, not alone through prayer and mystic experience, but necessarily through the creative and persistent application of human reason to the realistic problems of the human community. "Only by way of participation in human affairs and strivings are we to seek God." [3]

God is that which sustains us in the effort to achieve a world in which men may live in dignity and fulfill their highest potentialities as human beings. God is that which drives us to pursue peace, even when the cause seems hopeless or impossible. God is the assurance we have, despite the horrendous magnitude of evil of which man is capable, that the sources of moral and spiritual existence are built into man and nature by the creation and that these qualities can, by devoted study, empirical testing, and faithful nurture be identified and used for good. The magnitude of evil is a function of modern day technology but the moral crisis involved in man's need for decision-making remains a matter of both despair and hope, as it has always been for us. Despite the adverse testimony of the angels of peace and truth, God created man, our tradition insists. Despite their decision that man should not have been created, our rabbis agreed that man must look to his works. It is this function we see for modern-day religion. It must, without reference to supernatural intervention, direct us to those human resources that actualize the divinity within us. Religion—the awareness of the moral and spiritual consequences of power and knowledge—must be reconstructed so that it will direct our use of science and technology, or else we shall destroy ourselves.

In the past, the Jewish people, by teaching the world of a God in control of natural forces, by insisting on the priority of righteousness in the service of that God, by demanding their right to be a people particular and unique—in the past the Jewish people, by holding firmly to such beliefs, became the target of pagan man, the object of hatred of arrogant men, the victim of Christian contempt. We still draw to ourselves the anger of every tyrant, the enmity of every extremist group whether to the left or right. The very attention focused upon us by Hitler's rage, the changing strategies of East-West politics, the evil inherent in modern day nationalisms, provide us with the occasion to bring yet another revolution in spiritual thought.

For the Jewish response to evil, our own comprehension of the meaning of our existence, the way we reconstruct our theology, worship, and structures of organization will, once again, speak to the minds of men. The role of Jews in the crises of freedom and the problems of participatory democracy at home and power politics in Israel can bring light to the world. We are once again in position to be a teacher for humanity.

It must become our purpose, therefore, to show the world how religions can be used in "improving human character and promoting international peace." Dr. Kaplan, in his book written four years ago, *The Purpose and Meaning of Jewish Existence,* has suggested that the very purpose of our evolution was exactly this, to become "an instrument for moral and spiritual humanization. . . . Though diverted again and again from that purpose," he added, "through their own ineptitude and through the hostility of nations, the Jewish people is still being haunted by it." [4]

The establishment of the State of Israel, the renascence of Jewish life there and the ongoing threat to Israel's survival, have without doubt stimulated many of us to realize that throwing our lot in with the Jewish people ought to mean "living for that which might save mankind from impending doom, and which might render human life itself worthwhile."

"We Jews, therefore, have to transpose our traditional religion . . . by tracing its ethical strivings to laws inherent in the cosmos. In doing so, we shall effect the same kind of spiritual and moral revolution as our ancestors did when they proclaimed that there was only one God, and that it was He alone they and all the rest of mankind should acknowledge as God. That is henceforth to be our vocation . . . to become a people in the image of God." [5]

NOTES

[1] Mordecai Kaplan, *The Meaning of God in Modern Jewish Religion*, 1937, New York: Reconstructionist Press, p. 353.

[2] *Ibid.*, p. 225–227.

[3] *Ibid.*, p. 30.

[4] Mordecai Kaplan, *The Purpose and Meaning of Jewish Existence*, 1964, Philadelphia: Jewish Publication Society, p. 306.

[5] *Ibid.*, p. 317.

BEYOND THE APOLOGETICS
OF MISSION

Daniel Jeremy Silver
Editor, CCAR Journal
Rabbi, The Temple
Cleveland, Ohio

Apologetics is an art form when it is not an outright con game. Its validity depends more on skillful communication, on playing the right emotional stops, than on logical impeccability. That is why even the most brilliant apologetics sound strained and tinny when a generation exchanges the conventional wisdom of its parents for other assumptions. To say that the familiar rhetoric of the mission of Israel no longer is compelling is not to say that it has been proven false—it was never strictly true—rather, it is to state that the existential assumptions of our times differ radically from the more confident and self-assertive attitudes of the mid-nineteenth century.

I asked a Seminar recently to comment on Micah 5:6, "The remnant of Jacob shall be in the midst of many peoples, as dew from heaven, as rain upon the earth." I got back discussions of the liberal voting patterns of American Jews and impressionistic analyses of the Jewish contribution to civilization. Everyone had discarded the Bible's theological frame of reference for a sociological or an historical one. No one suggested that Micah had prophesied that God would send the Jews into the Diaspora as he offers the dew to the earth in order to invest the world with some special divine grace; yet this is one clear application of the text and precisely what Samuel Usque understood when he justified Jewish survival to the generation which had suffered the death throes of Iberian Jewry.

Degraded and crushed though you are, blessings come to the world because of you, as Micah says, you alone re-

329

ceive heaven's favors. These words bear witness to it: "The remnant of Jacob shall be in the midst of many peoples, as dew from heaven, as rain upon the earth." . . . the world receives benefit from your existence.[1]

Such experiences suggest to me that any contemporary discussion of the significance and purpose of Jewish survival must address itself to functional questions rather than to theological affirmations—to interest this generation we must answer "What's in it for God?" Quote Deutero-Isaiah's classic and once compelling statement: "This people I have formed in order that I may make known my greatness" (43:22), and you may be met, as I was once, with a smart "Why can't God handle his own public relations?" And who, in the generation of the Holocaust, will accept the once familiar justification that God scatered his people and allowed them to suffer so that in the End of Days, through a miraculous redemption, God might prove to the world the fullness of His power? "No thank you, God."

I doubt that many of us really accept any image of Israel as the lynch-pin of civilization. There can be a world without Jews and there is no proof that such a world would not further refine the uncertain enterprises we call civilization. Unless I misread the early prophets, they did not assume that God had also to destroy the rest of mankind if and when He rooted out and pulled down the kingdoms of Israel and Judah. China and India represent great civilizations built without any significant Jewish contribution. Albert Schweitzer and Martin Luther King, Jr. stand for the legion of decent and courageous men who were nurtured in non-Jewish homes on the milk of non-Jewish ideas. Rabbis can no longer say to their confirmation classes: "He who separates himself from the Jewish people commits spiritual suicide."

Nor can we put forward with any hope of being convincing the rabbinic argument that being Jewish puts one on the way to salvation. כל ישראל יש להם חלק לעולם הבא.[2] One asks "What is salvation?" Another says "I thought only Christianity claimed the keys to the kingdom." Certainly the one minority Talmudic opinion the average contemporary Jew can cite is the brotherhood week standard: "The righteous among the non-Jews has a place in the world to come." Furthermore, the generation that waits for Godot does not await God's Messiah. No one I know tells his children they must remain Jews so that at the appropriate time the *Mashiach ben David* can be born of our best bloodline.

To be sure most moderns will agree that Jews and Judaism have made and continue to make certain useful contributions to mankind's development; but it is one thing to claim to be useful and quite another to claim to be indispensable. The Journal of the Academy of Arts and Sciences pointedly is entitled *Daedalus*. Daedalus contrived artful wings, but when his son flew too high those wax wings melted. The contemporary mood has no patience with those whose rhetoric outreaches their flight plan.

Interestingly, the contemporary emphasis on tailoring apologetics to size has helped many of us to read Deutero-Isaiah in his own terms and not as a resounding social gospel editorial straight from *The Christian Century*. We can now appreciate that in his famous "Light to the Nations" speech (trotted out so routinely as a proof text for any and every version of the mission of Israel) Deutero-Isaiah spoke not as a twentieth-century secular liberal, but much more in the vein of a turn-of-the-century European Zionist. He was Theodor Herzl reading aloud his Utopian novel, *Altneuland,* happily daydreaming about the attractiveness of a redeemed Zion. Herzl foresaw that architects and social workers from many small nations would visit Zion in order to transfer and reproduce her achievements. To be sure Herzl's vision was economic, while Deutero-Isaiah's vision was theocratic. The ambassadors and sages of the pagan world would visit Zion, not to tour kibbutzim, but to see *in situ* the laws and disciplines which helped make gracious the life of this kingdom of priests and this holy nation. Both Herzl and Deutero-Isaiah believed that good would come to the world because of Zion. Neither insisted, as far as I can tell, that the world would collapse without a redeemed Zion. Do we? Our earth throngs with more than two billion people. What can

thirteen million really accomplish? I thank God daily that ours
is not the only community eager for righteousness.

Some of our apologetes seem to claim that Jews must survive
for the ideals of Judaism to survive. Presumably, if there were
no Jews the world would forget the Commandments and
the prophets. History offers no clear support for this assumption. For long periods in the Middle Ages, the Catholic
Church banned the reading of the Old Testament despite
the presence of Jews. The impact of a symbol depends
entirely on the mental set of the beholder; and today a
billion Asians and an increasing number of the religiously indifferent in the West see in the continued existence of Jews no
more than the continued existence of Jews. This argument also
suggests that Judaism encloses a reserved wisdom whose special
insights are required by a convulsed and confused world. We
hope our pulpits and our writings refract judgment and some
wisdom, but how many would argue that Judaism envelopes
an arcane doctrine which men could never have puzzled out
unaided? The Talmud already suggests, "Had the Torah not
been given, we could have learnt modesty from the cat, sexual
regulation from the dove, manners from the rooster, and respect
for the property of others from the ant" (Erubin 100b). If
there were in Judaism such a gnosis, as rabbis presumably we
would be its guardians; if so, Dr. Glueck, unfortunately, for-
got to whisper it to me on Ordination Day. The Ark in my
synagogue contains only the Torah which, I have been taught,
speaks in everyday Hebrew בלשון בני אדם. To be sure the cabbalists
came close to transforming Judaism into a mystery cult. The
Torah was not language, but fire—black fire on white fire: Yet
the central tradition pondered the utility of the *mitzvot*, וכל מה
שאתה יכול לתת לו טעם, תן לו לעם and proclaimed that although the
revelation was infinitely profound, it was an open book, the inheritance of the whole congregation of Israel.[3] The *Mishpatim* had
a self-evident function. The *Hukkim* were not so clearly utilitarian but they were not capricious. As Maimonides put it: רוב דיני
התורה אינן אלא עדה מרחוק מגודל העדה לתקן העדה ולייישר המעשים .[4] "Most
of the laws of the Torah are counsels of deep meaning given to
us by God (the Great Counselor) in order to set right our

knowledge and to set all our deeds on the right path." Saadyah wrote a treatise on *Shemuoth*—those commandments which rabbinic tradition assumed men would never have deduced or inferred if they had not been revealed by God. Saadyah's treatise has been lost, and its fate is symbolic of the contemporary attitude towards any claim of possession of an esoteric truth— whatever credence such views may have had has been completely lost. Judaism encloses many fine insights, but we have no copyright on any of them. The fundamental insights have become part of the universal intellectual patrimony and would continue to be available in a world without Jews.

What then does one gain by conversion? One gains the עול המצווה and the עול מלכות שמים , an opportunity of participating fully in a special history, of obeying fully a unique discipline, and of relating familiarly to a specific spiritual literature. Conversion is a passage from ideas to identification; from analysis to affirmation; from being an observer to the excitement of the game.

Deutero-Isaiah suggested the value of religiously observant Zion as an advertisement of God's law. Philo agreed and assumed that obedience to the Torah law would lead to the golden age, for these laws "are venerable and of God-like character." [5] We must reassess these confident assumptions for not only are there deep divisions within Judaism as to the operative prescriptions of the Torah law; but the many ask if Jewish life, as it really is, represents a compelling inducement for others to adopt the Torah way. Our age takes no one and no group at its self-image. What is there in the private life of a suburban American Jew or of an Israeli farmer-soldier which can lay claim to a unique standard of holiness? What rabbi really guides a *kehillah kedosha*?

This much seems clear: (1) The transcendental idiom is out of style. Quote "You are my witnesses," and someone will say, "Who me?" and another, "How?" and a third, "Are you telling the truth, the whole truth and nothing but the truth?" (2) The existential mood emphasizes encounter, the deed, doing your thing, and finds revelation within the context of relationship. The young are quick to separate rationalization from reason, and in such an age the keepers of the flame do well to take to heart Deutero-Isaiah's cautionary preface to his "light of the nations" speech. "You shall not cry, nor lift up, nor cause His voice to be heard in the street." (3) We cannot rest our case on any claim of special virtues presumedly displayed by Jews. As an impressive sheaf of sociological analysis learnedly proves, all Jews are not learned and saintly, but then all Jews have never been learned, saintly, and proper examples for their children. This was true when Isaiah named his son *Shear Yashuv* (after "a saving remnant") and was equally true when the Hassidim spoke of the saintly 36 (the *Lamed Vovniks*) who keep our world together and who were obviously anonymous because everyone knew none of his neighbors qualified. It is not the individual and routine failings of individual Jews which endangers Jewish survival (as some rousing sermons would seem to indicate) so much as the vagueness, the emptiness, and the limpness of what passes for a corporate Jewish way of life. To blame the disinterest of the young on the ordinary vices of their ordinary parents is to mistake a symptom for a disease. (4) There must be a distinctive Jewish way of life—a specific focus—a unique perspective—a particular history for there to be a compelling thrust toward Jewish survival. Jewish experience will attract if the Jewish people do their thing; light lights, build a State, speak Hebrew, seek learning, retain their calendar, remain sensitive and stiffnecked, remain rooted in history and, therefore, marginal to any contemporary ideology, and seek holiness and God in the ordinary and the everyday.

No static or theoretical answer will satisfy. I have often marveled at Abraham Heschel's appeal to the campus. It's not the power of his argument; mysticism is in any case served better by feeling than logic. His spell is a function of his personality, his midrashic style, his clear pleasure in being a Jew, and his record of political courage which preconditions a liberal audience. His listeners know that deep within he draws the water of joy from the wells of salvation. They are thirsty and it is that thirst which will keep them Jews if we can provide the institutions, the experiences, the vital insights and the genuine article to which they can relate and through which they can mature and develop.

One Sunday morning last June, I turned on television and watched a taped panel discussion on the vanishing American Jewish youth. The panel found little that was hopeful or sanguine to report. I dressed and went down to Case-Western Reserve to a meeting of Jewish students at the Hillel House. Two hundred and fifty undergraduates, one of every three Jews enrolled in the college, volunteered that morning to spend his or her summer in Israel helping out during the emergency. Here was a patently urgent piece of business and they stood up and were counted.

I find myself emphasizing again and again the terms tangible, real, visible, urgent, significant; and in my limited way seeking ways of shaking and awakening the organized Jewish community. My own experience leads me to this position. I am a Jew because my home was palpably Jewish. I am a Jew because as a child I visited the threatened communities of Europe with my parents, and shivered in the cold light of impending martyrdom; and because I was taken to visit grandparents who were part of the beleaguered *yishuv,* and took my first lesson in courage from the daring of a people willing to lay siege to history. Buber once wrote: ". . . the book still lies before us, and the voice speaks forth as on the first day."[6] I came to listen to the book and to hear the voice, but I know I might not have paused to listen, I might have read without being receptive, if I had not encountered the tangible spirit, the real article, the pulsating history.

Men will affirm only that which they believe to be significant. Jews will not remain Jews simply for the sake of Sunday School classes for their children, or High Holy Day catharsis for their guilt feelings, or even because our Reform theology is neat and pristine. Indeed, I often think that the Reform movement has spent too much time tidying up our theology. Men do not breathe pure oxygen or drink pure alcohol. For my part the *Union Prayer Book* need not be theologically or philosophically consistent—the *Siddur* certainly was a theological hodgepodge.

What it must be, and is not, is electric and captivating. Among a passionate people abstractness and aridity are deadly sins, and a people without passion already has one foot in the grave. Jews will remain Jews for the sake of Israel, to spite a hate-filled world, to strengthen the significant institutions of a visibly useful community, to join a vigorous search for a contemporary philosophy, to enjoy a colorful pattern of celebrations, to add one's sacrifice to a sacred history; to sense, however indistinctly, that they are partners with God in the work of creation or because they believe that there are legends still to be made; but not for the sake of a neat syllogism or a finely spun moralism or even because their rabbi makes a fine appearance at the local Rotary. When the liturgy speaks of Torah as our life and our longevity, חיינו ואורך ימינו , it refers not to the scroll or its columns of text or the latest scholarly emendation, but to the world become the context—the structure—of a God-serving community. Saadyah said as much when he wrote "Israel is a people only by virtue of the Torah," and the mystics underscored this argument with their famous observation "God, Israel and the Torah are one."

In my youth the Jewish people were a reality. As I grew older Judaism as a body of wisdom and a way of sanctification became increasingly significant. I came to recognize that the Torah provided me with a frame of reference against which to weigh the various political and philosophical gospels of the day. When men cried, "The State's the thing, Central Planning is the way, The individual is nothing," I, unconsciously, recalled reading with my Hebrew teacher the story of Nathan pointing his finger at King David. Later, when men encouraged me to believe that the world is an utterly ugly place and life a hapless enterprise, I was so busy recruiting specialists for the Haganah, that I unconsciously dismissed black pessimism and latched on to Zechariah's image of Israel as a prisoner of hope. The Holocaust shattered my innocence and took me beyond tears. Zionism shattered my despair and took me beyond joy. The faith shattered my contemporaneity and took me beyond cynicism. The world, as I know it, is a cold and bruising place. Judaism and Jewish people, as I know them, have helped me to accept this world and to sense a hope beyond futility, a power beyond the obvious confusions, and a spirit beyond the mechanical passage of time. I do not dismiss or hold insignificant the value of our literature as an inducement to be or to remain a Jew, but I know that in my experience the consciousness of a vibrant people preceded my consciousness of the value of the tradition. נשמע preceded נעשה . Revelation resided within the deed itself.

NOTES

1 Usque, Samuel, *Consolation For The Tribulations Of Israel,* translated by Martin A. Cohen, JPS (Philadelphia, 1965), p. 234.

2 *M. Sanhedrin* 10:I.

3 *M. T. Temurah* 9:13.

4 *M. T. Temurah* 4:13.

5 Philo, *On The Life Of Moses,* 2:3:16, Loeb Classical Library, Philo, Vol. 6, p. 457.

6 Buber, Martin, *Israel and the World,* p. 245.